O Jerusalem!

O Jerusalem!

The Story of St. George's College

STEPHEN W. NEED

Foreword by
Hosam Naoum

WIPF & STOCK · Eugene, Oregon

O JERUSALEM!
The Story of St. George's College

Wipf & Stock
An Imprint of Wipf and Stock Publishers
199 W. 8th Ave., Suite 3
Eugene, OR 97401

www.wipfandstock.com

PAPERBACK ISBN: 979-8-3852-3759-3
HARDCOVER ISBN: 979-8-3852-3760-9
EBOOK ISBN: 979-8-3852-3761-6

VERSION NUMBER 02/06/26

In memory of
John Wilkinson

I was glad when they said to me,
"Let us go to the house of the Lord!"
Our feet are standing within your gates,
O Jerusalem. (Ps 122:1–2)

Contents

List of Maps and Photographs

Foreword

The Most Rev. Dr. Hosam Naoum,
Anglican Archbishop in Jerusalem,
and Primate and President Bishop of the Province
of Jerusalem and the Middle East

It is with great delight that I write this foreword for *O Jerusalem! The Story of St. George's College*, written by my longtime friend and former colleague at St. George's Cathedral, the Rev. Dr. Stephen W. Need. As not only Anglican archbishop of the Episcopal Diocese of Jerusalem but also president of the college's governing board, I am grateful to him for his many years of diligent research and long hours of writing that have now led to the publication of this splendid history of St. George's College, Jerusalem.

As the reader will discover from the text, Stephen is the perfect person to have written such a comprehensive and definitive volume. Beginning as a student at St. George's in the 1980s and then continuing in the new millennium as course director and later dean, he was personally involved in several stages of the college's history. Indeed, Stephen not only knew many of the foundational figures from the institution's earliest decades but was himself involved in the college's evolution in its later ones—even as he continues to be among its most earnest supporters to this very day.

What results from this personal association is a detailed and engaging account that transports the reader into the St. George's Close during both the formative years leading up the college's official establishment in the early 1960s, and the ones that followed when it finally opened its doors to students from around the world. As the reader will also see, because of the political turmoil that has so often engulfed Jerusalem during much of this journey, the process has not always been a linear one. Successes were often followed by setbacks.

One thing that has remained a constant throughout, however, has been the commitment of all involved to cultivating within the college's student-pilgrims a deeper faith in our own Christian beliefs and practices, while simultaneously promoting a greater understanding of other spiritual traditions. The college has done this through a ministry of education, personal encounter, and worship—all in the very land where our Lord Jesus Christ himself served during his earthly ministry prior to offering up his life for the salvation of the world.

As we often say in this part of the world: "Jerusalem belongs to everyone." For so many pilgrims, St. George's College has served as their first gateway to the Holy City, transporting them to a new level of spiritual relationship with the living Lord, as well as a closer partnership with the "living stones" who continue to uphold that faith in the very place where it all began.

Whether your association with St. George's College has been a long one or is brand new, I pray that its story as presented here will be a blessing to you and will encourage you to commit yourself to making periodic pilgrimages to the Holy Land. And if you do indeed choose for yourself such a spiritual discipline, I think that you will discover in these pages that there is no better place in which to do so than at St. George's.

++Hosam E. Naoum
Feast of the Holy Cross, 2025
St. George's Cathedral, Jerusalem

Preface

ABOUT TEN MINUTES' WALK north from the Damascus Gate or Herod's Gate in the walls of the Old City of Jerusalem—through the vibrant color of local Palestinian shops and markets—you come to the junction of Nablus Road and Salahedeen Street.[1] You are outside the Old City in East Jerusalem. Nearby, you see the characteristically English tower of St. George's Cathedral raising its head proudly through a sprawling cluster of buildings. Modeled on Magdalen College, Oxford, and dating from the beginning of the twentieth century, St. George's Cathedral tower is a landmark on the Jerusalem skyline, signaling the Anglican presence in the city. Inside the grounds of the cathedral, you find St. George's College, an institution serving the worldwide Anglican Communion as well as the Anglican diocese of Jerusalem. This book tells the fascinating story of how the college was born, grew, and developed into what it is today.

St. George's College, Jerusalem, is an international, ecumenical institution in which participants from many different countries and Christian denominations around the world take part in shorter and longer courses throughout the year. It is a facility through which pilgrims retreat from their ordinary lives in prayer, study, and travel. The roots of the college go back to the nineteenth century, and are embroiled in the political and religious developments of that period. The college building dates from 1962 but was thoroughly renovated and extended in the 1980s. It includes student and staff accommodation, offices, a lecture room, common room, chapel, and library. From the beginning, the college's focus has been the land of the Bible, the Bible itself, and the local people: Jews, Christians, and Muslims. Today, St. George's continues to offer a unique experience to all who pass through its doors.

1. There are different spellings of this name. This is one popular rendering. The street is named after the twelfth-century Muslim leader Salaḥ el-Dīn.

Because of its location and purpose, the college is unique. It might be likened in some respects to other institutions such as the Anglican Centre in Rome, but its location and purpose make a significant difference. Jerusalem is the mother city of Christians. It is the location of Jesus' death, burial, and resurrection. It plays an important role in the New Testament, not only as the physical location of the last days of Jesus' life but also as a theological symbol of the revelation of God in history. The city is also crucial to the Jewish understanding of God and of faith, and is central to the Hebrew Bible or Christian Old Testament. For Muslims, it is the third holy city after Mecca and Medina. Capturing the heart, soul, mind, and imagination, Jerusalem is like nowhere else on earth. It has been fought over endlessly, and destroyed and rebuilt constantly. It is the only place where three monotheistic faiths—Judaism, Christianity, and Islam—find their roots as well as their ultimate destiny.

The fact that St. George's College is situated ten minutes' walk from Jerusalem's Old City walls and about twenty minutes from the Church of the Holy Sepulcher containing the tomb of Christ gives it an unparalleled opportunity for education, pilgrimage, spiritual growth, and political awareness. It has been said repeatedly that St. George's College courses "transform lives." They certainly change and renew perspectives, refocus faith and awareness, and enable participants to grow in understanding of their own and others' faith and practice.

Part 1 of this book exposes the roots of St. George's College deep in the complex political developments of the Middle East from the middle of the nineteenth century onward. Tracing a historical outline beginning with the activities of Napoleon Bonaparte in Europe, it shows how political and missionary activity helped establish a consulate in Jerusalem and eventually an Anglican church in the Old City. It tells the story of several bishops and their contributions, and how one of them changed direction and built St. George's Cathedral outside the Old City. It was alongside this cathedral that St. George's College was eventually built. This part of the book shows that, from the beginning, there was an educational dimension to the vision of the Anglicans in Jerusalem.

Part 2 moves the story forward through the upheavals of the 1948 and 1967 wars when the political landscape of the area as it appears today was laid down. This section shows how, following early summer schools and other activities for pilgrims and visitors in the cathedral complex, a building was erected and St. George's College as it is known today was born. The lives and contributions of three of the "founding fathers" of the college, John Wilkinson, Gilbert Sinden, and John Peterson, are outlined along with details of the original building and its renovation in an exciting "Comes of Age" project. This section also shows how the ethos of St. George's as a center of education and pilgrimage was established and developed.

Part 3 of the book relates the college's life "on the ground" through a look at its staffing and management structure and through following some of its main courses out in the field. This section takes you out into the Holy Land itself, and indeed to several other countries, to many of the sites and experiences which over the years have become part of the essence of St. George's courses. That essence is a blend of pilgrimage and study, of history and faith, and of devotion and discussion that St. George's has always offered and enabled. Hopefully, as you read, you will feel something of the characteristic element of the St. George's College experience: the combination of worship, study, pilgrimage, and community formation.

Part 4 tells the story of Kids4Peace (K4P)—a movement spearheaded by the college—which brought together Palestinian and Israeli youth in a series of summer camps. There is also an account of Rekindling the Spirit, the college's 2009 reunion in the US. The first real interfaith course also features in this section, along with developments up to the time of writing. Throughout the book, the contributions of numerous individuals are related, showing the richness of the college's staff, and the wide experience its leaders brought, over the years, to this unique institution.

Part 5 is an independent chapter offering a theology of St. George's College courses. There has never been an official statement of educational or theological philosophy for the college, so I offer one here. The combination of head and heart in St. George's courses has always been a characteristic feature, and sometimes the resulting tension has triggered challenges for course participants. In this final section, therefore, I offer the suggestion that course members are pilgrims who embark upon a journey of "faith seeking understanding," following the expression associated with St. Anselm of Canterbury in the eleventh century. The pilgrim journey involves a "conversation" between the many different layers of knowledge and understanding that arise as God is experienced in new ways. The overall view is one of pilgrims rooted in faith but searching for greater understanding wherever it may lead. In this way, they grow both in faith and in understanding. The basic idea here is developed by use of the theology of icons, a fundamental element in Orthodox spirituality.

Part 6 is a collection of relevant documents from the college's history, including a list of college deans and diocesan bishops, two college constitutions, details about the supporting regional committees, aims and objectives of courses, and examples of course calendars. These appendixes are intended to provide a historical record of legal and formal aspects of the college. Finally, in this section, there is a note on the traditions surrounding St. George, after whom the college and cathedral are named.

A collection of photographs showing elements of the college's history, as well as its appearance today, will be found between parts 2 and 3.

In the twenty-first century, St. George's College offers a stunning variety of experiences and opportunities to those who sign up for its courses: studying the Bible in the land of the Bible, visiting archeological sites and holy places, and encountering the peoples of the land. Participants meet a dizzying variety of Christians from the local churches, experience and appreciate something of the richness of Eastern liturgies and theology, and meet local Jews and Muslims, Israelis and Palestinians, hearing their views and sharing some of their experiences. Location and purpose come together in everything the college offers.

O Jerusalem! The Story of St. George's College is the result of several different lines of investigation: historical research, interviews with people who have been at the college either as staff or students or both, and a good deal of my own personal experience of being at the college on and off for over forty years. Because of the multidimensional nature of the college, the book covers historical detail on how it all came about and developed, personalities that played a key part in furthering its purpose, and day-to-day experiences of courses, including management of the college and travel in the Holy Land and beyond. Because of these different lines of approach and the various dimensions of the college's history and life, the mood and voice change occasionally in the book, especially in part 3 where something of a "travel journal" style comes into play with the intention of capturing the moving, experiential, pilgrimage dimension of the college's courses. Overall, the book is the story of the origins, growth, and development of St. George's College, of what it has been in the past, and of what it continues to be today. My hope is that reading this account will itself be a pilgrim journey, reflecting something of the college's essence, character, and identity.

I would like to thank the following for their help and assistance while writing this book: the Borthwick Institute for Archives at the University of York for material relating to Brother Gilbert Sinden in its Society of the Sacred Mission (SSM) archive, and for permission to quote some of it here; the Jerusalem and the Middle East Church Association (JMECA) and its staff in the office in Farnham, Surrey, for access to its *Bible Lands*[2] archive, and for permission to quote material from it here, as well as for a Kenneth Cragg Travel Grant which enabled a trip to Jerusalem in the later stages of

2. *Bible Lands* is the magazine of JMECA. First published in 1899, it has been one of the main sources for this book.

writing; the staff at the Middle East Centre (MEC) at St. Antony's College, Oxford, for access to its *Bible Lands* archive; the British Regional Committee (BRC) of St. George's College for support and encouragement along the way; Jennifer Johnston at Inspirit Cartographics for creating the maps; and the staff at Wipf and Stock publishers for their expert guidance. I am also grateful to those in Jerusalem who have assisted in different ways at various stages: Dean Richard Sewell and the staff at St. George's College for their help and hospitality, as well as for permission to quote material from the St. George's College archive; and the Rev. David Pileggi at Christ Church.

I would also like to thank: the Rev. Canon John Peterson for originally suggesting that I write a history of St. George's College, and for his constant support and encouragement; the numerous people who agreed to be interviewed for the book, in person, by Zoom, or through email; and those who read drafts of the manuscript and offered constructive comments at various stages: Clare Amos, Don Binder, Andrew Mayes, Angela Murray, John Peterson, Stephen Platten, Clive Handford, and especially Meg Booth who helped with American spelling and punctuation, as well as overall style. I cannot thank Meg enough. Many thanks also go to Archbishop Hosam Naoum for writing the foreword. Any inadequacies and inaccuracies are, of course, my own.

My wife, Jill, played an important part in the life of St. George's College during my time as dean and I thank her for her patience, understanding, and support during those years and throughout the period of writing.

It has been impossible to mention everyone who has ever passed through the doors of the college or even been on its staff—they run into large numbers. This account includes those who played a key part, as well as some others. My apologies to any who think they should have been mentioned here and have not been.

The photographs are reproduced with thanks to St. George's College.

Finally, I dedicate this book, with respect and admiration, to John Wilkinson, whose vision and commitment played such an important part in the early stages of the college's life.

Stephen W. Need
Bexhill-on-Sea
East Sussex
England
October 2025

Abbreviations

BIBLE

Gen	Genesis
Exod	Exodus
Num	Numbers
Deut	Deuteronomy
Josh	Joshua
1 Sam	1 Samuel
1 Kgs	1 Kings
Neh	Nehemiah
Ps	Psalm
Song	Song of Solomon
Isa	Isaiah
Ezek	Ezekiel
Matt	Matthew
Phil	Philippians
Col	Colossians
Rev	Revelation

OTHERS

ABM	Australian Board of Missions
ACC	Anglican Consultative Council
AMB	Australian Missionary Board

ANZC	Australia/New Zealand Committee
ANZRC	Australia/New Zealand Regional Committee
ARC	Australia Regional Committee
BC/AD	Before Christ/Anno Domini (after the Lord)
BCE/CE	Before the Common Era/Common Era (used as a secular alternative to BC/AD)
BM	Bachelor of music (degree)
BRC/BC	British Regional Committee/British Committee
BSAJ	British School of Archaeology in Jerusalem
CDSP	Church Divinity School of the Pacific
CMJ	The Church's Ministry Among Jewish People
CMS	The Church Missionary Society/Church Mission Society
DBE	Dame Commander of the Most Excellent Order of the British Empire
DD	Doctor of divinity
DMin	Doctor of ministry (degree)
ECUSA	Episcopal Church in the United States of America
GTS	General Theological Seminary (New York City)
JMECA	Jerusalem and the Middle East Church Association
K4P	Kids4Peace
LJS	London Jews Society
LTh	Licentiate of theology
MDiv	Master of divinity (degree)
MEC	Middle East Centre (St. Antony's College, Oxford)
NARC/NAC	North American Regional Committee/North American Committee
NCCUSA	National Council of Churches of the USA
NECC	Near Eastern Christian Council
NEST	Near East School of Theology (Beirut)
NRSV	New Revised Standard Version (of the Bible)
PEF	Palestine Exploration Fund

PNCC	Palestine Native Church Council
SEITE	South East Institute of Theological Education
SPG	Society for the Propagation of the Gospel
SSJE	Society of St. John the Evangelist
SSM	Society of the Sacred Mission
USPG	United Society for the Propagation of the Gospel
VTS	Virginia Theological Seminary (Alexandria, VA)
WCC	World Council of Churches

PART 1

Background and Origins

I

Background

The roots of St. George's College, Jerusalem, are entangled in the shifting political sands of nineteenth-century Europe and its interests in the Middle East.[1] It was political and economic ambition that led the British to want control in the Middle East and which eventually resulted in them setting up a consulate and a cathedral in Jerusalem. The surrounding political context was crucial to the college's origins and has remained central to its story ever since. Moreover, the Middle East has seen constant political upheaval, and this has played its part, over the years, in shaping the college's identity.

But there are three other important areas which must also be noted at the beginning of this study. First, mission.[2] Politics was mingled with religion in a strong wave of missionary zeal which helped motivate British interest. A variety of missionary groups went out to the Middle East to spread Christianity and establish churches, some to convert Jews. Even where mission seemed a priority, political elements were still at work. Next, archeology.[3] There were archeological explorers whose eyes turned to the Middle East in the same period. The eighteenth and nineteenth centuries saw the birth of archeology and the beginning of collecting artifacts in museums. It was an exciting period of archeological exploration and discovery, and the British were among those who led the way. And finally, pilgrimage.[4]

1. I am indebted in this first part to Tibawi, *British Interests*, aware that his emphasis on politics over religion in this saga has been criticized. See Cragg's review of *British Interests* in *Bible Lands* 14:18 (Jan. 1962) 318–19. In studying the Middle East, of course, politics and religion must never be separated.

2. See Neill, *Christian Missions*.

3. See Cline, *Biblical Archaeology*; see also Moorey, *Century*.

4. See Hunt, *Holy Land Pilgrimage*.

The Middle East, and especially Jerusalem, has long been a place of pilgrimage for Jews, Christians, and Muslims. From the fourth century onward, Christians made their way to the Holy Land to visit the holy places, and, although this is not a particularly British phenomenon, the British joined in a revival of pilgrimage and travel to the Middle East in the nineteenth century, not least under the auspices of the tour leader Thomas Cook.

These four tributaries, politics, mission, archeology, and pilgrimage, flow into the history of St. George's College, forming significant characteristics of its origins, development, and continuing identity. In this first chapter, we consider them in turn.

POLITICS

To understand the origins of St. George's College, we must first find out something about the original historical and political context into which it was born. What were the British doing in the Middle East in the nineteenth century, and what gave rise to the building of an Anglican cathedral in whose grounds a college was eventually established? Why did the British want a presence in Jerusalem? What were their interests and hopes for the region? This section focuses on these questions.

The political roots of the Anglican presence in Jerusalem might be traced back to events triggered by the French Revolution beginning in 1789. In a period of radical upheaval and reorientation, the French, under the dynamic leadership of Napoleon Bonaparte, demolished their monarchy and set up a new-style Republic. Thinking himself to be another Alexander the Great, Napoleon's vision for himself and his country spread well beyond France to Egypt and Syria and ultimately to India. Napoleon rose to power rapidly and imagined himself ruler of a new empire. At the same time, the developing British Empire had expanded in an easterly direction. Having lost their colonies in America, the British now looked east and gradually took over significant new territories. Already, in 1599, they had founded the East India Company, a business mechanism through which they did trade with India in the much-loved teas, spices, materials, and opium of that country.[5] The increasing control of the British in India during the next two centuries eventually saw them establishing their own rule in India in 1858. During this entire period, it was crucial for Britain to control the routes to India, as well as India itself. Political and economic ambition, therefore, lay at the heart of the British interest in the Middle East during these years.

5. For a scintillating account of the whole enterprise, see Dalrymple, *Anarchy*.

Another political influence upon British interest was the powerful Ottoman Empire that ruled the East, including Palestine from 1517 to 1917. The Ottoman Turks were threatened from several sides, including Russia farther east. They needed the support of allies in Europe, and Britain became one of them. With pressure coming from France in the west, it was inevitable that the British would protect the interests of the Ottomans who controlled Egypt. Good relations with the Ottomans secured their own position. When Napoleon decided to move east with his army to Egypt, taking Malta on the way, the British saw that if he controlled the route to India, he would soon control India itself. Thus, protecting Ottoman interests in the area, as well as their own, the British, under Horatio Nelson, faced Napoleon in Egypt, defeating him at the Battle of the Nile in 1798.

But Napoleon was not deterred. He continued east to the coast of Palestine. If he could take Jerusalem in due course, and Syria, he imagined he would secure the corridor to India and defeat the British trade and business interests there. He could then effectively be the ruler of Europe. He made his way, therefore, farther east through the Mediterranean to the coast of Palestine at Acre, the famous Crusader port. However, the British were waiting for him under the leadership of Sir Sydney Smith. Napoleon did take Jaffa, and some of his men even made it to Mount Tabor, but he himself was defeated at Acre in 1799, his vision of taking Jerusalem and the rest completely frustrated. The remains of many of Napoleon's ships lie sunk under the Mediterranean to this day. In this encounter, the British had supported the Ottomans once again, this time in Palestine, and in their victory were reassured of their own control along the route to India.

A second opportunity for the British to assert themselves in the area came several decades later when, in 1831, Mehmet Ali of Egypt saw similar opportunities to the French before him. Ali was one of the most dynamic figures of the nineteenth-century Arab world, and is known today as the founder of modern Egypt. Albanian by descent, he was in charge of Egypt under the Ottomans. However, he sought to assert his power and authority over the Ottomans and set out to overthrow the sultan in Constantinople. Though he had been defeated by Napoleon in the earlier events described here, he had military power and experience, and spurred his army, led by his son Ibrahim Pasha, to take the whole area of the Levant including what is known today as Israel-Palestine and Syria.

Mehmet Ali was relatively successful in his campaign, taking Gaza, Jerusalem, and Acre. He planned to press on to Constantinople itself but the Ottomans responded with Russian support, which once again attracted European and particularly British interest. The sultan was pleased to have the British on his side, and the combined forces were successful in driving the Egyptians back. A few years later, Ali had another go with a similar outcome. The turmoil was not quelled until a war in 1840 when Ali was defeated, though with certain arrangements designed to appease his anger. It was clear to the British that they needed to stay in alliance with the Ottomans to retain the stability of the developing empire. Queen Victoria succeeded to the throne of England in 1837 and a new era began. The British wanted to reinforce their presence in the Middle East as securely as possible. As the years went by, they became increasingly determined to control the routes to India, as well as India itself. Things went largely to plan: the British Raj, or rule, in India was established in 1858, and in 1877 Queen Victoria was proclaimed "Empress of India" thus consolidating British presence and power in that country. In 1869 the Suez Canal was opened, raising further questions about control of sea routes to the east: the British purchased the shares in 1875.

Furthermore, during the first half of the nineteenth century, certain political and religious roles played an important part in the gradual establishment of the British in the area. It is worth noting what some of these were. The roles were occupied by different individuals at different stages but an appreciation of what they were helps clarify the events leading to the establishment of a British presence in Jerusalem by the middle of that century. From the perspective of Jerusalem there was, first, the sultan, head of the Ottoman Empire based in Constantinople. Palestine was in the Ottoman Empire and ruled by the Ottomans. Then, there was the British ambassador to Constantinople, also residing in Constantinople. There was the king or queen of England: for much of the time with which we shall be concerned, Queen Victoria. There was also the prime minister of England, a position occupied by various individuals during this period. There was the Ottoman ruler of Palestine, and eventually the British consul, both in Jerusalem. There were also the leaders of the missionary societies that helped establish the Anglicans in Jerusalem—and eventually the Anglican bishop in Jerusalem. Different personalities came and went, but all these roles played a continuing part in the story of how the British rose to preeminence in the Middle East and how the Anglican Church came to be in Jerusalem.

MISSION

The political side of the various campaigns we have mentioned is clear enough. But, as always, religion played a part. The nineteenth century was a time of religious renewal and revival, as well as of political ambition. Several missionary societies were founded in this period, including ones that would play an important part in the establishment of the Anglican bishopric in Jerusalem in 1841. But first let us consider the overriding context in which they emerged.

British Christians, especially those of the churches emanating from the Reformation in Europe in the sixteenth century, knew of the importance of the lands of the Bible. The events of ancient Israel had been played out there, and the life, death, and resurrection of Jesus himself were focused on Jerusalem. Christian religious interests in the area, therefore, were inevitable and strong. But the driving religious interest in the land of the Bible and in the Holy City of Jerusalem in these times focused upon the Jewish people in particular. Napoleon, whose activities in the Middle East we have outlined in the previous section, had himself spoken of his wish to see the Jewish people return to their land.

For many Protestant Christians, the Reformation slogan *sola scriptura*, or "the Bible only," was key. For them, the Bible showed that the Jews were the ancient people of the land. They were the chosen people of God and had been given the land of Israel. They knew that the Jews had lost that land to the Romans in AD 70.[6] Now, in the nineteenth century, the view developed that the time had come for them to return to their rightful home. Many Christians felt that God was calling the Jews back to their land as part of ushering in the second coming of Christ. Indeed, political events had started to point to this possibility. It all seemed to be there waiting in Scripture, especially in the book of Joshua and in the Old Testament prophets. The fact that the same individuals who saw this inevitable working out of God's plan for the Jews also had a good deal of political power and influence meant that the idea of a Jewish return to the land was a possibility that could be brought into reality.

The notion that the Jews in Europe might look for a homeland spread widely and found articulate expression in several Jewish thinkers of the period. In 1896 Theodore Herzl published his most famous work, *The Jewish State*.[7] His trigger was the anti-Semitism he encountered in school in Budapest, where he was born, and later in Europe, especially Paris, where he worked. Known today as the "Father of Zionism," Herzl and his friends considered several different possible locations for a Jewish state. It was not at first thought that this might be the ancient land of Israel itself. But increasing enthusiasm and support turned interests toward the Middle East, and the focus gradually turned to Palestine, as it was then known. The

6. I have kept BC and AD for dates. For their meanings and alternatives, see the list of abbreviations at the beginning of this book.

7. Herzl, *Jewish State*.

World Zionist Congress met in Basel, Switzerland, in 1897, and gave birth to the idea of a homeland for the Jewish people in Palestine. What began in Europe in the nineteenth century later became the Zionism of the twentieth century. Herzl's contribution was fundamental and, with the support of European governments, his influence was ultimately to play its part in the establishment of the state of Israel in 1948.

Two important elements of this thinking are summed up in the title of Barbara Tuchman's famous book *Bible and Sword*.[8] Biblical prophecies of the Jews returning to their land could be brought to fulfillment through political maneuvering. So this sense of the "restoration" of the Jewish people to their homeland became a key feature in the vision of Christian mission to the area as well as in political aspirations. The founding of key missionary groups during the period and the power of particular individuals with significant influence in the British government brought an influential combination of politics and religion into British interests in Palestine. Theology and biblical ideology started to become political reality. George Eliot's 1876 novel *Daniel Deronda* popularized some of this restorationist ideology in narrative form.[9]

The religious interests in the Middle East in this period, therefore, were Jewish as well as Christian. It is important to appreciate that the Jewish, Christian, and Muslim populations in the land itself were very mixed at the time when Christian missionaries started to arrive, and the new arrivals found themselves faced with considerable challenges. The Jewish population was largely Orthodox and conservative, with many shades of difference among and between them. The Muslims were Sunni, but again with a variety of types. The Christians were even more varied. Until the nineteenth century there were no Protestants in the Holy Land. Many of the Christian groups had been there since the fourth century when they arrived as pilgrims. They were largely Orthodox Churches including Greeks (the dominant group), Armenians, Syrians, Copts, and Ethiopians. The Reformation had played an important part in European religion and politics from the sixteenth century onward, but it had not so far affected the Middle East.

The Greek Orthodox Church in Jerusalem had a good deal of religious and political influence in the country. The Roman Catholic Church, or the "Latins," had arrived in the area when Western "Roman" Catholics had gone to the Holy Land during the Crusades, following the Great Schism between East and West in 1054. The Latin patriarchate based in Jerusalem was part of the Latin Kingdom of Jerusalem (1099–1187), and lasted until

8. Tuchman, *Bible and Sword*.

9. Eliot, *Daniel Deronda*.

the country was taken back by the Muslims under Saladin. From that time the Latin patriarchate was dissolved until it was reestablished in 1847 and the Greek patriarch was in exile for centuries in Constantinople.

The result of this was that in the early nineteenth century, though the Orthodox and Catholic Churches in the Holy Land were strong, they had no local patriarchs in Jerusalem, leaving a vacuum in local leadership. The local Arab Greek Orthodox Churches were overseen by the Russian Orthodox patriarch in Moscow, and the Catholics were overseen by the Catholic Church in France. Long-standing Russian and French interests in the area, therefore, continued to play a part. When Protestants started to arrive in the land as missionaries, they found themselves to be a new and largely alien breed, facing varied and contrasting communities of Jews, Muslims, and Christians.

Thus, by the middle of the nineteenth century, Jewish interests in the Holy Land joined with Protestant Christian missionary zeal and political ambition in focusing on the land of the Bible. Religious leaders, as well as politicians, looked east to see how they might bring about the restoration of the Jews to their land and help usher in the second coming of Christ. Several missionary societies were already being set up in England during this period. Two of them deserve our particular attention. The first is known today as the Church's Ministry Among Jewish People (CMJ), while the second is the Church Mission Society (CMS).[10] Both were founded in London and both played key roles in setting up and developing the Anglican bishopric in Jerusalem. Both still exist today and continue their missionary work in the area.

CMJ was originally the London Society for Promoting Christianity Amongst the Jews, and was founded in 1809 by Joseph Frey. It started off within another movement called the London Missionary Society (LMS), eventually became known as the London Jews Society (LJS) and then the Church's Mission to the Jews (CMJ), before taking its current title more recently.[11] Early on, it was based in buildings in Palestine Place, Bethnal Green, in the East End of London. The five-acre plot there had a chapel, a school, and a college. At first the CMJ involved Nonconformist Churches, as well as the Church of England. Soon it became solely Anglican. The movement began to attract enthusiasm in high places. The British foreign secretary, Lord Palmerston, and a man called Anthony Ashley Cooper, who became the seventh Earl of Shaftesbury (and who is usually known as Lord

10. The historical background of CMJ can be found in Crombie, *Jewish Bishop*. For CMS, see Stock, *History*; Cragg, "Being Made."

11. To avoid confusion, I shall refer to it, hereafter, as CMJ.

Shaftesbury) became strong supporters. With their political connections, the idea of establishing a significant Protestant presence in the land of the Bible took root in the British government.[12]

In the mid-1820s a Dane called John Nicolayson (originally Nicholajsen), who was to play a key role in the development of Anglicanism in Jerusalem, traveled in the Middle East with CMJ. He soon settled in Jerusalem and wanted an English "center" from which he could preach to the Jews and convert them to Christianity. In his vision, this would take the form of a church and a school in Jerusalem, and would be under the authority of a bishop. There would also be a British consul to cement the arrangement. Before long, Nicolayson was not only converting Jews but also drawing in Christians from the local churches, and alienating quite a few locals in the process. He was not to be deterred, however, and soon rented a room in Jerusalem for worship in Hebrew, Arabic, German, and English. He also bought land upon which he started digging, quite illegally, in order to lay foundations for a chapel.

Coming into the picture slightly later than CMJ, although founded slightly earlier, was CMS: the Church Missionary Society. This started life from an organization known as the "Clapham Sect," a group of like-minded individuals including the Rev. John Venn, rector of Clapham in south London. William Wilberforce, the famous political activist and campaigner against slavery, was also among them. A solely Anglican society, CMS was founded in 1799 following a suggestion to Wilberforce from the East India Company that a missionary society be set up. Originally it was known as the Church Missionary Society for Africa and the East, but was changed later to the Church Missionary Society. As recently as 1995 it changed its name again to the Church Mission Society (still CMS). CMS went to Palestine in 1820 in the person of James Connor, who wrote a journal describing some of the schools he saw. Various other CMS missionaries operated in the region and in Palestine. Later, the work of CMS expanded considerably under Samuel Gobat, one of the Anglican bishops.

In short, both CMJ and CMS played a crucial part in taking Protestant Christianity to the Middle East. Both societies helped form and influenced the setting up and the development of the Jerusalem Anglican bishopric. They both continued to play a part in the various layers of Anglicanism that evolved in Jerusalem in subsequent years. As we shall see, although it was CMJ that played the primary role in the original setting up of the Anglican bishopric, it was CMS that influenced its later development. Over the years, the Anglican Church in Jerusalem and the Holy Land moved

12. For a lively account of the whole story, see Crombie, *Love of Zion*.

from its restorationist origins in CMJ (still evident today at Christ Church in the Old City of Jerusalem) into a new identity, the broader evangelical Christianity of CMS.

CMJ and CMS are two of the main veins in the development of Anglicanism in the Holy Land. Both societies were committed to preaching the gospel and to providing education to the local people to whom they ministered. Both established schools and the provision of health care. And both encountered the same challenges: namely the interface not only with local Jews and Muslims but also with local Eastern Christians. In order to understand the landscape in which the Anglican bishopric was born and grew from 1841 onward, it is important to appreciate the contribution and continuing activity of these two missionary societies.

ARCHEOLOGY

Another important strand in the British interest in the Middle East in the nineteenth century, and indeed in the background of St. George's College, is the development of archeology in the Holy Land. This is a fascinating story in its own right but it is noteworthy here because archeology attracted British explorers to the Middle East, sometimes with political agendas. Later, archeology became central to St. George's College courses. The roots of archeology in the Holy Land are American, with the British joining in a little later. And there are many different layers, including political, religious, geographical, and biblical.

The "founding father" of biblical archeology is usually thought to be the American Edward Robinson. Until the nineteenth century, the Holy Land lay undiscovered and unexcavated in terms of archeology. Edward Robinson was not the first to travel to the Holy Land in search of the background to the Bible but he was the most significant of the early archeological explorers. His own background lay in the American Presbyterian Church in Connecticut, where his father was a minister. Robinson trained as a teacher and went to Andover Newton Theological Seminary in Massachusetts. He excelled in biblical languages and worked on Hebrew and Greek texts as a professor. He was eventually appointed professor of biblical literature at Union Theological Seminary in New York.

Before taking up this position, Robinson decided he wanted to visit the lands of the Bible and set off with his colleague Eli Smith on a four-month trip to Palestine in 1838. The magnetic draw of the biblical lands was in the air at the time, and the trip is now legendary in biblical archeology. The two men traveled through Egypt and Jordan, and then to Jerusalem and on to Galilee and Beirut. They traveled the land on horseback, visiting over a thousand biblical sites, though of course these were not yet known or marked. Robinson's aim was to identify biblical places in the land by searching for connections between modern Arabic place names and the biblical Hebrew place names. Using simple tools including a compass, a telescope, maps, and a few relevant texts, they sought to locate the places of the Bible. Robinson focused on geography and history, while Smith, himself a well-seasoned traveler in Arab countries and a scholar of Arabic, focused on language and local customs. Their concentration on topography, languages, and sites in association with the Bible was their overall strength. The results of this pioneering work and of a follow-up visit in 1852 were published later as *Biblical Researches in Palestine, and the Adjacent Regions.*[13]

The discipline of archeology was relatively new at this time, and the visit of Robinson and Smith to the lands of the Bible marks a turning of interest to the Middle East. Robinson's journey stands in the background of all subsequent journeys of archeologists searching for the biblical past. Indeed, at the Wailing Wall at the Temple Mount in Jerusalem today there stands Robinson's Arch, an arch that Robinson himself located and identified and which is named after him. He will always be associated also with the Siloam Tunnel in Jerusalem, and with Jerusalem's "Third Wall," as well as with the synagogue in Capernaum in Galilee, because of the role he played in their identification and subsequent excavation. It was Robinson who, through a telescope from a boat on the Dead Sea, identified Masada as the palace of Herod the Great and as the location of the suicide of the Jews against the Romans in AD 70–73. Because of Robinson's limited knowledge at the time, he did, of course, make many errors of judgment during his investigations and failed to identify places that have since been certified. But he drew a significant line in the sand and helped establish an influential discipline.

Many others followed in Robinson's footsteps and the British soon became involved. Key among them was George Adam Smith whose *Historical Geography of the Holy Land* is a classic in the field.[14] Smith was a professor of Hebrew and Old Testament in Scotland, and first went to Palestine in 1880. The book was published soon after his first visit and he returned several times around the turn of the century. There were also other books on Jerusalem as well as an atlas. Along with Robinson's work, Smith's book has come to symbolize the nineteenth-century interest in exploring the region and recording artifacts found. The combination of travel to the places of the

13. Robinson and Smith, *Biblical Researches.*

14. Smith, *Historical Geography.*

Bible with the interest in geography, history, texts, and maps contributed enormously to the overall discipline now known as "biblical geography."

Many of the great names in the history of archeology in the Holy Land were not archeologists or academics in the strictest sense of the words. They were explorers, artists, engineers, and others who with striking stamina and commitment took the discovery of Jerusalem and other places to new heights. In particular are those associated with the Palestine Exploration Fund (PEF) founded in England in 1865, and whose aims were to explore the land of Palestine though not particularly from a biblical point of view.[15] Several key people were involved, including Arthur Stanley, dean of Westminster, well known later for his book on Palestine;[16] Henry Tristram, the orientalist; and George Grove, of the *Grove Dictionary of Music and Musicians*,[17]who also had an interest in the Bible.

It was the work of Charles Wilson, however, that formed the basis of numerous waves of work under the PEF. Again, the concentration was on mapping, geography, natural history, and archeology. Like Robinson, Wilson worked in Jerusalem at the Temple Mount area, giving his name to an arch at the northern end of the Western or Wailing Wall. Another PEF explorer was Charles Warren, who worked underground at the City of David and the Gihon Spring. His name is well known from Warren's Shaft in that area. Claude Conder and Lord Kitchener also undertook work with the PEF. Eventually, the results of PEF projects were published in the *Survey of Western Palestine* in seven volumes (1884).[18]

The second half of the nineteenth century saw the further development of archeological work in Palestine and witnessed the establishment of several major institutions in Jerusalem, which helped cement work already done and prepare the way for that which followed in the twentieth century.[19] These institutions also signified the continuing political interests in the area and their establishment helped strengthen the presence of European governments in the region. The British School of Archaeology in Jerusalem (now the Kenyon Institute) was established in 1919. It was to have major archeologists at its helm in the twentieth century, including the well-known British Kathleen Kenyon who worked in Jericho and Jerusalem.[20] Other

15. The PEF continues today, based in Greenwich, London.

16. Stanley, *Sinai and Palestine*.

17. Sadie, *New Grove*.

18. Warren et al., *Survey*.

19. For more background on some of the British institutions in the Holy Land, see Gibson, "British Archaeological Institutions."

20. In years to come, Kenyon's work would be mentioned regularly on St. George's College courses. For an illuminating biography of this amazing lady, see Davis, *Dame*

important archeological institutions were also established during this period: the French École Biblique et Archéologique Française (the well-known Dominican monastery and library on Nablus Road, close to St. George's), 1890; the German Protestant Institute of Archaeology (now on the Mount of Olives), 1900; and the Albright Institute of Archaeological Research (on Salahedeen Street, close to St. George's and originally called the American School of Oriental Research), 1900. Although established later, these schools continued the work begun earlier by various explorers, focusing on geography, history, archeology, maps, and surveys, as well as on biblical texts.

Another example of British interest in the Holy Land linked with archeology in the nineteenth century is the story of Gordon's Calvary and the Garden Tomb.[21] This is a fascinating story in its own right but can only be outlined here. There had always been scholarly and popular debate about whether the Church of the Holy Sepulcher in Jerusalem was really the site of Jesus' death and burial. Around the middle of the nineteenth century a local landowner found a tomb just north of the Damascus Gate near the École Biblique, an area peppered with tombs of various types. German and American scholars were soon involved and it was thought that this tomb might be the tomb of Jesus.

But it was the British General Gordon, known as Gordon of Khartoum because he had been a soldier there, who, while living in Jerusalem in the late nineteenth century, popularized the view that the tomb of Jesus had been found outside the walls of the Old City. This view was supported by the fact that the rocky terrain near what is today the East Jerusalem bus station, looked uncannily like a skull. Through complex biblical and archeological calculations, Gordon maintained that what looked like a skull must be the "place of a skull," or Golgotha, where Jesus died, and known to us from the Gospels (e.g., Mark 15:22). The fact that the tomb already mentioned was nearby completed the picture, and Gordon convinced many that this was indeed the place. The property was sold to the British who formed the Garden Tomb Association, and it has been in their hands ever since. Discussion about its authenticity continues.

From the beginning of biblical archeology there was always the question of how discoveries in the land related to the text of the Bible. This question was to permeate the whole history of the discipline, but at first there was a good deal of expectation that the archeological discoveries would help "prove" the biblical accounts. It is often said that the early archeologists

---

Kathleen.

21. See Frantzman and Kark, "General Gordon"; Walker, *Weekend*.

worked with "the Bible in one hand and a spade in the other." Eventually, of course, there were disappointments when text and spade contradicted each other. A very well-known case is when Kathleen Kenyon's excavations at Jericho in the 1950s led her to believe that the walls of Jericho had fallen long before the time of Joshua as recounted in the book of Joshua (5:13; 6:27). Gradually, over the years of the twentieth century, both the purpose and the results of this discipline became minefields of scholarly disagreement.

Overall, these individuals and organizations represent another layer of European interest in the Middle East, and in particular in the land of Palestine.[22] They show another level of the political and religious interest in establishing a center in Jerusalem. It is certainly clear that the interests were not always purely archeological: political ambition motivated archeological excavation. Archeological projects helped establish foreign presence in the land. Most importantly here, the archeological explorations outlined in this section set the scene for one of the dimensions of learning that was to play a key part in St. George's College when it was eventually established. In days to come, the story of archeology in the Holy Land would play a significant part in college courses, and pilgrims and students would study the connections between the land and the Bible through visiting archeological sites.

PILGRIMAGE

The final area of background interest in this introductory chapter is pilgrimage. Among other things, a pilgrim is one who travels to a holy place for the strengthening of spiritual life. Pilgrims to holy places are often at a turning point in their lives, and in their awareness and experience of God. To some extent, it might be said that all travelers to the Holy Land are pilgrims. Although participants in St. George's courses have often been thought of primarily as students, they have also been thought of as pilgrims, and the theology of pilgrimage has frequently influenced the college's sense of its identity and purpose. It is, therefore, worth considering some of the background elements of Holy Land pilgrimage here in order to help introduce St. George's College.

Pilgrimage to Jerusalem features in Judaism and Islam, as well as in Christianity. In ancient times, Jewish pilgrimage to Jerusalem was focused on the temple. Jerusalem was the location of the great temples of Solomon and Herod. Many of the psalms are songs written for and by pilgrims.

22. For further examples and details, see Ben-Arieh, *Rediscovery*; Silberman, *Digging*.

"Going up" to Jerusalem to the holy place, to God's house, was something all faithful Jews did at the major festivals of the year. The Psalms of Ascent (120–134) include Ps 122: "I was glad when they said to me, 'Let us go to the house of the LORD!' Our feet are standing within your gates, O Jerusalem" (Ps 122:1–2). Those who went up, went to offer sacrifice, to pray, and to worship in the presence of God in his own house. The temple in Jerusalem was the place of sacrifice and was the religious and political center of the Jewish nation. Pilgrimage to Jerusalem has remained important in Judaism down to the present day.

In Islam, pilgrimage became a defining feature of the faith, in fact rather more so than in Judaism and Christianity, the main pilgrimage, of course, being to Mecca. And pilgrimage is a requirement in Islam, not an option, constituting one of the so-called five pillars of the faith. All Muslims must make the hajj pilgrimage at least once in a lifetime, if wealth and health permit, according to the Qur'an.[23] Those who have been to Mecca have carried out what is required of them and use the title *hajji*. There are three holy places in Islam: Mecca where Muhammad was born, Medina where he is buried, and Jerusalem where he ascended into heaven on a white horse called Buraq. Jerusalem is certainly a place of pilgrimage for Muslims, but only after the other two places.

Christian pilgrimage to Jerusalem began in the second century.[24] The business of going to Jerusalem, and of marking places in which Jesus had been, probably began very early on. But we know that in the second century Melito of Sardis went to Jerusalem, and others soon followed. Christian pilgrimage to the Holy Land began in earnest when the religion became legal and official in the fourth century, and when the new Christian emperor, Constantine the Great, and his mother, Helena, began to build churches in the Holy Land. His famous churches in Jerusalem were magnets for Christians: the Church of the Holy Sepulcher and the Church of the Eleona on the Mount of Olives, as well as his Church of the Nativity in Bethlehem and his basilica at Mamre, near Hebron. In the fourth century, Christian pilgrimage to the Holy Land flowered and bloomed, and has continued throughout Christian history.

We know that in AD 333 a pilgrim went to Jerusalem from Bordeaux in France. But the most well known of the fourth-century pilgrims was a lady usually known as Egeria or Etheria. Possibly from a religious community in Spain, she traveled in the Holy Land between 381–384 and left

23. See Dawood, *Koran*, e.g., 19, 20, 40, 224.

24. If the Gospel passion narratives were written in the context of liturgy focusing on holy places, this might constitute the first-century origins of pilgrimage. See Trocmé, *Passion*.

behind a journal, known today as *Egeria's Travels*, in which she describes the places she visited and the things she saw. She was in Jerusalem during Holy Week and described the services she attended in the Church of the Holy Sepulcher and elsewhere.

The text of *Egeria's Travels* is incomplete and has lost its beginning and ending. The surviving account starts in the Sinai desert and moves north through the Holy Land to Constantinople. Most fascinating is Egeria's description of what she saw in numerous places and what went on there. She is one of the earliest sources for pilgrim travel, and the earliest full account for our sense of liturgy in the holy places of Jerusalem during Holy Week in those years. She describes the Jerusalem liturgies and the behavior of pilgrims in fascinating detail, and so the work is a key source on the development of pilgrimage and of liturgy. The man who translated into English and edited *Egeria's Travels* in the twentieth century was the Rev. John Wilkinson, dean of St. George's College. We shall encounter him and Egeria in more detail in the next chapter.[25]

There are many other pilgrims, too, who over the centuries made the journey to the Holy Land. Some left behind their itineraries or other material. An important one was St. Jerome who lived in Bethlehem for thirty-eight years in the fourth century, founded a religious community, and translated the Bible into Latin. In AD 570 a pilgrim from Piacenza in Italy made the journey. And in later centuries there were Arculf (seventh century) who traveled widely in the area and on his way back was driven by a storm onto the coast of Britain at Iona, where he met Adomnan[26] and dictated to him an account of what he had seen in the Holy Land; and Willibald, an Englishman (eighth century), who became bishop of Eichstätt in Germany, and whose travels were written up by a nun called Hugeburc. Following the Muslim conquest of the Holy Land in the seventh century, Christian pilgrimage slowed down considerably but flourished again in the Crusader period (1009–1291) with figures such as Saewulf, Fulcher, and the Abbot Daniel.

In addition to pilgrimage as such, it is worth mentioning here the nineteenth-century developments in travel. Thomas Cook began his trips across Britain and Europe in the 1860s, and operated his first trip to the Holy Land in 1869. It went by ship to Sidon and then by horse to Jerusalem, camping in tents and traveling for many hours a day. Gradually, Thomas Cook and Son established themselves as the predominant tour leader to

25. Wilkinson, *Egeria's Travels*. See also McGowan and Bradshaw, *Pilgrimage*. There have also been translations into other languages.

26. Biographer of St. Columba.

many destinations, and by World War I were leaders in the field, traveling by rail as well as horse. From that time onward until its sad collapse in 2019, Thomas Cook operated internationally. Alongside actual travel to the Holy Land during this period, travel writers played a significant part in encouraging interest in the lands of the Bible. The work of Mark Twain in the US[27] and H. V. Morton in England[28] come readily to mind. Thus, pilgrimage to the Holy Land expanded and developed with many different ideas about the journey, and many different itineraries. Thousands of pilgrims eventually made their way to Jerusalem, many of them to St. George's College.

The importance of pilgrimage, the spirituality of pilgrimage, and the itineraries that we know from across the centuries, all play an important part in coming to a full appreciation of St. George's College which stands in the tradition of pilgrimage, and which in the modern period has flourished on easy travel and available flights. Because of its location, pilgrimage has always featured in one sense or another in what the college has offered. Through the second half of the twentieth century the ease and speed of travel were such that shorter trips were possible and more could be seen in less time. St. George's played a significant part in enabling many pilgrims to experience Jerusalem, and pilgrimage became a key element in the college's own understanding of its identity and mission, as well as in the subject matter of its courses.

This chapter has provided four broad brush strokes on an enormous canvas: politics, mission, archeology, and pilgrimage. Through setting the scene politically, we have shown how the British came to be in the Middle East in the first place. Through attending to mission, we have seen how CMJ and CMS began to establish Anglican Christianity in the Middle East, showing some of the roots of the Anglican bishopric. Through looking at the beginnings of archeology in the Holy Land, we have shown the continuation of British interests through a discipline which focused on engaging with the land but which was often also political. And finally, through noting briefly the tradition of pilgrimage to the Holy Land from ancient times to modern, we have underlined another element in the motivation of travelers to the area.

Albeit in a variety of different senses, these four crucial elements still constitute some of the defining characteristics of St. George's College today. There is always a political context, and the life of St. George's has been affected and influenced constantly by local political events in the Holy Land and the wider region. In a rather different sense from that of the nineteenth

27. See Twain, *Innocents*. Originally published in 1869.

28. See Morton, *Steps*. Originally published in 1934.

century, the college is still focused on its mission and purpose, largely through its educational programs and its role in the Jerusalem diocese. Archeology is the local national sport, and always plays a key part in the college's programs through visits to biblical and other sites. And pilgrimage has not only been part of why people have traveled to Jerusalem and to St. George's but has also been part of the college's own sense of its purpose and aim. From the beginning, these four characteristic traits have played an important part in the college's curriculum and daily life.

From the early 1960s onward, St. George's College has had a building in Jerusalem which has provided a comfortable base for all its operations. From the early years, the work of the college has spread through numerous countries, drawing students from across a wide range of Christian denominations and traditions. The college has become international, ecumenical, and even interfaith. Before telling that story in part 2, however, we turn first to the establishment of the specific historical context into which the college was originally born: the Anglican bishopric in Jerusalem.

2

Origins

THE DECADE FROM 1831 TO 1841 is crucial, to say the least, in the story of the evolution of the Anglican bishopric in Jerusalem. As we have seen, at the beginning of this period Mehmet Ali of Egypt occupied Palestine and Syria. He continued in power until the war of 1840. During this period (despite a harsh regime for some locals), foreigners, local Christians, and missionaries were treated kindly. This enabled movement in favor of the idea of setting up a permanent Anglican presence in Jerusalem. Those who helped the Ottomans during this period (the Russians, the French, the Austrians, the Prussians, and the British) looked for opportunities to cement their relations and to secure their benefits in the region. At this point, the last two in this list, the Prussians and the British, become the focus of our interest. Both hoped to secure and develop their presence in Jerusalem and the wider area. The Ottomans had accepted their support in war, and by the end of the decade these important allies felt that their own visions for the future should be taken seriously. During the long decline of the Ottoman Empire, maps were redrawn and countries reconfigured. New possibilities came into view.

The Prussian Empire was itself developing in Europe during this period. In 1840 Frederick William IV became king. Following the events of the sixteenth century, much of Europe was Protestant, including Prussia. Christianity in Prussia was Protestant—Lutheran, and a mix of various Protestant denominations under the United Evangelical Church of Prussia. There was already a united and uniting church, and the new king sought to strengthen unity and development both within his country and farther afield. Like many other countries, therefore, Prussia looked to the Middle East for such development. As we have noted, the Orthodox Churches in Palestine (largely Greek) already enjoyed the protection of Russia, while the

Catholics enjoyed the protection of France. There was no official Protestant presence in the Middle East although, as we have also seen, there were Protestant missionaries and explorers. Frederick William looked at the British interest in Palestine and saw new opportunities for Prussian growth.

AN ANGLICAN BISHOPRIC

The British interest in Palestine grew considerably during this formative decade. The developing empire, the idea of a Protestant presence in the area, the powerful wave of restorationist thinking among British Christians, and the overall support from people in power in the British government all meant that eyes were turned on Jerusalem. In England, the foreign secretary, Palmerston, and Lord Shaftesbury were very keen on establishing a presence in Jerusalem. With the Prussians also interested, the scene was set. And so it was that King Frederick William sent an envoy, Christian Charles Bunsen, to London to discuss the matter with a future Prime Minister, William Gladstone, as well as with Shaftesbury and Palmerston. Sir Robert Peel (Prime Minister, 1834–1835 and 1841–1846) also looked favorably on the idea.

Gradually, with the support of all these players who maintained that the hand of God was behind it and that headway could be made swiftly, the idea of a Protestant presence in the Middle East, and more specifically an Anglican bishopric in Jerusalem, became firm. CMJ had the support of key players in England. Queen Victoria was approached about the matter, and approved. Owen Chadwick says, "At bottom this plan was part of British and German policy in the middle east. The powers were manoeuvring for the loot which lay about as Turkey collapsed."[1]

Other events also affected the developing situation. By 1839 the British had opened a consulate in Jerusalem.[2] The presence of John Nicolayson with CMJ had played a big part in enabling this. Palmerston wanted it and had sought permission from the Ottoman authorities as well as from Alexandria under whose direct authority Jerusalem fell. It was emphasized that a consul should be there to look after and protect British travelers in the area. So far, there had been no other consulate in the region—the British was the first. Legal permission was granted by the sultan and the first vice-consul (as he was known), William Young, went to Jerusalem. It was made clear that he would be responsible for protecting local Jews and Protestant Christians.

1. Chadwick, *Victorian Church*, 189.
2. Today's Rectory at Christ Church is the original consulate building.

In 1840, as we have seen, the Egyptian occupation of Palestine came to an end and the power reverted directly to the sultan. This changed the climate but the British had played such an important role that the Ottomans accepted their ideas. It was thus seen that a permanent British presence in Jerusalem was possible and the idea of a Protestant building in the city came to the fore. Nicolayson had rented buildings and purchased land. He was already holding Protestant services in Jerusalem. But the situation was complex. Permission was needed. And there was an Ottoman law that no new buildings were allowed to be erected by Christian groups. In spite of these obstacles, and against local opposition, Nicolayson dug down to bedrock on the land he had purchased inside the Jaffa Gate in Jerusalem, and started to lay foundations. There was so much local opposition, however, that the process soon stalled.

There were also objections in England to the whole idea of an Anglican bishop in Jerusalem. Key among them came from leaders of the Oxford Movement. In 1833 John Keble preached his famous *National Apostasy* sermon in the University Church of St. Mary the Virgin in Oxford.[3] The sermon was prompted by the British government's plan to suppress ten bishoprics in Ireland, then part of the United Church of England and Ireland. Keble's objection was that this intervention by Parliament flew in the face of the church's own authority given to it by Christ and maintained by the church across the centuries through its succession of bishops. Keble believed that the Church of England was the Catholic Church in England but rejected the notion that Parliament could act alone in matters of the church. "Parliamentarianism" or "Erastianism,"[4] he maintained, was unacceptable. There were several different phases in the Oxford Movement but the group that followed Keble in the early period included other well-known figures of the day, namely, Edward Pusey and John Henry Newman. Pusey was Lord Shaftesbury's cousin. Newman was vicar of St. Mary's University Church in Oxford. It was Newman who later marked Keble's sermon as the beginning of the Oxford Movement. And because the movement published its views in "tracts" it also became known as "Tractarianism."[5]

In addition, other issues of the time such as Catholic Emancipation (1829) and the Reform Bill (1832) had raised the likelihood of the British Parliament ceasing to be entirely Anglican. Because the Church of England is the state church, the danger for Keble and others was that a

3. Keble, *National Apostasy*. The same basic point is made in Newman's first tract. See Newman, *Tract One*. For the wider story, see Rowell, *Vision*.

4. So named after the sixteenth-century Swiss theologian Thomas Erastus who maintained that the state has rights over the church in decision-making matters.

5. The Oxford Movement's emphasis on sacraments, liturgy, and ritual came later.

not-entirely-Anglican Parliament might be left influencing decisions in the church, especially if it acted without any consultation with the church. A constitutional crisis was breaking, primarily political but also theological: the Church of England was losing its Catholic pedigree. Those who followed Keble's lead soon saw that an Anglican bishopric in Jerusalem, decided upon by the British government in partnership with the Protestant Lutheran Church in Prussia, was irregular. The subject provoked deeply-felt emotion and soon became extremely divisive.

Furthermore, those following Keble said that the real bishop of Jerusalem was the Greek Orthodox patriarch of Jerusalem and that Anglicans had no business establishing an episcopal figure of their own there. A more general point was that the whole idea seemed back to front: a bishop was to be created before there was a community for him to look after. Such a situation seemed to put the cart before the horse and was theologically unsound. Later, in 1845, Newman left the Church of England to join the Roman Catholic Church claiming that the creation of the Anglican bishopric in Jerusalem had been the last straw for him.[6]

But the idea had taken hold, and those in favor, including Palmerston, Shaftesbury, and CMJ won the day. There would now be an official joint arrangement between the United Church of England and Ireland, on the one hand, and the United Evangelical Church of Prussia, on the other. Behind this ultimately were Queen Victoria and King Frederick William IV. The twentieth-century writer Bishop Stephen Neill calls the development, "one of the strangest episodes of modern Church history."[7]

The proposed arrangement would look like this: the two countries would alternate in choosing the bishop—British, Prussian, British, Prussian, and so on. The bishop in Jerusalem would be under the archbishop of Canterbury who would have the power to veto any nomination, Prussian or British. Prussian nominees for the position would need to be reordained as Anglican, as would any Prussian clergy working under them. They would need to accept the teachings of the Church of England including the "Thirty-Nine Articles" of the *Book of Common Prayer*. Everyone felt that it was desirable that the candidate should be of Jewish descent, that he would be of the Church of England, and that he would be well educated. From the beginning, and with sensitivity to the other churches in Jerusalem, it was

6. See Newman, *Apologia*, 135–40. He says of the Jerusalem bishopric, "It brought me on to the beginning of the end" (140). See also Newman, *Letters and Diaries*. During the early 1840s, Newman commented regularly on the development of the bishopric calling it, for example, "fearful" (288), "hideous" (289), "atrocious" (297), and "most unhappy" (312).

7. Neil, *Christian Missions*, 304.

decided that the Anglican bishop would be known as the "Anglican Bishop 'in' Jerusalem," not "of" Jerusalem.

The question of Anglican bishops abroad was relatively new and it is important to note that the idea of the Jerusalem bishopric had to pass through Parliament before it could be implemented on the ground. There had been two Acts of Parliament already in 1786 and 1813 which allowed the Church of England to have bishops abroad. CMS had sent a bishop to Calcutta in 1814. Now, in 1841, another Act known as the "Bishops in Foreign Countries Act" or the "Jerusalem Bishopric Act" was passed. This legitimized the idea of an Anglican bishop in Jerusalem. In the same year the "Colonial Bishoprics Fund" was set up to help fund such ventures, but as Palestine was outside the British Empire at the time, it did not qualify for support. The "Jerusalem Bishopric Fund" was then established.

One of the best ways of appreciating the origins of the Anglican diocese of Jerusalem, and therefore ultimately of St. George's College, is to look at the succession of bishops of the diocese, especially in the early period.[8] They were all educated and enterprising men whose determination and influence enabled the gradual evolution of the Anglican presence in the Holy Land. These were men who had received an above average level of education in their own home contexts and were committed to the same thing for others when they arrived in the Holy Land. Their background in higher educational pursuits illustrates an important layer in the birth of the idea of an Anglican college in Jerusalem.

CHRIST CHURCH

CMJ led the way in favor of the bishopric in practical terms and the first British nomination was the Rev. Alexander McCaul who turned it down. It was then offered to the Rev. Michael Solomon Alexander, a converted Jew who had been ordained in the Church of England.[9] He accepted and was consecrated on November 7, 1841, in Lambeth Palace Chapel by the archbishop of Canterbury (William Howley), with Bishop Blomfield (of London), Bishop Muray (of Rochester), and Bishop Selwyn (of New Zealand) also taking part. Among those present were Bunsen, Shaftesbury, Stratford

8. The following sections are indebted to Farah, *Troubled Waters*, the only history of the Anglican diocese of Jerusalem in English. Farah also wrote a history in Arabic. On the Anglican Church in the Holy Land in the early period, see also Cragg, "Anglican Church."

9. See Crombie, *Jewish Bishop*; Corey, *Rabbi to Bishop*.

Canning, and William Gladstone. Alexander McCaul preached the sermon. The stage was now set for further development.

Thus, Michael Solomon Alexander became the first Anglican bishop in Jerusalem.[10] He was in post for nearly four years. Born in Schönlanke in the region of Posen in Prussia in 1799, he was the son of a rabbi, and well educated in Hebrew and in Judaism generally. As a young man, Alexander traveled to England where he found work teaching Hebrew in Colchester, Norwich, and Plymouth. He worked as a rabbi at first but soon came under the influence of the recently founded "London Jews Society" (LJS, later CMJ) with its agenda of converting Jews to Jesus. As we have seen, CMJ hoped for the restoration of the Jewish people to their land, and focused on prophecy and messianic hopes in the Hebrew Bible. It saw these hopes fulfilled in Jesus and read the New Testament largely in that frame of mind. Alexander soon found himself reading the New Testament with them and before long became convinced that Jesus was indeed the Jewish Messiah as they said he was.

On this basis, Alexander converted to Christianity in Plymouth where he was baptized at St. Andrew's Church in 1825. He married Deborah Levi, and at first there was enormous pressure on them to separate but they stuck together and she was also baptized. After a period in Exeter, they moved to Dublin where Michael got a job with CMJ. He became more and more involved with the Anglican Church and its structures and was eventually ordained deacon and then priest. After a period working in Germany on missions with CMJ he returned to England and to London where, in addition to his responsibilities with CMJ, he became professor of Hebrew at King's College, London. He played a significant part in the translation into Hebrew of the New Testament and the Church of England's *Book of Common Prayer*.

After his election and consecration, Alexander and his wife and six children set sail for Jerusalem, accompanied by a chaplain and a doctor. The boat chosen for their journey was named *Infernal* and Alexander felt uncomfortable and objected. The replacement was called *Devastation* which they took! They sailed via Gibraltar and landed at Beirut where they were joined by the consul-general, Colonel Hugh Rose. They then traveled to Jaffa and on to Jerusalem arriving on January 19, 1842. They were amazed at the crowds that were out to greet them, learning only later that the celebrations were for the end of Ramadan! The Alexanders now began the complex process of settling into the Jerusalem community and establishing

10. See *Bible Lands* 14:18 (Jan. 1962) 294–97. See also *Bible Lands* 14:19 (Apr. 1962) 314–16.

important relationships with locals and expatriates. Following CMJ, their aim was to convert Jews to Christianity. They had been instructed specifically not to interfere with local Christians.

Jerusalem finally had an Anglican bishop, even though there were very few Anglicans living in the city. Relationships in the community would be crucial and it is important to note again here who some of the various parties were. The local Jews and Arabs were of course central. The Arabs were largely Muslims but some were local Greek or other Orthodox or Latin Christians. Alexander also had John Nicolayson and others of CMJ in Jerusalem and London to keep happy, as well as the representatives of CMS which continued its missionary work in the area. In addition, there were the political leaders: the British vice-consul in Jerusalem (William Young), the Prussians, both in Prussia and in Jerusalem, and the Ottoman authorities in Jerusalem and in Constantinople where Sir Stratford Canning was now British ambassador. The role of the new bishop was complex and tough but Alexander was eager and enthusiastic.

The Alexanders soon gathered around themselves a small community of people through baptisms and weddings. Their worship centered on a regular Eucharist celebrated in Hebrew. Michael was keen on education and learning, and soon established a "Hebrew College," a small group of people to whom he taught various languages.[11] With the help of his doctor, furthermore, he set up a hospital and offered medical aid to locals. He traveled in the wider area, setting up small medical stations in Bethlehem, Hebron, and Safed in the north, and went to Beirut and Baghdad. His diocese was supposed to cover the vast area of Syria, Chaldea, Egypt, and Abyssinia, as well as Palestine.

The challenge for Alexander was tough and he became increasingly embroiled in difficulties arising in the local communities. On the Jewish front, he quickly found that he was not welcome among local Jews who were less than eager to embrace his version of Christianity. The few he did manage to convert became alienated from their own communities, sometimes with dire consequences. On the Christian front, the locals were curious but suspicious, with similar results. Relations with local Christians inevitably developed, however, and seeds of later work under Alexander's successor, Samuel Gobat, were soon sown with conversions from the Orthodox Churches to Anglicanism. There were also inevitable tensions in relations with local Muslims.

11. This "college" has been thought of by some as effectively constituting the roots of the later St. George's College.

A significant challenge for Alexander was that it proved harder than he had hoped to get permission to erect a building for worship, and even though Nicolayson had started the process, permission had to be secured from the Ottomans who were not forthcoming. Now that Jerusalem was back under direct Ottoman rule, it was necessary to get a decree from them. But the law forbade Christians from building new buildings, and even though there were cases of others (Greeks and Russians) carrying out building projects, and even though sometimes hints were given that it was acceptable, an official *firman* (decree) from the sultan was needed and took some time to get. It was not until 1845 that a *firman* was granted and building work was continued and very gradually completed. Despite many setbacks, the process and the actual building project proved fundamental to the gradual establishment of the Anglicans in Jerusalem.

One continuing problem which deterred progress somewhat was illness in the Alexander family. Several of the children died during their time in Jerusalem, and Michael himself was never in good health. His condition vacillated and his work was often interrupted because of this. During those times Jerusalem was not free from disease, sickness, and early death. In November 1845 the bishop set off with his wife and others on a visit to Egypt, traveling through the Sinai desert. On the journey, he suddenly became quite ill and was taken to a tent near Ras el Wady, where he died. He was forty-six years old. His body was taken immediately to the CMS property in Cairo where it was encased in three coffins—a wooden coffin, inside a metal, inside a wooden. Then, draped in a black cloth on two poles between two camels, it began its long journey back to Jerusalem via Gaza. The journey ended with a burial ceremony on November 23, 1845, in the Protestant Cemetery on Mount Zion. His tomb can still be seen there today.

Alexander had been Anglican bishop in Jerusalem for nearly four years. He was a visionary man with energy and optimism, and, above all, commitment to the Jewish people and to the church and others in the Holy Land. With the help of those around him he had launched the Protestant bishopric in Jerusalem, and he firmly believed that this would enable the "restoration" of the Jewish people to the land and their ultimate conversion to Jesus Christ, the Messiah. He had made a start in education and medical care, as well as in nurturing a small nascent community of Protestant Christians. He had fought many a local setback and tackled many controversies, believing firmly that the hand of God was guiding the whole operation. In many ways, much had been achieved. There was now a small Anglican community in Jerusalem, the CMJ and CMS still in support, a British vice-consul, and the beginnings of a church building. Alexander's death was, of course, a blow to the momentum that he had helped develop but now the scene was set for future growth. The question was, who would succeed Alexander in this established role? It was the turn of the Prussians to nominate.

A successor was soon found in Samuel Gobat from Switzerland.[12] Born in 1799 in Crémines in the Canton of Bern, he was a very different candidate from Alexander. Gobat was a Lutheran minister who, as we have mentioned, had worked with CMS. He was an educator and a linguist who knew French, German, and English, as well as the biblical languages, Hebrew, Greek, and Latin. Having been in Abyssinia (Ethiopia) he knew Ge'ez and Amharic. He had also been in Paris and London. For several years he was vice-principal of the CMS college in Malta, during which time he had helped with the translation of the New Testament into Arabic. Furthermore, he had already spent time in Palestine, Lebanon, and Syria as a missionary with CMS. Gobat was zealous and energetic about missionary work and education, and was therefore a good candidate for the Jerusalem job. Though he was not Jewish, he had all the other qualifications and King Frederick William IV, therefore, recommended him as the first Prussian nominee. As it had been decided that Prussian candidates should take Anglican orders, Gobat was ordained deacon and priest in Fulham Palace, and then consecrated bishop in Lambeth Palace Chapel, London, (like his predecessor) by the archbishop of Canterbury (William Howley) in July 1846.[13] He then set off for Jerusalem with his wife, Marie. Gobat's reign was to be very much longer than Alexander's, at over thirty years. It was also to be very different in style, direction, and achievement.

The tenor of Gobat's episcopate changed the direction of the Jerusalem bishopric. He had come from CMS not CMJ. His focus, therefore, while still including the conversion of Jews was not limited to that. Gobat's outlook was broader, and he was to take both his role and the new Protestant community in Jerusalem in a different direction. His emphasis was on mission, and throughout his time in office he focused on preaching, education, and building schools. In the end, his emphasis turned away from converting Jews to converting local Christians. Although the agreement had always been that the Protestant bishop would not interfere with local churches, Gobat, frustrated by Jewish indifference and hostility, gradually turned toward local Christians, some of whom, for numerous reasons, turned to him.

At first the local Christian interest in the Anglicans began naturally and without any proselytizing on Gobat's part. Sometimes local Christians

12. For more information, see *Bible Lands* 15:1 (July 1962) 11–16.

13. His initial Anglican ordinations were planned for St. Paul's Cathedral in London but there were objections and demonstrations against him and the Jerusalem Anglican bishopric.

felt neglected by their own churches and approached Gobat for instruction and Bible study. For the Anglican bishop, it was often a matter of whether to turn such people away or respond to them hospitably. Gradually, the borders between the various groups blurred, and during Gobat's time there were many conversions from the local churches to the new Protestant community. Often the movement was because of opportunities in education or medical care or something to do with perceived social betterment. But convert they did, and the Protestant church grew significantly in numbers. This did not happen without local tension and bad feeling.[14] But Gobat was an adamant and single-minded individual who largely ignored local and even CMJ and British concern about the situation.

In 1849 the Protestant church building begun by Nicolayson just inside the Jaffa Gate of the Old City was completed and consecrated by Gobat. Its name was "Christ Church," as it has remained to this day.[15] The bishop also ordained the first local Arab clergy. Pursuing his long-standing interest in CMS, he also encouraged that society to set up its own presence in Palestine, which it did in the 1850s. Gobat's own work in mission continued under the auspices of CMJ, but he was frequently at odds with them and their leaders.

During his long term in office, Gobat's concentration on schools saw the establishment of many in the region. Probably the best known was the Bishop Gobat School on Mount Zion.[16] This opened originally inside the Old City, but then moved outside to Mount Zion and became known to generations of Arab Anglicans as one of the best places for educating young people in Jerusalem. Gobat also opened schools in Bethlehem, Beit Jala, Nazareth, Jaffa, Lydda, Ramleh, Nablus, Zababdeh, Shefa 'Amr, Nisf Al-Jbal, Burqin, Rafidiah, and Salt in Jordan, among other places. The list gives a good impression of the scope of Gobat's influence and achievement. A great deal of time and energy was spent establishing these schools, but unfortunately numbers of staff were often limited and standards were often low.

Gobat's work with the local Arabs led to another shift of "tectonic plates" in the Protestant landscape. His at first imperceptible switch from concentration on Jews to concentration on local Christian Arabs gave way to a split with CMJ and their leaders. Gobat moved more toward the CMS and their local missionary endeavors, with the result that those who attended Christ Church and its services in Hebrew, Arabic, German, and English

14. However, it seems that from the early days the Armenians in Jerusalem always made the Anglicans feel welcome in the city.

15. On the wider background and development at Christ Church, see Crombie, *Love of Zion*; *Restoring Israel*; and *Prophetic Property*.

16. Today's Jerusalem University College.

began to feel somewhat estranged. Eventually, the growing community of Arab Anglicans of gentile Christian origin and background (mostly from the Orthodox or Latin communities) began to want independence, separation from the Jewish emphasis of CMJ, and a church of their own. And so it was that one was eventually built for the Palestinian Arab Anglican Christians in West Jerusalem. This is the Church of St. Paul, not far from the main highway that runs today along the so-called Green Line that separated Israel from Jordan between 1948 and 1967. Gobat consecrated St. Paul's in 1874, and in so doing established another layer in the developing Anglican presence.

Thirty-three years passed and Gobat became a major figure in the leadership of the Anglican Church in Jerusalem and the Holy Land. He continued teaching the Bible and languages throughout this period, and was committed to educating all who came to him. But at seventy years of age, he began to slow down. For the last decade of his life things moved slowly, and he died in Jerusalem in 1879, aged eighty. He is buried close to Alexander in the Protestant Cemetery on Mount Zion.[17] His presence towers over the history of the Anglican diocese of Jerusalem. During a long reign, he had embarked upon a new path that left CMJ and Christ Church somewhat isolated, and saw the diocese moving forward into the future with a more specifically Arab identity.

Following Gobat's death, it was once again the turn of the British to nominate a candidate. Canon Henry Tristram, the well-known orientalist and ornithologist of Westminster Abbey, was offered the position but turned it down. He recommended the Rev. Joseph Barclay, another very different character, who accepted.[18] Barclay was born in 1831 near Strabane in County Tyrone, Northern Ireland, and was of Scottish descent. Like his predecessors, he was a linguist with several languages, including the biblical ones, to his name. He worked on the Hebrew text of the Talmud. Ordained in 1854, he served as parish priest in several parishes in England and at one point looked after St. Margaret's next to Westminster Abbey in London. After offering his services to CMJ as a missionary he went to Constantinople in 1858. He had been committed to missionary work from his early youth, and had been in Jerusalem with the CMJ as incumbent of Christ Church from 1861 to 1870, during Gobat's time. This gave him great familiarity with the situation in Jerusalem, but he resigned in 1870 because CMJ refused to increase his salary. In 1865 he married Lucy Andrew, one of the daughters of William Wayte Andrew, vicar of Ketteringham in Norfolk. At

17. Sadly, Gobat's grave was vandalized in early January 2023.

18. For more information on Barclay, see *Bible Lands* 15:2 (Oct. 1962) 29–32.

the time of his appointment as bishop in Jerusalem, Barclay was rector of Stapleford in Hertfordshire.

Barclay was consecrated on July 25, 1879, by the archbishop of Canterbury (Archibald Campbell Tait) in St. Paul's Cathedral, London. His contribution in Jerusalem was significant in that, like his predecessors, he was committed to education. His missionary interests meant that he saw the importance of the schools founded by Gobat and did his best to consolidate the infrastructure laid down by his predecessor. Barclay's contribution was to try to improve conditions and raise standards. When he arrived in Jerusalem, there was something of a division in the Anglican community, but he encouraged CMJ and CMS to work more closely together. He inherited some of the other, largely financial, problems from Gobat but, again, tried to smooth out difficulties. He established a weekly meeting for pilgrims visiting Jerusalem, and generally encouraged everyone to work together in harmony. In 1880 he was awarded a doctor of divinity degree (DD) from his alma mater, Trinity College in the University of Dublin, acknowledging his commitment to education and learning. Unfortunately, Barclay died suddenly in 1881 after pains in his chest. He was fifty years old and had been bishop for less than two years. He is buried with his predecessors in the Protestant Cemetery on Mount Zion in Jerusalem. His wife died four months after him.[19] Like Alexander, Barclay's time in office was short but he built up a certain amount of security and confidence among those with whom he worked.

The first forty years of the Anglican bishopric in Jerusalem had been eventful and busy. Three bishops had held office and there had been a great deal of laying of foundations and building upon them. Three very different characters and personalities had been at the helm. Three different men had given themselves to leading locals and foreigners, as well as travelers and pilgrims, in the area. Three very different men had worked with the various parties involved, with varying degrees of success. Each reign can be seen to have had its own ethos. But a good deal had been achieved, largely through the forceful character of Bishop Gobat. The other reigns were distinct but short.

In sum, the British and Prussian Protestants were now in Jerusalem. The bishopric was established with two buildings, several churches around the land, many schools and hospitals, and a presence among the Jerusalem

19. There is a memorial monument to the Andrew family on the wall inside Ketteringham church bearing Barclay's name. It reads as follows: "In fond remembrance of . . . Lucy Agnes Tryphosa . . . widow of Rt. Revd. Joseph Barclay DD LLD Bishop of [*sic*] Jerusalem." The story of Lucy's father and the local squire is told in Chadwick, *Victorian Miniature*.

communities that was becoming familiar and gaining respect. Tensions, of course, remained. CMJ and CMS continued to vie for control. Locals and expatriates pulled and pushed. Wider political interests and dynamics remained alive and kicking. The next challenge was to appoint a new bishop who would take up the reins and lead things forward. Unfortunately, the tensions between factions were making the Anglo-Prussian alliance itself quite fragile, and things now took a surprising lurch in a new direction.

ST. GEORGE'S

Following the death of Bishop Barclay, there is a long gap in the list of Anglican bishops in Jerusalem.[20] Relations between the British and the Prussians had not always been as smooth as had been hoped for. British appointments had been bound up with British interests and Prussian with Prussian. In particular, the detail of the arrangements over the reordination of the Prussian clergy and the archbishop of Canterbury's veto were not generally well received by the Prussians. Even though Bishop Gobat had been in office for over thirty years, he had not cemented the relationship with the British that well. Also, despite Gobat having been the Prussian candidate and having had a long term in office, the Prussians themselves felt alienated by him and pushed out. So it was that, after Barclay's death, the Prussians pulled out of the deal completely, leaving the situation in a mess. It was the Prussian turn again after Barclay but they wanted no more to do with it.

Inevitably the situation gave rise in England to the revoicing of old objections to having an Anglican bishop in Jerusalem in the first place. The Tractarians again raised objections, and a great deal of further discussion ensued until the Prussians finally pulled out in 1886. There was no appointment to Jerusalem until 1887, with the Prussians gone and the British in it on their own. In due course, the Lutheran community went its own separate way, building churches, schools, and hospitals of its own throughout the Holy Land. The Lutheran Church of the Redeemer in the Old City of Jerusalem was opened in 1898 by Kaiser Wilhelm II.

The next appointment to the now solely Anglican Jerusalem bishopric was significant, and marks another key turning point in the story. In 1887 George Francis Popham Blyth was appointed Anglican bishop in Jerusalem.[21] He held office for twenty-eight years. Blyth was British through and through. Born in Beverley in Yorkshire in 1832, he became a student

20. On this period, see *Bible Lands* 15:3 (Jan. 1963) 46–52.

21. For more information on Blyth, see *Bible Lands* 15:4 (Apr. 1963) 72–78. See also *Bible Lands* 15:5 (July 1963) 94–96.

at Lincoln College, Oxford. (His experience of Oxford was later to influence his work in Jerusalem.) Blyth emerged from Oxford with a doctorate and worked in several parishes. Eventually he went to India and Burma where he was an archdeacon in Rangoon. In India he married Mary Anne Crommelin.

In 1886 the archbishop of Canterbury (Edward White Benson) approached Blyth about taking the Jerusalem job. After brief hesitation, he accepted the challenge. Blyth was an Anglo-Catholic, and there were objections from CMJ and CMS, both of which were largely evangelical in their churchmanship. The old objections from the Tractarians were aired yet again: the real bishop of Jerusalem was the Greek Orthodox patriarch and the cathedral was the Church of the Holy Sepulcher. Even in this new climate with no Protestant Prussians to complain about, such voices maintained that the whole enterprise of Anglicans in Jerusalem, and the way in which the bishopric had been established, was an anomaly. Even Blyth himself thought that the Anglican bishop in the Middle East should perhaps reside somewhere other than Jerusalem.

In the event, Blyth was consecrated in Lambeth Palace Chapel on March 25, 1887, by the archbishop of Canterbury (Edward White Benson) and set off for Jerusalem. He was installed at Christ Church, but from the beginning felt seriously isolated. Christ Church belonged to CMJ and they were very much in charge there. The many schools established by Gobat were now in the hands of CMS. The local Arab Anglican clergy were now largely controlled by CMS and had formed their own Palestine Native Church Council (PNCC). Blyth was committed to working with all parties, furthering mission and education, but often felt he had no real authority. The role of the bishop had become marooned amid competing leaders and interests. Blyth's vision was to develop Christ Church into a significant base for Anglican mission, evangelism, and education in the region. His idea was to extend the complex of buildings inside Jaffa Gate, creating a "Collegiate Church" with a dean (himself) and canons under his direction. In addition, there would be a training college for the local Arab Anglican clergy and teachers. Blyth was also committed to working among the local Jews and Muslims. It was not long, however, before his vision was rejected by CMJ who foresaw loss of authority and control over their own project. Blyth would have to think again—and he did.

As an alternative, he established the "Jerusalem Bishopric Mission Fund" to support his wider work in the region, helping clergy and building new churches.[22] He did not give up on his idea of a Collegiate Church,

22. Also known as the "Jerusalem and the East Mission" (J&EM), it established a

however, and soon thought of the possibility of a major new building project, this time outside the Old City walls to the north. The idea of establishing an independent Collegiate Church apart from Christ Church, Blyth thought, looked promising. It would be independent of CMJ and CMS, even though Blyth himself would still work with both. During the next few years, the idea took off and the Collegiate Church of St. George the Martyr[23] was built on a property bought for the purpose at the junction of Nablus Road and Salahedeen Street to the north of the city.

The complex was designed by the British government architect in Cyprus, George Geoffrey, and in addition to the church, in English Gothic style with stone arches and a wooden ceiling, there were offices and a bishop's house.[24] The buildings were in local limestone and based on New College, Oxford, with a quadrangle around the church entrance. Dedicated to the patron saint of England, St. George (thought to be originally a local Palestinian saint[25]), the complex was consecrated by the bishop of Salisbury (John Wordsworth) on St. Luke's day, October 18, 1898, just over ten years after Blyth arrived. Celebrating the event a hundred years later, *Bible Lands* reprints some details from its first edition in 1899, including the following about the building and the service: "The Church is of stone with a fine groined roof of timber. The style is transitional from Early English to Decorated. There is an ambulatory which runs entirely round the Church, giving ventilation, coolness, and easy access to the sittings, as well as to the choir."[26]

The bishop's throne, given by the bishop of Salisbury, is mentioned, as are the litany desk and the font, given by Queen Victoria. The splendor of the occasion is also noted as follows: "The consecration of the church on St. Luke's Day was a service most solemn and dignified; all were impressed by it. There were present representatives of every Church, except the Latin, (who gave their sympathy but were not allowed to be present) which is episcopally represented at Jerusalem. The Orthodox Prelates, Armenian and Syrian Bishops, Coptic and Abyssinian dignitaries were there. The leading

Trust (J&EMT) in 1929 which still exists today. One of the charities operating under it is the Jerusalem and the Middle East Church Association (JMECA), which was established in 1976 when the province of Jerusalem and the Middle East was formed. *Bible Lands* magazine, started in 1899, is now published by JMECA. Blyth also established the "Good Friday Offering," an annual collection in the Episcopal Church in the USA, which is still given to the diocese of Jerusalem.

23. Officially known as St. George's Cathedral since January 6, 1976, but often referred to as such before that date.

24. See Kroyanker, *Jerusalem Architecture*, 136–39.

25. On St. George, see appendix F.

26. *Bible Lands* 24:7 (Easter 1998) 315.

Lutheran clergy attended."[27] The writer of the account comments that, "As an ecclesiastical pageant the scene was striking and successful, all the details of management and ceremonial having been carefully rehearsed. But the spiritual effect was still more satisfactory. Those present were greatly impressed."[28]

By 1910 Blyth realized that the church needed to be bigger and an extension was consecrated by the bishop of London, the Rt. Rev. Arthur Foley Winnington-Ingram.[29] Queen Victoria died in 1901 and a bell tower named after her successor, King Edward VII, was added in 1912. Based on the tower of Magdalen College, Oxford, it stands separate from the cathedral due to the relatively high likelihood of earthquakes in the area.[30] The whole project illustrated Blyth's interest in taking Oxford to Jerusalem, and reflected his vision perfectly: a British establishment for education, learning, and the pursuit of scholarly work in the Holy City. St. George's would be an Oxford College in Jerusalem, complete with chapel. Also, Blyth envisaged four canons: scholars in Arabic, Hebrew, church history, and education. It would be known as the "Collegiate Church of St. George the Martyr, Jerusalem," keeping an eye on the Church of the Holy Sepulcher as the cathedral of Jerusalem and the patriarch its bishop. The local Arab congregation eventually grew around the new St. George's and included many from St. Paul's Anglican Church nearby.

Blyth worked tirelessly for twenty-eight years developing his vision with all the parties involved, reinforcing the contributions of his predecessors in both the Palestinian and Jewish communities. His vision and energy continued, and with his love of learning, languages, and music he excited and inspired everyone around him. In 1899 he opened a new boys' school nearby, St. George's School, which still today provides education for local Palestinian Anglicans and others.[31] In addition to the work at St. George's, Blyth built churches around the diocese and encouraged the evolution of a

27. *Bible Lands* 24:7 (Easter 1998) 313.

28. *Bible Lands* 24:7 (Easter 1998) 314. See also the original account in *Bible Lands* 1:1 (July 1899) 1–4. For illustrations and a plan of the building, see *Bible Lands* 3:34 (Oct. 1907) 17–20.

29. See *Bible Lands* 3:33 (July 1907) 2–3; *Bible Lands* 3:47 (Jan. 1911) 226–30, 241–42.

30. On the bell tower, see *Bible Lands* 3:47 (Jan. 1911) 230–31. For a picture, see *Bible Lands* 4:52 (Apr. 1912) 52. See *Bible Lands* 4:49 (July 1911) 20–21, for a report on progress on the bell tower. Other pictures appear in these volumes.

31. There are many famous Palestinian alumni of the school including Edward Said and Sari Nusseibeh. The Rev. W. Awdry, creator of the Railway Series and Thomas the Tank Engine, taught in the school from 1933 to 1936.

new diocese in Egypt under a new bishop, Llewelyn Gwynne.[32] Thus, Blyth took the Jerusalem diocese into a different phase with its new buildings and the Collegiate Church.

But although Blyth's dream had come true, things had changed on other fronts. At Christ Church, CMJ had gone its own way. Because of Blyth's Jerusalem Bishopric Mission Fund, St. George's became separate, even from CMS, in terms of funding. Blyth had gotten his own way and still worked with both societies. But tensions remained and he often found himself still without authority over the local Arab Anglican clergy and others. In addition to cultural clashes, such crises of authority between locals and expatriates have remained part of the dynamic of St. George's ever since. But times were changing, and in 1914 Blyth was eighty-two years old. He retired from Jerusalem and returned to London, to Kensington where he died in the same year just after the war began. His funeral was held at St. Paul's Church, Hammersmith. Blyth's time in Jerusalem is captured beautifully by his daughter Estelle in her book *When We Lived in Jerusalem*.[33]

From the point of view of this study, Blyth's time as bishop constitutes a key development in the emerging story of the Anglican diocese of Jerusalem, and so also in the story of St. George's College which would be built later, near St. George's Collegiate Church. The beginnings of Anglicanism in the Holy Land were at Christ Church, but it was Blyth who built St. George's and provided the geographical and physical setting in which the college would later spring up and in which it would play out its significant role in the years to come. In this section of the book, however, we shall continue the story of the development of the diocese through several more episcopal officeholders to illustrate further the background to the college over the ensuing years. If Bishop Blyth had been responsible for the building of St. George's Collegiate Church, the following years were ones of consolidation and development of his basic vision. Blyth had retired at the beginning of the war in 1914. There was, of course, no Prussian candidate now and the British chose Canon Rennie Miles MacInnes to succeed Blyth.

MacInnes was born in Rickerby, Northumberland, in 1870, to a family involved in politics. They were evangelical Christians and devoted to mission. Rennie went to Trinity College, Cambridge, and trained for the ministry at Ridley Hall in the same city. He served a curacy at St. Matthew's, Bayswater, and worked in several other parishes. In 1896 he married Janet Waldegrave Carr. By the time of his appointment to Jerusalem, he

32. On appointing a bishop for Egypt, see *Bible Lands* 2:17 (July 1903) 6. On the later appointment of Gwynne (1920), see *Bible Lands* 6:87 (Jan. 1921) 95–98.

33. Blyth, *When We Lived*.

was already a canon of St. George's because of his missionary work in Cairo and the East. From his missionary standpoint, he was committed to building good relations with Jews and Muslims and with the local Christians. MacInnes was the right man for the job and was consecrated by Archbishop Randall Davidson in Westminster Abbey on October 28, 1914. However, he was unable to go to Jerusalem until the war ended in 1918, operating from Cairo for the first four years of his time in office.

The sands of the Middle East had been shifting rapidly during the years since the foundation of the diocese in 1841, and, through all the developments, the British interests in Palestine had grown and consolidated. They had supported the Ottomans all along, keeping an eye on the trade route to India and helping to strengthen the Ottoman Empire lest some European power usurp it. When the Ottoman Empire weakened during the First World War, the British stepped up their interest.[34] In 1917 the British issued the Balfour Declaration which supported the idea of a homeland for the Jewish people in Palestine. This changed the political climate in the Middle East forever. In the same year, British rule in Palestine (turning later into the British Mandate) began and lasted thirty years.

On December 11, 1917, British General Edmund Allenby dismounted his horse and entered the Old City of Jerusalem on foot through the Jaffa Gate, symbolizing a peaceful regime to come.[35] It was an occupation nevertheless, and the British were to control Palestine until 1947. This thirty-year period further solidified British presence in the region. Jerusalem now had a consulate, a bishop, and a diocese with churches, schools, and hospitals in different places around the country. As bishop, even though in absentia, MacInnes was directly involved in what was going on in the early stages of the war. When it ended in 1918, he arrived in Jerusalem in a new situation within a new political matrix. There were opportunities as well as challenges, and he had much to offer.

The new bishop soon saw what needed doing at St. George's for Bishop Blyth's vision to be fully realized. Like Blyth, MacInnes was a builder and erected several buildings in the diocese. In Jerusalem he continued the project at St. George's by adding accommodation to the complex and providing living space for St. George's staff as well as for pilgrims and visitors. These buildings are now the St. George's Cathedral Guest House. MacInnes also saw that the educational side of the vision needed cementing into the complex. He created two roles that would be significant in this educational

34. It was during this period that T. E. Lawrence ("Lawrence of Arabia") joined the Arab revolt against the Ottomans. See Lawrence, *Seven Pillars*; Asher, *Lawrence*.

35. See *Bible Lands* 5:75 (Jan. 1918) 215–20. The deal was signed with the Ottomans at St. George's Cathedral on a table which is still there in the archbishop's office.

provision. First, soon after arriving, he appointed the Rev. Stacy Waddy as a canon of the cathedral and as archdeacon of Palestine. Waddy was given responsibility for education in the diocese. He had been a headmaster in Sydney, Australia, and brought with him all the necessary skills. He developed the St. George's Boys' School, as well as the British Girls' High School and the CMS College, also known as the English College. The latter had played a part in educating Arab clergy and teachers in the diocese. Waddy's job was to expand the institutions and raise educational standards all around.

The second appointment was of the Rev. Herbert Danby, a Hebrew scholar from Keble College, Oxford.[36] MacInnes hoped Danby would be instrumental in providing locals and foreigners with serious opportunity to study the Bible, languages, and archeology in the Holy Land. In addition to his actual work at St. George's, Danby is remembered today for several scholarly publications including, first, his translation (with introduction and explanatory notes) of the Mishnah from Hebrew to English. The Mishnah is the most important Jewish text after the Torah, and was completed originally in about AD 200. Danby finished his translation in 1933.[37] And second, his contribution to an English-Hebrew dictionary[38] based on the work of Eliezer Ben-Yehuda, the creator of modern Hebrew. With these appointments Bishop MacInnes envisaged postgraduate study at St. George's with students going out from England. The Oxford model of learning was now ready to be taken up in Jerusalem.[39]

Another significant appointment by MacInnes into the community at St. George's at this time was that of an American bishop's chaplain. One of the key holders of this office was the Rev. Charles Thorley Bridgeman, a dynamic character who also taught at the Armenian seminary or school in the Armenian Quarter in the Old City.[40] This tradition has continued until recently. All the chaplains contributed in some way to the educational profile of the Cathedral Close, which increased the emphasis on scholarly presence and activity, enabling something more of Blyth's vision to be gradually realized. The educational profile of St. George's was sharpening and the Anglicans were becoming better known in the wider Jerusalem community. Indeed, Bishop MacInnes was present along with Lord Balfour and

36. Danby was at St. George's from 1919 to 1936.

37. Danby, *Mishnah*. For a review, see *Bible Lands* 8:140 (Apr. 1934) 473–75.

38. Danby and Segal, *English-Hebrew*.

39. By 1920 educational provision was in place and it is this that formed the basis of the centenary celebrations at St. George's College in January 2020. See later, part 4, chapter 10 on this.

40. See Hummel, "Canon Bridgeman."

others at the official opening of the Hebrew University on Mount Scopus in Jerusalem in 1925.

MacInnes's time as bishop lasted until 1931 when he died and was buried in Burgh near Carlisle in England. He had furthered Bishop Blyth's vision and brought about the next stage of completion of buildings and the laying of an educational infrastructure by appointing scholarly canons. The idea of an Oxford College in Jerusalem had taken shape and was moving forward. In addition to providing instruction for locals, including some mostly short-term theological education for Arab seminarians, the idea of providing summer schools for Anglican clergy from England also developed. These began as short courses at St. George's—initially in the bishop's house and using the accommodation provided by MacInnes. It was these "summer schools around the year" that were the seed of what later grew into St. George's College, with the need for its own buildings and space in the Cathedral Close.[41]

The commitment to education on the part of the Jerusalem Anglican diocese was continued by MacInnes's successor, George Francis Graham Brown.[42] He had been principal of Wycliffe Hall, Oxford, and a lecturer at Wadham College. He took with him to Jerusalem many educational and management skills. Born in China of missionary parents, he had the missionary spirit in his blood. Educated in Glasgow and at Trinity College, Cambridge, he was married to Jane Paisley Hay. While serving in the forces in France during the First World War he suffered injuries and returned to England, where he became a school teacher at his old school in Monkton Combe, Somerset. He was consecrated in St. Paul's Cathedral in London by the archbishop of Canterbury (Cosmo Gordon Lang) on June 24, 1932, in a rare joint Anglican-Old Catholic consecration service.[43] Like his predecessors, Graham Brown worked on raising the standards in education in schools in the diocese as well as improving health and medical care. He founded the Bishop's School in Amman, Jordan, and arranged conferences for school teachers and leaders in the diocese.

Graham Brown held office for ten years during the lead-up to the Second World War but died suddenly and tragically during the war in November 1942. Traveling back by car from Lebanon and Syria, where he had been on diocesan business, and crossing a railway line at el-Zeib in today's West Bank, his car was hit by a train and he was killed instantly. He was

41. See *Bible Lands* 14:13 (Oct. 1960) 211–12, where Archbishop Campbell MacInnes writes of his father's hope for courses in Jerusalem in 1926 and of his own in 1946.

42. "Graham Brown" was his unhyphenated surname.

43. See *Bible Lands* 8:133 (July 1932) 248–58, for details of Bishop Graham Brown.

taken back to Jerusalem and buried alongside Bishops Alexander, Gobat, and Barclay in the Protestant Cemetery on Mount Zion.[44]

It was during Graham Brown's time as bishop that the Rev. Kenneth Cragg appeared in the diocese. Cragg went to Beirut to teach at the Shimlan Bible School and later at the American University. He founded St. Justin's House, a hostel for students at the university. In due course, he became a significant player in the diocese, a bishop in Egypt, and an internationally renowned scholar in Christian-Muslim relations. We shall encounter Cragg again later, as he was to play an important role in developing summer schools at St. George's.[45]

Following Graham Brown's death in 1942, Weston Henry Stewart was appointed bishop. He was born in 1887 in Bakewell, Derbyshire, and educated at Oriel College, Oxford. In 1932 he married Margaret A. Clapham, the daughter of a Cambridge economics professor. By the time of his appointment, Stewart had already been a chaplain at St. George's Cathedral as well as archdeacon in Palestine, Jordan, and Syria. He was consecrated by Archbishop William Temple in Westminster Abbey on September 21, 1943, and went to Jerusalem straightaway. He had a legal mind and did much to develop the constitutional and synodical structure of the Jerusalem diocese. He appointed Charles Thorley Bridgeman archdeacon and made other appointments to canonries at St. George's, developing further the sense of a Collegiate Church. Looking forward, he saw the potential of the Jerusalem diocese, its likely growth, and the possibility of inaugurating a Jerusalem archbishopric and developing a wider set of Anglican dioceses around it. Indeed, this structure was to come into place under his successor Archbishop Campbell MacInnes.

But the surrounding landscape changed dramatically in 1948.[46] After thirty years of British rule in Palestine, and following the Second World War and the Holocaust, the eye of the world, and especially of many Jews, turned once again to Palestine as a possible homeland for the Jewish people. The rise of Zionism from the nineteenth century onward, the growth of restorationist views, and the turn of political events all contributed toward the United Nations supporting the establishment of a Jewish state in Palestine.

The British Mandate had brought its own problems locally. The British had established their presence in the Middle East after over a century

44. For the *Times* obituary and other details, see *Bible Lands* 10:175 (Jan. 1943).

45. Cragg also later wrote numerous important books, including *Call of the Minaret*, *Sandals*, and *Arab Christian*. See also Thomas with Amos, *Faithful Presence*.

46. See Bunton, *Palestinian-Israeli Conflict*; Chapman, *Whose Promised Land?*; Cohn-Sherbok and El-Alami, *Palestine-Israeli Conflict*; and Harms, *Palestine-Israel Conflict*.

of trying, but they had grown tired of the task of uniting various factions under their rule. There had been much violence from both Jewish and Arab groups, one of the most well-known incidents being the bombing of the King David Hotel in Jerusalem by the Jewish Irgun in July 1946.[47] In 1947 the British felt that it was time to hand over the Mandate to the United Nations. The UN forged a deal which was considered inadequate by many, including the Arabs, but it passed through the General Assembly. After much uncertainty, David Ben Gurion and others signed a Declaration of Independence setting up the Jewish state of Israel on May 14, 1948, after which a war between the Zionists and the Arabs broke out. The date has been celebrated ever since as a triumph for the Jewish people, but remembered by the Palestinians as a catastrophe (*Nakba*): roughly seven hundred fifty thousand were displaced. Those who ended up inside Israel became "Israeli Arabs." From the point of view of the decline in "British interests" in the Middle East, it should be noted that the British withdrew from India in 1947.

The establishment of a new state in the region changed the political context of the diocese of Jerusalem considerably: from British Mandate Palestine to the new state of Israel. One of the many outcomes of the change was that, while most of the country became Israel and some of it became Jordan, Jerusalem was divided, with the western part of the city falling under Israel and the eastern part falling under Jordan. East Jerusalem was the area in which St. George's Cathedral stood and where St. George's College would later be built, in a divided city. Bishop Stewart steered the diocese through a great deal of upheaval following 1948, and stayed until 1957 when he retired and returned to England, to Rutland, where he became rector of Cottesmore, as well as being assistant bishop in the diocese of Peterborough. He died in 1969 and is buried in Exton near Oakham, Rutland. The diocese of Jerusalem had taken an important structural turn during Stewart's time.

Stewart was succeeded by Angus Campbell MacInnes, son of Rennie MacInnes who we have already encountered as bishop in Jerusalem (1914–1931). Born in Cairo when his father was a missionary there, Campbell MacInnes was another dynamic character in the development of the Jerusalem diocese. He had lived in Jerusalem, of course, when his father

47. The hotel housed the British military headquarters. One of the ninety-one people killed in the incident was Brian Conway Gibbs. His wife, Joan Gibbs, was a frequent participant in St. George's College courses in later years. I am very grateful to Dr. Oliver Hersey, president of Jerusalem University College, for tracing Brian's details. The Irgun (Hebrew: organization) was a Zionist group that fought for the establishment of a Jewish state before 1948.

was Anglican bishop. He had been in the army there, and a CMS missionary, and knew the area well. Educated at Harrow and Trinity College, Cambridge, he had trained for the ministry at Westcott House, Cambridge, and worked in Peckham in South London. He had married Joy Masterman and been archdeacon in Palestine and principal of the Bishop Gobat School on Mount Zion. He had been rural dean of St. Albans and bishop of Bedford (an assistant in the diocese of St. Albans). He was, therefore, already a bishop when he was appointed to Jerusalem in 1957.

Campbell MacInnes played a key role in developing the diocese as well as encouraging the idea of St. George's College. Arab nationalism, the growth and development of the diocese so far, and the sense of its importance and significance led to the feeling that the Anglican bishop in Jerusalem should be an archbishop. And so, Campbell MacInnes was appointed "Archbishop and Metropolitan." Another development also came to a head at this time. During the Second World War a sense of the indigenous Arab Anglican Church had grown stronger and it was felt that there should be an Arab bishop in the area to lead the local Arab Anglicans. And so, Archbishop MacInnes spearheaded the process of electing the Rev. Najib Cubain as bishop of a new diocese which included Jordan, Lebanon, and Syria. Cubain had been active in the PNCC and was the region's first Arab bishop. Appointed in 1958, he threw himself into the task with energy and enthusiasm. The Anglican Church in the Middle East had been growing and consolidating. The diocese of Iran was founded in 1912, and in 1961 the Rev. Hassan Dehqani-Tafti was consecrated in Jerusalem as the first indigenous Anglican bishop for Iran. Furthermore, MacInnes set up an Episcopal Synod with an eye on developing a stable structure for the Anglican Church in the wider region. From this point onward, the roots of what would later become the province of Jerusalem and the Middle East (1976) can be discerned.[48]

Archbishop MacInnes also sought to develop the idea of a Collegiate Church in Jerusalem as established by Blyth. He elected John Zimmerman, the biblical scholar, as a canon. The two well-known Every brothers also became involved: Edward who lived in Jerusalem, and his twin brother George, a member of SSM, who visited. George was the author of theological books and was very well known. Another significant person at St. George's at this time was Harold Adkins, a keen musician and choir director

48. In 1962 John Zimmerman wrote that, "the diocese became the seat of a province on 8th July 1957, and several dioceses hitherto supervised directly by the Archbishop of Canterbury, were assigned to the new metropolitan." This must be distinguished, however, from the later 1976 province which still exists. See Zimmerman, "Jerusalem Archbishopric," 420.

who was headmaster at St. George's School. He became sub-dean and later dean of St. George's Cathedral. And then there was Kenneth Cragg, already mentioned, who now became more involved.

It is worth following Cragg's contribution in some detail here as he is, in a particular sense, a background "founding father" of St. George's College. From Cragg's time onward, the roots of the later college can be seen growing. Cragg studied in Oxford and was trained for ordination at Tyndale Hall in Bristol.[49] He stood firmly in the Church of England's Evangelical tradition. Having been in Beirut in the 1940s, and Hartford Seminary, Connecticut, in the early 1950s, he was appointed a residentiary canon of St. George's Cathedral in 1956, and given the stall in the cathedral associated with the study and teaching of Islam. He was there three years and developed a series of significant summer schools focusing on Christians living in Islamic contexts. There was a conference in 1956 organized by the Near East Christian Council (NECC), and then further conferences over several years. The conferences sometimes attracted over a hundred participants, including locals. They went from all over the Middle East and were housed at St. George's Guest House, Christ Church, and the Sisters of Zion on the Via Dolorosa in the Old City. Sessions were held in the MacInnes Hall[50] at St. George's, with worship in the cathedral. Trips out to holy places were part of the program. In addition, and at other times, Cragg led short courses in different locations across the Middle East.

Quite early on in all this, *Bible Lands* speculates that Cragg's work "may result in the establishment somewhere in the Middle East of a Muslim Centre or Institute."[51] It was soon hoped that a more formal situation would emerge, and other staff were brought in to help. By 1960, however, Cragg had moved to St. Augustine's College, Canterbury, England, where he continued his work on Islam through organizing similar summer schools. But he maintained his involvement with St. George's. The summer schools in Jerusalem became popular, and gradually the dream of a building became part of the vision. It was at this time that the notion of "St. George's College" started to emerge clearly. During this period, Archbishop MacInnes wrote in *Bible Lands* about the desire for "a centre of theological studies"[52] at St. George's, and of "the building which will be needed."[53]

49. Later part of Trinity College, Bristol.

50. A large hall in St. George's Close, built by and dedicated to Rennie Miles MacInnes, Bishop in Jerusalem (1914–1931).

51. *Bible Lands* 13:12 (Oct. 1956) 176.

52. *Bible Lands* 14:14 (Jan. 1961) 227.

53. *Bible Lands* 14:15 (Apr. 1961) 241.

The idea grew, and by early 1961 Cragg himself, writing of the upcoming summer school in Jerusalem, comments that "it is expected that the 1961 summer venture will be a sort of preliminary canter for the new St. George's College before it begins its own programme proper in the autumn."[54] Cragg's 1961 summer school was called The Care of the Churches and included the Rev. John Wilkinson and Kathleen Kenyon among its speakers. Wilkinson was teaching at St. Augustine's College, Canterbury, and Kenyon was an internationally-known archeologist and director of the British School of Archaeology in Jerusalem. Overall, such summer schools were aimed at locals across a wide area, in addition to others from English-speaking countries. As well as attracting laity, there were opportunities for local and foreign ordination candidates, and refresher courses for clergy. Subjects included Islam, mission, biblical studies, and Christian writing skills, among other things.

Recalling his involvement with the Jerusalem diocese years later, Cragg makes the following comment in one of his many books: "Jerusalem (the Old City, then in Jordan) was always the venue for summer Schools, the first of which convened in July, 1958, to be continued every year until 1967 (After 1959 I shared in them from Canterbury) Some sixty gathered every year from the whole dispersion. Variously housed, they combined some 'pilgrimage' dimension with lively Biblical study, Islamics and Christian theology in tandem."[55] In this recollection, the author shows something of what was going on by the late 1950s and early 1960s, and of what would soon turn into St. George's College.

As the short courses became more and more popular, students of all sorts started to appear. Some might be on their way to other events. A report from an SSJE brother (R. Dalby) tells of a course for participants on their way to a WCC conference held in India in 1961.[56] First, he says, "At the end of 1960 it was announced that an Anglican centre for theological study and research would be set up in Jerusalem during 1961, to be known as St. George's College, whose work would be in some respects similar to that now being done by St. Augustine's College Canterbury, for the whole Anglican Church. The personnel for this College are now in residence at St. George's Hostel, alongside the Anglican Cathedral in Jerusalem, but so far its buildings exist only on paper, with no material embodiment."[57] He then

54. *Bible Lands* 14:15 (Apr. 1961) 242.

55. See Cragg, *Faith and Life*, 122. I am grateful to Malcolm White for drawing my attention to these comments.

56. See *Bible Lands* 14:18 (Jan. 1962) 298–99.

57. *Bible Lands* 14:18 (Jan. 1962) 298.

goes on to describe the course including Edward Every's lectures on the Eastern Churches, following the stations of the cross along the Via Dolorosa, visiting Jericho, Qumran, the Temple Mount in Jerusalem (including the Dome of the Rock and the Al-Aqsa Mosque), Bethesda, the Chapel of Abraham at the Church of the Holy Sepulchre, and other sites. It is clear that Cragg's influence continued as the Anglican institutions in Jerusalem and Canterbury developed in similar fashion. Some of the basic characteristics of the later St. George's College courses can certainly be seen emerging in these summer schools.

As the idea grew, it was realized that more staff would be needed. Archbishop MacInnes writes, "In my view it is no good waiting for buildings and students; we must begin by finding a staff who are prepared to start from scratch." And so he appointed the Rev. Felix Boyse (who had been in Oxford) as principal, in order to give the educational opportunities at St. George's even more solid grounding.[58] *Bible Lands* reports the planning that Boyse and others were doing at this time.

> The principal has thought out a most attractive programme of courses for next year, and copies of this were handed out at the Assembly of the W.C.C. at New Delhi to those who would be interested, and received warm commendation for the provision made for such different types of students. For priest students and ordinands, a semester from January to April and again from October to the end of the year; short courses in February for the clergy of the jurisdiction; in June, for those concerned with Christian writing, translation and literature in the Muslim world; in July, dealing with the Christian in a non-Christian society; in September, a three-week course for Anglican missionaries, the history and archaeology of the Holy Land, and discussion on the changing pattern of missionary activity; and a summer term in August for visiting ordination candidates, on biblical, archaeological and historical questions in the Holy Land, with a survey of the Eastern Churches, their history, liturgies and customs.[59]

We shall meet Felix Boyse again in part 2. Suffice it to say here that plans to develop a college were now really moving forward.

As more and more students showed up in Jerusalem, it was realized that St. George's was a tremendous resource for Anglicans locally and worldwide. The possibilities were enormous and the focal subjects were clear: the

58. *Bible Lands* 14:13 (Oct. 1960) 212; *Bible Lands* 14:14 (Jan. 1961) 227.

59. *Bible Lands* 14:18 (Jan. 1962) 297–98.

Bible and the land, archeology, the local Christians, and the other faiths. As the idea grew and the students continued to arrive, it was felt increasingly that there wasn't enough room. A special building was definitely needed. It would enable more organization, more teaching space, offices and accommodation, and the better management of the entire exercise. Courses would be possible throughout the year and a full staff could be appointed. It was now looking increasingly likely that the vision for a college building at St. George's would be realized.

With significant people around him, Archbishop Campbell MacInnes was able to move the collegial community forward. The building bricks that had been supplied by Bishop Blyth can now be seen moving into place under MacInnes. As we have noted, from the very beginning of the idea of an Anglican bishopric in Jerusalem, there had been a commitment to education. The archbishops of Canterbury had always hoped that there would be some sort of a college in Jerusalem. Archbishop Howley had spoken of this in 1841. It had been Blyth's vision and dream. Interestingly, A. L. Tibawi, writing in 1961, notes that the roots of all that was happening in his time went back to 1841 when Bishop Michael Solomon Alexander sought to establish a college at Christ Church in Jerusalem with five Jewish students.[60] The whole idea now became clearer, as MacInnes saw the need for a more stable educational infrastructure. He had seen this in his days as archdeacon, and he now tried to implement it at various levels in the diocese and in the Cathedral Close. A college was an obvious and now inevitable development.

The story of the physical building of St. George's College and the growth of its staff takes us into part 2 of this book and into the main part of the story. But it is worth glancing back to be reminded of what had already happened by 1960. The seeds had been sown through all the years of establishing the Anglican bishopric, and now some real achievements could be seen. The Protestant bishopric, which had been set up against many odds and in a complex and changing political context, was now realizing one of the key strands of its vision. There had been turbulent relations. There had been clashes of personality and leadership. There had been lives cut short and delays because of war. But, at last, something concrete was happening specifically to bring about a facility that would enable a unique provision for Christian education for Anglicans and others in Jerusalem and the Holy Land. All the bishops so far had been men of learning and education, and had put their individual stamp upon the process. There was still a long way to go, but a great deal had already been achieved.

60. *Bible Lands* 14:15 (Apr. 1961) 242–43.

EXPANDING HORIZONS

Before moving on to tell the story of the appearance of a building for St. George's College and the emergence of more organized courses, however, we will first explore some of the developments that took place in the surrounding context, including the continuing development of the Jerusalem diocese. Even though a building enhanced the college courses from 1962 onward, war struck Jerusalem again later in that decade. As we shall see in part 2, in June 1967 the Israelis occupied East Jerusalem, the Golan Heights, the Gaza Strip, and the Sinai Peninsula. This meant that St. George's College, hitherto under Jordanian rule, was now in territory occupied by Israel. The Israeli occupation of the area has remained unchanged down to the present day and has affected the life of the college ever since, at every level, including its staff and course participants.

Archbishop MacInnes encouraged and inspired all the early staff and leaders. But after the 1967 war it was unclear what would happen next and how things would turn out practically and financially. MacInnes retired in 1968 and returned to England where he became an assistant bishop in the diocese of Salisbury. He died there in 1977 and is buried in the Cathedral Close. He was succeeded by Archbishop George Appleton in 1969.

Appleton was a man of considerable stature.[61] He would draw some important lines in the sand during his time in office in Jerusalem. He took with him a wide and deep experience in the Anglican Church. Born in Windsor, England, in 1902, he was educated at Selwyn College, Cambridge, and St. Augustine's College, Canterbury. He became vicar of St. Botolph's Church, Aldgate, in London and later archdeacon of London and residentiary canon of St. Paul's Cathedral. He spent twenty years in Burma (Myanmar) with USPG, and had important experience in mission. In 1929 he married Marjorie Alice Barrett in Burma. He was later archbishop of Perth in western Australia for four years. In 1968 the archbishop of Canterbury, Michael Ramsey, invited Appleton to be the next Anglican archbishop in Jerusalem with a view to making some significant changes. Appleton accepted and soon set up a commission to look at establishing a proper constitution for all the churches under his care.

We have seen that, during the time of Archbishop Campbell MacInnes, the Anglican Church was growing and developing locally and regionally.

61. His obituary, written by Kenneth Cragg, appeared in the *Guardian* on September 4, 1993. It was reprinted with permission in *Bible Lands*, along with reflections by Hassan Dehqani-Tafti and Edward Every, and an address given by Bishop Samir Kafity at a Service of Thanksgiving at St. George's Cathedral, Jerusalem, on September 17, 1993. See *Bible Lands* 22:8 (Winter 1993) 394–401.

Now, during Appleton's time in Jerusalem, two important changes were agreed in principle. First, that there should be a "province" holding together the Anglican dioceses in the area (now "Jerusalem," "Egypt," and "Jordan, Lebanon, and Syria") and operating under a united synodical government. Second, that the office of Anglican bishop in Jerusalem should be indigenized. These two concerns came to a head and Appleton oversaw a great deal of the legal work involved. The task of implementing the new province on the ground was huge, not least in legal, financial, and practical terms in all the countries concerned. After much negotiation, in 1976 the "province of Jerusalem and the Middle East" was born. It included Jerusalem (now including "Jordan, Lebanon, and Syria"), Egypt, and the diocese of Cyprus and the Gulf (1976).[62] It also included the diocese of Iran. The existing diocese of "Jordan, Lebanon, and Syria" under Bishop Cubain was now closed.

During the establishment of the new structure for the province, politics interrupted again. On the one hand, the October War of 1973 struck in Israel. The Egyptians and the Syrians attacked Israel in an attempt to retake the territory lost to the Arabs in 1967. At stake were the West Bank, the Golan Heights, the Gaza Strip, and the Sinai Peninsula. In the event, this Yom Kippur War (so called because it took place at the time of the Jewish festival of Yom Kippur, or the Day of Atonement) lasted three weeks in October. One of the later outcomes was that Israel gradually withdrew from the Sinai in stages between 1979 and 1982. On the other hand, the war in Cyprus in 1974 resulted in the division of the island, changing the landscape and history of that country. From this time onward Cyprus was divided between Greeks and Turks. Even so, in the general scheme of things, in spite of political upheaval and disruption of life in the wider region, nothing changed significantly for St. George's College as a result of the wars of the early 1970s.

But simultaneously with all this, many locals and expatriates in the Holy Land felt that the Anglican bishop in Jerusalem should be a local Arab. This was encouraged by Archbishop Appleton. As we have seen, the first Arab bishop in the area had been the Rev. Najib Cubain who looked after a separate diocese. Now it was thought that decisions about matters in the diocese of Jerusalem should be made in Jerusalem and not in London or Canterbury. The bishop should be chosen by the local people, from among the local people, for the local people.

During all the discussions led by George Appleton, the Rt. Rev. Robert Wright Stopford, the bishop of London, played a key role representing the archbishop of Canterbury. When Appleton retired in 1974, Stopford was appointed to replace him as "vicar-general" for two years, to oversee

62. See Murray, *Anglican Diocese.*

and implement the final stages of the constitutional revisions and the indigenization of the bishop. Stopford had been bishop of Peterborough as well as of London, and had held a number of educational and secretarial positions. He was well suited to the position in Jerusalem and moved things forward effectively in his short time in office.

When Stopford himself left Jerusalem in 1976 after nearly two years, Faik Ibrahim Haddad became the first Palestinian bishop of the new diocese which included Jerusalem, Israel, and the Palestinian territories, as well as Jordan, Lebanon, and Syria in a new configuration. Bishop Haddad came from Tul-Karem in the West Bank, and had been a student at the Bishop Gobat School in Jerusalem as well as at the Near East School of Theology and the American University in Beirut. He was ordained priest by Bishop Graham Brown in 1940, and provided a good deal of stability through property management and finance. Haddad was consecrated in 1974 but took office in 1976.[63] Married to Sophie, he was bishop until 1984.

During the years that followed and until today, the Anglican bishops in Jerusalem have all been Palestinian Arabs, some from inside Israel and some from the West Bank. There have been five so far, including Faik Haddad. The others are: Samir Hanna Kafity, originally from Haifa in Israel (1984–1998), who was also president bishop of the province and married to Najat; Riah Abu el-Assal (1998–2007), an Israeli Arab who was rector of Nazareth for twenty years before becoming bishop. He was married to Suad. Next, Suheil Salman Dawani (2007–2021), a West Banker from Nablus who transformed the diocesan office buildings in Jerusalem. In 2014 Bishop Dawani was given the title archbishop as a result of a vote in the province that the historical importance of Jerusalem meant that the bishops in Jerusalem should always have that title. He was married to Shafeeqa. Most recently elected (2021) is Hosam Elias Naoum (another Israeli Arab), born in Haifa, who had been dean of St. George's Cathedral for several years (2012–2020).[64] Naoum became primate of the province in 2023. He is married to Rafa. These Palestinian bishops all brought their individual gifts and strengths to the diocese and supported St. George's College in various ways, not the least in their role as chairman of the college foundation, or governing body.

The Anglican diocese of Jerusalem has developed in many different directions over the years under several different leaders and now lies at the

63. It is the usual practice in the diocese of Jerusalem for a new bishop to serve up to two years as a "coadjutor" bishop (i.e., assistant or helper), usually overlapping with his predecessor.

64. Hosam Naoum was consecrated as coadjutor bishop on June 14, 2020 and took office in 2021.

heart of the wider province of Jerusalem and the Middle East.[65] It should be noted that the diocese has always been the immediate context for St. George's College, even though the college's wider reach has gradually become global.

SUMMARY

At the beginning of the nineteenth century there was very little significant British activity in the Middle East. In the first part of this book, we have seen how such activity took root and grew into the establishment of an Anglican diocese and province. Waves of interest, motivated by politics, mission, archeology, and pilgrimage rose to a considerable height as a consulate was established in Jerusalem, and a converted rabbi, Michael Solomon Alexander, was consecrated first Anglican bishop. For a while a partnership was held between England and Prussia, but this was relatively short-lived. Even so, in the early years a series of highly educated and motivated bishops took up the reins and spread the Anglican version of Christianity out into the wider region. They built churches, schools, and hospitals. They taught languages and studied the Bible. They preached the message of the gospel and welcomed converts from surrounding faiths and Christian denominations. Through their vision and hard work, the Anglican Church gradually became established in the Holy Land.

From the beginning there was a strong thread of interest in education in the vision of the Anglicans in Jerusalem, especially in men such as Gobat, Blyth, and Campbell MacInnes who laid the infrastructure for later development. By the middle of the nineteenth century, the Anglicans had built Christ Church in the Old City, and by the end of that century, St. George's Collegiate Church, or Cathedral, north of the city. In the first half of the twentieth century the British took greater control in Palestine under the so-called British Mandate (1917–1947). Eventually, even though significant upheaval changed the political landscape, new dioceses were born and an overall province was created to hold them all together.

In the years following the official inauguration of St. George's College in 1962, it operated within the context so far described in this chapter. But from that time onward, it fell specifically under the guidance of a dean who was responsible for its day-to-day running, the appointment of staff, and

65. On June 29, 2020, the province of Jerusalem and the Middle East was reduced in size when the diocese of Egypt and North Africa left and joined the newly formed Episcopal province of Alexandria, consisting of Egypt, North Africa, Ethiopia, and Gambella.

the operation of courses. The college has, of course, always been under the auspices of the Anglican diocese of Jerusalem and its bishop, and this context must not be forgotten. But from the beginning the bishops delegated leadership to the college deans and their staff.

The focus of the story in part 2 of this book, therefore, turns to our main concern: St. George's College under its deans and staff. We shall see the emergence of its building, the vision of those who established further infrastructure, both physical and intellectual, through a "Comes of Age" project, and the birth of some of its unique courses. We shall also see how the college burst its local and regional boundaries and became an internationally-known institution of the developing worldwide Anglican Communion and global church.

PART 2

Building and Coming of Age

3
Building

SINCE ITS HUMBLE BEGINNINGS as short courses and summer schools, as described in part 1, St. George's College, Jerusalem, has grown into an internationally respected place of pilgrimage and learning, serving the entire Anglican Communion and beyond. Developing its various strands of influence over the years, it has become a unique institution. In addition to its main offering of "study-pilgrimages" to Christians around the world, it also provides retreat and educational opportunities for local Palestinian Christians through the Anglican diocese of Jerusalem. In the first part of this book, we saw something of the background, origins, development, and context of the college, how the vision was born and developed, and how some of the key players worked to bring it all about. Now, in part 2, we take up the story from the building of a special facility in Jerusalem in the early 1960s, down to the completion of its renovation in 1990, and beyond.

Today, the college is a flourishing ecumenical educational institution on a bustling street in East Jerusalem only a few minutes' walk from the Old City. Its current mission statement says, "St. George's College, Jerusalem, is an Anglican community of education, hospitality, pilgrimage, and reconciliation. Through study, site visits, engagement with the local Christian community, prayer and reflection, lives are transformed and faith renewed."[1] The college is a center of pilgrimage and study. Anyone may sign up for its courses. The original subjects still guide the programs: the Bible and the land, the local Christians, and people of other faiths in the area. Visits to archeological sites and holy places are interspersed with study of the Bible and of history. Participants follow in the footsteps of pilgrims who have gone before them over the centuries. Prayer and study are truly

1. From the St. George's College webpage.

ecumenical and many different Christian traditions have been represented. More recently, Jews and Muslims have also taken part. St. George's College courses draw students into multiple layers of experience, awareness, faith, and understanding. No wonder they are often said to be life-transforming.

LAYING THE FOUNDATIONS

Walking into the St. George's College campus in East Jerusalem today, you will find a modern building with modern appliances. It has most of the comforts expected by contemporary Western travelers and pilgrims. The building itself has a fascinating history, and tells the story of the development of the college in the second half of the twentieth century. The original, simple 1960s building was renovated during a "Comes of Age" project stretching throughout the 1980s when another floor was added.

Just outside the door of the dean's apartment, inlaid into the wall of the college, is the St. George's College foundation stone, carved in English and Arabic by the Rev. John Wilkinson in 1962. The inscription reads, "WITH THANKS TO GOD AND PRAYER FOR ST. GEORGE'S COLLEGE BISHOP STEPHEN F. BAYNE LAID THIS CORNER STONE 18 APR. 1962." Wilkinson was skilled in a variety of areas and the stone bears witness to his enormous contribution to everything that the college was to become. It marks a significant turning point in the college's history: the building of a facility in which to house students, staff, and administration, and in which to hold courses and to teach. To mark the progress and to establish the building, a stone-laying ceremony was held on April 18, 1962, in what is now the college car park.[2] The stone was put in position and the new college building was launched. Those present included Archbishop Campbell MacInnes, the Rev. Felix Boyse (first principal), the Rev. John Wilkinson, Mr. John Edwin Simpson (architect), representatives of the various Jerusalem churches, and a great number of local people. Bishop Stephen Bayne, who laid the stone, was the executive officer of the Anglican Communion. It was an immensely exciting time as the new building started to rise and new opportunities were born.

As we have already seen in part 1, during the middle decades of the twentieth century there was a growing sense of the need for a building in which to run courses. During the 1950s, the vision developed into a real hope that this would happen. Then fundraising and prayer had brought Archbishop MacInnes and many others to the point of seeing the operation through. At one stage, it was thought that a college building might be

2. The order of service is in the college archive.

located somewhere else such as Bethlehem, but Jerusalem was the obvious choice. Writing in *Bible Lands* in 1960, eighteen months before the laying of the cornerstone, Bishop Bayne encapsulates the vision as follows:

> For more than 30 years the dream and the hope has stirred in many people's minds that there might be at St. George's, in the heart of the Christian world, in the heart of Christ's world, a centre for study—not merely one more school, but that there might be a unique school which Jerusalem alone makes possible, a place to which might come men and women—clergymen, laymen and laywomen—for the specialized study in Biblical and archaeological history and liturgics, and the oecumenical life of the Churches of the world. That specialized study literally could not be given at the same depth or with the same strength anywhere else in the world. It catches the imagination of every person who has ever spent any thoughtful time in Jerusalem.[3]

Before any building commenced, Archbishop MacInnes appointed a principal for the new college. He chose the Rev. Felix Vivian Allan Boyse from England. Alongside Boyse, he appointed the Rev. John Wilkinson as tutor. Boyse had an interesting career before arriving in Jerusalem, as he continued to have after leaving. He had been vice-principal of the Theological College at Cuddesdon near Oxford in England. Studying first at Corpus Christi College, Cambridge, and training for the ministry at Cuddesdon, he had served a curacy in Derby. After Jerusalem he served in parishes in Southwark and London, and was later preacher at Lincoln's Inn, London, and later still, chaplain at the Royal Hampton Court Palace Chapel in London. Boyse brought administrative skills to the college, as well as academic teaching, and was well equipped to take the new institution through its early stages.

The story of the building of the college is told in stages through fascinating reports in *Bible Lands*, for the years concerned. Having appointed scholars to take care of teaching in the Cathedral Close (Every, Adkins, Zimmerman, and Wilkinson), the archbishop realized how quickly things were growing. In the first years of the 1960s, word spread that the project had been launched. The vision of an Anglican college building in Jerusalem had caught the imagination of many around the world. Now it was becoming a reality. Once a building was up, further educational opportunities would emerge. In October 1960 Archbishop MacInnes writes, "I trust that in the days to come we may not only have students, but also teachers from

3. *Bible Lands* 14:13 (Oct. 1960) 213.

all parts of the Anglican Communion."[4] In July 1961 he writes, "Now that we have the staff, we realize that the present buildings are not going to be adequate."[5] The "present buildings" are the existing cathedral complex.

Of course, the new building was some time in the planning.[6] Funds had to be raised, and there was a huge campaign encouraging those who knew Jerusalem to donate. There was an early appeal for fifty thousand pounds based on costs of about forty thousand pounds, and then more funds to help move forward.[7] In January 1962 the archbishop writes, "The plans have now been worked out in detail and an application has been made to the municipality for a permit to build."[8] He adds, "In the meantime the architect has gone on with all the detailed drawings and specifications, so that the plan may go out to tender with no delay. Bishop Stephen Bayne has accepted the invitation to lay the foundation stone, and it is hoped this can be done on the Wednesday in Holy Week, 18th April, 1962."[9] Fundraising continued throughout the proceedings. By April 1962 the archbishop writes, "The permit to build the college has been received, the plans are complete, the lowest tender accepted, and the contract signed."[10] Progress was spasmodic, but by April 1962 the land to the south of the cathedral had been bought, the groundwork had been mapped out, and work had begun.

Felix Boyse's tenacity in taking the project forward, through thick and thin, is clear. Archbishop MacInnes says, "Undaunted by the delays in receiving the necessary permits to build, Canon Boyse got courses arranged and the College started, notably a much-appreciated short course for delegates passing through Jerusalem on their way to the World Council, entitled 'The Centre of Christendom.' The syllabus of courses for 1962 was widely distributed at New Delhi. Also, Canon Cragg held his annual Summer School in July, on the theme 'The Care of the Churches,' with 57 registered members."[11] The archbishop also says, "The cost is going to be a good deal more than we had expected, and we shall have to depend greatly on the generosity of our friends if the work is to be fully carried out."[12]

4. *Bible Lands* 14:13 (Oct. 1960) 212.

5. *Bible Lands* 14:16 (July 1961) 261.

6. For the wider picture, see *Bible Lands* 14:13 (Oct. 1960) 211–14, which includes Archbishop MacInnes's annual report. See also *Bible Lands* 14:15 (Apr. 1961) 241, on funds coming in.

7. In 2025 this would equal about £1.5 million and approaching $2 million.

8. *Bible Lands* 14:18 (Jan. 1962) 289.

9. *Bible Lands* 14:18 (Jan. 1962) 297.

10. *Bible Lands* 14:19 (Apr. 1962) 308.

11. *Bible Lands* 14:19 (Apr. 1962) 320–21.

12. *Bible Lands* 14:19 (Apr. 1962) 308.

But carried out it was! The new college attracted support from many directions. In December 1962 the archbishop of Canterbury, the Most Rev. Michael Ramsey, wrote in the Diocesan Notes for the diocese of Canterbury, "A new project of great interest to all of us Anglicans is St. George's College in Jerusalem. This offers places for students who would study both the world's religious [*sic*] and the problems of Christian Unity, for Jerusalem is indeed a place of confluence for religious [*sic*] and for diverse Christian traditions. I commend the appeal which St. George's College is making to any parish which will direct part of its giving to a worth-while Anglican enterprise."[13]

Many years later, to mark the fiftieth anniversary of the new building, Boyse wrote the following in the British Regional Committee's news magazine:

> When I was asked by Archbishop McInnes and the Jerusalem and the East Mission to set up St. George's College, in 1961, the challenge was quite considerable. I was then a member of the Southwark Diocesan Missions Committee, and had previously been in the Holy Land, but only as a visitor, so to live and work in the Arab world was a new experience.
>
> At that date the border between Israel and the Hashemite Kingdom of Jordan was very close: in fact, the Anglican school, just across the road from our Cathedral and the site of the College, had its western windows bricked up, as they faced directly into Israel. Normally life was peaceful, but there was only one frontier crossing, which could be used only by tourists (on two passports), United Nations officials, and consular representatives. In all the time I was there, I got a double-crossing permit only once—to sort out a library that had landed up on the wrong side of the border in the previous hostilities. I still have a rifle bullet which struck my flat in the finished college a year or so later, when an "incident" occurred on the border; it might have been fired from Israel, or could have come from a trigger-happy Jordanian soldier.
>
> When I arrived in April 1961 to start things going, there were of course no college buildings; and a lot of discussion had to take place to decide on the precise plans. Until the building was up and functioning, residential courses were not an option, and we lived some distance away near the St. John's Ophthalmic Hospital. Just about a year later, in April 1962, the College was beginning to take shape, and Bishop Stephen Bayne, the Executive Officer of the Anglican Communion, came to lay the

13. *Bible Lands* 15:3 (Jan. 1963) 42.

> foundation stone. The lettering, in English and Arabic, had been skilfully chiselled by the Reverend John Wilkinson, who succeeded me.[14]

Boyse also mentions two other things worthy of note: that four Ethiopians went to the college at the instigation of Emperor Haile Selassie, and that he remembers the pope arriving in Jerusalem—Paul VI's famous visit during the Second Vatican Council in 1964. Boyse left Jerusalem in the same year.[15]

During 1962 and 1963 work on the building continued while courses were held in the close. One course in 1962 included, among others, students from King's College, London, and was entitled a "vacation term." Reporting in *Bible Lands* after what was clearly a formative experience, one of the participants relates his experiences. There were nineteen participants from quite a wide variety of countries. They had gone to St. George's, he says, to take part in the first summer vacation term for ordination candidates to be held at the new college. The building was not complete, however, and they stayed in St. George's School where they were well fed by the matron. They came from a dozen different theological colleges around the world. He writes of the incredible experiences of visiting the holy places and then adds,

> All these experiences were backed up by a great variety of lectures, some given by the staff of the College, others by outside speakers. The Archbishop's dining room was our lecture room, and from outside came the continuous chipping of stone as the Arab builders hastened on with their task of building the new College. While we were there the roof was laid, with much ceremony, and before we left, Canon Boyse was able to show us round the uncompleted building. It was exciting to feel that we were among the first to walk round a building that will, we believe, be of primary importance for Anglicans in the years ahead.[16]

A moment in time is captured in that account of the college building coming into being. *Bible Lands* for October 1962 reports the following: "The College buildings have sprung up rapidly and the whole of the outer shell is now complete. There seems every prospect that the staff will be able to move in by Christmas time, and that we shall be able to accommodate students

14. Felix Boyse, in *St. George's Update* (Jan. 2012), 5, St. George's College archive.

15. He died in 2020 at the age of 102.

16. *Bible Lands* 15:3 (Jan. 1963) 43.

early in the New Year."[17] It continues, "The building is finely placed, and seems to fit in well with its surroundings. St. George's is likely to be in the very centre of the Arab part of the town, for big new Government offices and an office for His Majesty the King are shortly to be built."[18] Things now progressed at speed and *Bible Lands* of January 1963 reports, "The new St. George's College building is now complete, except for a few last touches, and it should be in occupation by the time this letter reaches you."[19] During the building process, workmen had become aware of a Roman cistern under the college grounds. This remained unused until the renovation completed in 1990 when it became the Benshoof Cistern Museum.[20]

On February 25, 1963, the college was dedicated and opened in a ceremony with Archbishop MacInnes presiding. The building consisted of two floors with simple accommodation for thirty-two students. There were communal bathrooms, office space, a common room, and a lecture room with a small library. There was also accommodation for the dean and other staff. In April of the same year, *Bible Lands* reports,

> During the last few days of February there was a meeting of representatives of Theological Colleges of the Middle East, discussing the matter of textbooks. It is the second meeting of this sort which it has been possible to hold in the College. We took the opportunity of our visitors being present to have a short dedication ceremony, and blessing of the rooms now in use. The builders have now removed their hut, and though there is still some tidying-up of the grounds to be done, the work is to all intents and purposes completed and the College in full swing.[21]

As the college building was completed and streams of visitors and students flowed in, further gifts arrived, completing the appeal, as well as books to boost the library. Among those who went to the college at that time were two longer-term residents from Egypt. They stayed a year in training for ordination. One of them was Ghais Abdel Malek, later bishop of Egypt and primate of the province of Jerusalem and the Middle East. The other was Aziz Wasif.

St. George's College, Jerusalem, was finally built, students were attending courses, and it was becoming widely known. The vision had become a

17. *Bible Lands* 15:2 (Oct. 1962) 22–23.

18. *Bible Lands* 15:2 (Oct. 1962) 23. It seems that the area in which the college was to stand was still developing following the 1948 war.

19. *Bible Lands* 15:3 (Jan. 1963) 37.

20. This will be discussed in the next chapter.

21. *Bible Lands* 15:4 (Apr. 1963) 60.

reality. However, by the mid-1960s important questions about the purpose of the college were being asked. MacInnes writes in *Bible Lands* as follows:

> People have often asked me about the College and what exactly it is meant to be. One of the things we have been trying to avoid is calling it a Theological College, even though we trust that a certain amount of theology is taught there. The buildings have often been used as an overflow from the Hostel. Equally the Hostel has often been used as an overflow from the College. We have been able to use the two buildings, especially when there have been important Conferences where we have people to house. Now the intention of the College was partly in order that we might provide a place where ordinands from Arab lands could have a part at least of their training, but one of the things that is sometimes forgotten by people outside is the fact that in the neighboring countries, say, Jordan, Lebanon, Syria and Egypt, there are only 14 Arabic-speaking clergy, and with only 14 in that area the amount required of replacement is naturally very small. Most of the men will go to the University in Beirut for their preliminary training and then after taking their degree will come to St. George's for a year, and we have had men doing that, but the actual numbers at any one time are likely to be very small indeed.
>
> There is, however, another purpose for which the College is intended and that is in order that people from various parts of the world—parts of the Anglican Communion but not necessarily members of the Anglican Communion—may be able to come to take advantage of the many things that Jerusalem has to give . . .[22]

Although there were seminarians, or ordinands, at St. George's, there were never very many. This was not a seminary or theological college as usually imagined in Europe or the US, and its appeal soon started to broaden beyond ministerial training. Clergy were arriving on sabbatical; laity and students from other Christian denominations were participating in courses. And, in general, the trend was in the direction of short courses for mixed takers and conference space offered to a wide variety of people and organizations.

From the beginning, the essential characteristics of St. George's College courses grew out of local opportunities. The college was in Jerusalem and in the land of the Bible. Already the cathedral staff had specialists in biblical languages and archeology, as well as in Judaism and Islam. These

22. *Bible Lands* 16:11 (Summer 1966) 2–4.

areas all naturally became part of an emerging curriculum. The new building had classrooms, as well as accommodation and administrative offices. But a key defining factor, which remains one of St. George's characteristics today, was trips out into the field. Clearly, students didn't go to Jerusalem simply to sit in a classroom or library. The context offered the possibility of fieldwork, of visiting archeological sites, of encountering local Jews, Christians, and Muslims, of forming a traveling community, and of becoming pilgrims focused on prayer and devotion in the holy places. Students were based in Jerusalem but they could travel easily, south to Bethlehem and north to Galilee. The riches of the land were spread out around the college and were waiting to be drawn upon by participants in St. George's courses. The combination of academic study in the classroom with field trips out to archeological sites and prayer in holy places became characteristic of the courses offered at the college.

One interesting feature of college life in the early days is the existence of a college hood. It looks as though the practice was short-lived and quite flexible, but awarding an academic hood was known at St. George's as far back as 1904. Writing in *Bible Lands* in January 1963, Archbishop MacInnes says that the two Egyptian students already mentioned received hoods when they left the college.

> Just before the two ordinands left Jerusalem, I presented them with certificates and vested each with the hood of an Associate of St. George's. The first reference to this we have found is in our records of 1904, when there appeared a list of Associates of St. George's College who were entitled to wear a black hood with white lining and a red band on the edge. We have not been able to find much information about the Associates of St. George's College, apart from knowing that Bishop Blyth created this honour which was to be given to Arab clergy and others, including laymen, who served within the Jerusalem Bishopric. No new Associates have been appointed since 1914, but I am now proposing to renew the practice of making such appointments and to give the right to wear the hood of an Associate of the College to those who have completed a full course of study and are working within the Jerusalem Archbishopric. It may also on occasion be given to those who have served here faithfully, even if they have not actually studied in the College.[23]

Clearly this practice began long before the college building appeared, and there is no further evidence of the hood. However, its revival in the

23. *Bible Lands* 15:3 (Jan. 1963) 38–39.

early 1960s shows Archbishop MacInnes's commitment to marking a good standard of education once the new college building was up and running.

SHIFTING SANDS

In the early years, with the help of Felix Boyse, John Wilkinson began to craft courses that would later become the staple diet of the college. He laid down tracks, including all the elements that were to become his life's work. He was, without doubt, the right person in the right place at the right time. But more than that, he personally embodied what was needed at the time. The combination of study and pilgrimage, and the careful crafting of the main course, The Palestine of Jesus, were John's doing. He was essentially the architect of the courses, and over the early years his basic ideas were tried and tested. However, once the building had been constructed, there was inevitably a sense of completion and new beginnings, and in 1963 Wilkinson was appointed editorial secretary of the Society for the Propagation of the Gospel (SPG, and soon to be the United Society, USPG) in London. He left Jerusalem, with St. George's College in the hands of Felix Boyse, and returned to England. But Boyse himself left in 1964 and the college entered an uncertain period without a dean. With the help of cathedral staff (the Rev. John Zimmerman and the Rev. Clive Handford), Archbishop MacInnes oversaw the college but there were fewer courses and it was unclear what would happen next.

There were always questions about what the college would become and how it would be managed. There were numerous aspirations and speculations. But the departure of Wilkinson and Boyse reconfigured those questions. Who would be the new leader?[24] Where would students come from? And how would the college be managed and funded? St. George's College needed a constitution and a governing body. It needed to sort out where it stood legally, and in which country a governing body would be based. In fact, already in the early years of the college's life there was a discussion about the need for a constitution. And early on, an International Governing Body or Advisory Council was established under Archbishop MacInnes. It included faculty members of the Theology Department at King's College, London, and was chaired by the well-known dean of King's, the Rev. Canon Sydney Evans. The hope was to draw on the wisdom and experience of an

24. During this period, it was hoped by some that Sherman Johnson of CDSP (the Church Divinity School of the Pacific in Berkeley, California) would become the next dean of St. George's College but he declined. Johnson was a New Testament scholar who knew the Holy Land well. See Johnson, *Jesus and His Towns*.

international group that would hold responsibility for the college as efforts to establish its formal and legal side were made.

MacInnes and the staff also soon realized that more teaching space and rooms would probably be needed if the college was to become what everyone hoped in the future. More rooms were planned, and even the idea of another floor was discussed. From early on, St. George's was compared with local institutions such as the École Biblique and the American School of Oriental Research (now the Albright Institute). The hope was to complement rather than compete with them. Nor must we forget that following the visit of Pope Paul VI to the Holy Land in 1964, and at his suggestion, the Roman Catholic Church set up the Ecumenical Institute for Theological Research at Tantur near Bethlehem. Usually known simply as "Tantur," this institute was originally intended to attract individual scholars to do research. There was much concern on the part of St. George's College not to overlap with Tantur, much hope to work with the newly established institute, and much aspiration to establish good ecumenical relations all around. Another new institution in the region spurred the sense of global development at St. George's.

Questions of identity and direction at St. George's naturally continued, and it is clear from correspondence in the St. George's College archive that there was a growing sense of wanting to serve the whole Anglican Communion. Views emerged from both sides of the Atlantic about the college's purpose. Staff were needed; courses would be offered for clergy and laity on sabbatical. There was a growing sense that the college could be useful to those training to be teachers as well as to seminarians. Subjects would include the Bible, archeology, liturgy, local Christians, and other faiths. There were clearly challenges ahead but much hope and optimism as well. However, as discussions progressed and hopes soared, a catastrophic event occurred, sending the college's future into a spin. Without much notice, the cathedral and college staff, along with everyone in the region, suddenly became embroiled in the Six Day War of June 5 to 10, 1967.

It is worth understanding the background here. After the establishment of the state of Israel in 1948, regional tensions between Israel and the Arab countries had built up and were coming to a head. The presence of the state of Israel in the region had inevitably caused a good deal of friction with local Arab countries, not the least with the Palestinians. Following the Suez Crisis in 1956, relations between Israel and the surrounding nations deteriorated. As tensions grew, there were military threats and the assembling of troops and aircraft. In the event, Israel struck first at Egypt triggering a series of military events that saw Israel defeating Egypt, Jordan, and Syria. In a short time, Israel had defeated the three surrounding nations, occupying the Golan Heights, the West Bank, the Gaza Strip, and the Sinai Peninsula—and increasing its land size by about a third. Some three hundred fifty thousand Palestinians were displaced. West Bank residents were effectively rendered stateless.

The main outcome of the 1967 war for St. George's was that East Jerusalem ended up in territory occupied by Israel, leaving the cathedral and college not now in Jordan, as it had been since 1948, but in the Israeli-occupied West Bank. Until 1967, students and pilgrims going to the Holy Land and to St. George's Cathedral and College flew to Amman, Jordan, and went across the River Jordan to Jerusalem. Having visited the holy places in the Old City of Jerusalem, they would pass through the famous Mandelbaum Gate into Israel, and visit Galilee before flying out of Tel Aviv. In 1967 the college moved into occupied territory without shifting an inch! Travel became more difficult, movement was impeded, and, although the Mandelbaum Gate was demolished and the Israelis proclaimed a reunited Jerusalem, the country was again in turmoil and the city divided. At St. George's College, there was confusion and uncertainty about what would happen next.

As it turned out, the college closed its doors for over a year. *Bible Lands* indicates that this ran from May 1967 until April 1968. But it is also clear that reopening was partial and in stages, stretching well into 1969.[25] Some courses did run, and the building was used spasmodically and for a variety of other purposes too. But in an extremely trying and difficult period, staff were left wondering what the future might hold. Things were not returning to normal and the situation dragged on. Would the college survive? Following the departures of Wilkinson and Boyse, Archbishop MacInnes had overseen the college for several years. He kept a cool head during the events of 1967, and saw the war out in Jerusalem, but in 1968 he retired and returned to England.

In 1969, however, a new Anglican archbishop arrived and stayed five years: George Appleton who, as we have seen in part 1, was a man of noteworthy stature and experience. Obstacles were overcome and an exciting new chapter began. Also in 1969, John Wilkinson returned for six years. Following the war, therefore, it was Appleton and Wilkinson who spearheaded the reopening of the college. After a period of considerable uncertainty and fear about the future, hopes and aspirations were reignited and life at St. George's was soon up and running again.[26]

25. *Bible Lands* 17:3 (Summer 1968) 70–71; *Bible Lands* 17:8 (Autumn 1969) 243–44.

26. *Bible Lands* 17:11 (Summer 1970) 337.

FOUNDING FATHERS

Over the twenty-five-year period following the 1967 war, three men played key roles in developing St. George's College: John Wilkinson, Gilbert Sinden, and John Peterson. As we have seen, Wilkinson had already been on staff and had carved the foundation stone. He returned in the late 1960s to expand and develop courses. In fact, he consolidated the academic infrastructure that still gives St. George's College its unique identity today. Sinden was a British academic monk who became an Australian citizen and moved to Jerusalem for ten years. He developed the courses, reinforcing Wilkinson's combination of academic study and pilgrimage spirituality. Peterson was an American archeologist-priest who raised funds for a new floor on the college building, providing new facilities and possibilities all around. In this section we trace the backgrounds of these three important men, illustrating their specific contributions to the college's unique life and development during the next years.

John Wilkinson

John Wilkinson's years at St. George's College fall into two phases: the first was 1961–1963 under Archbishop MacInnes and with the Rev. Felix Boyse, when John helped establish the college and its courses through its first building. The second was 1969–1975, when he returned to Jerusalem under Archbishop George Appleton and consolidated what he had begun earlier. As we shall see, his contributions were varied. There are three areas in particular: first, his academic work and its impact on college courses; second, his design of a college logo; and, third, his work on the structure of the college including establishing a constitution, a governing body, and three regional committees.[27] Legal and financial matters also fall under this. First, John's return to the college and his academic contribution.

Archbishop Appleton was a wise and experienced man with an eye open to international concerns in the church. He could see that St. George's College could become a significant center of learning for the whole Anglican Communion and soon decided he would reopen its doors. His vision was inspired, and the wheels soon began to turn—especially when John Wilkinson wrote to Appleton in 1969 offering to help the college. Many years later (2012), reflecting on this time, Wilkinson wrote,

> A fortnight after I resigned from being Tutor of St. George's College I thought over what I had done. I determined to go back.

27. On the regional committees, see part 3, chapter 5, and appendix C.

My next job was with USPG. I was editorial secretary. I had to write a book a year under the experts on each region, who I must say dealt forgivingly with my mistakes. As a completely unexpected result of my work I came to know a great many Anglican bishops with dioceses outside the British Isles. I used my spare time to translate Egeria's Travels, an account by a pilgrim who had spent three years in Jerusalem, from 381 to 384.

There was a new Archbishop in Jerusalem, George Appleton, whom I knew slightly. He responded to a letter of mine by asking to see me. He suggested that I become head of St. George's College and I suggested that I should have a tour of the bishops I happened to know through USPG, in order for them to tell me what they would expect from the College, and for me to speak to them about my hopes. The year was 1969. So I missed the Israeli takeover of Jerusalem.

When I had done my tour of the Anglican Bishops I went back to Jerusalem. A great disadvantage was the overwhelming consciousness of the other staff of the recent invasion by Israel. Not having been through the war, I decided to treat the Arabs, whom I had known for a long time, and the Jewish newcomers on a purely humanitarian system—if they were annoying to me, I would blame them.

I had been a theological teacher before, but teaching politics was completely new to me. It was important for the students to make up their own minds. So they heard independent speeches by Jews and Arabs. Otherwise the courses were based on the exploration of biblical sites and the experience of different liturgies. Gradually this system formed into a manageable pattern. We had a long three-month course for clergy, for which we relied on scholarship money from abroad. I cannot speak too highly of Sam Van Culin, who guided me through these managerial challenges on his occasional visits from New York, nor of Ronald Metz, on the Archbishop's staff. I was joined later on by Ted Todd as tutor, who learned modern Hebrew, and later succeeded me as the head of the college.

The times were not always peaceful, and some of the courses had to be canceled. During these times I wrote *Jerusalem Pilgrims Before the Crusades*, with the invaluable help of the library of the École Biblique. It was just down the road, so should there be any emergency I could get back to the College. The short courses continued, and I specially remember the one from King's College London and an ecumenical clergy course under Norman Goodall, that seasoned ecumenist.

> The time came when I had supervised thirty short courses, and felt it was time to do something else. Looking back on my time in Jerusalem I had concentrated on teaching. I should have spent more time on making the building a better place to live in. But this was the destiny of the person who succeeded Ted Todd as Head, Canon John Peterson.[28]

This passage from John Wilkinson himself tells us something of the story of his involvement with the college following his return in 1969. His earlier years had concentrated on the building, and there were fewer courses then in comparison with later. But John turned out to be the chief architect of the courses during the first half of the 1970s. We turn now, therefore, to consider his life and interests, and especially his books, all of which reveal a great deal about the man and his work, as well as about course content at the college during those years.

John Donald Wilkinson was born in Wimbledon in 1929 and went to the Dragon School in Oxford and Haileybury College in Hertfordshire before national service in Malaya, and then Merton College, Oxford, where he read classics. His father was vice-principal of Cheshunt Theological College in Cambridge, England, and his mother was the daughter of a clergyman. John was all set to go into the church, and indeed trained for the priesthood at Cuddesdon Theological College near Oxford before serving a curacy at St. Dunstan's and All Saints' Stepney in London. By 1959 he had received an LTh (licentiate of theology) degree from the University of Louvain in Belgium. He was on the road to an academic career, and, as his interest in history and theology developed, he became fascinated by the Middle East and the lands of the Bible. After a short period teaching at Ely Theological College and at St. Augustine's College, Canterbury, he went to Jerusalem in 1961 as tutor at St. George's College under Felix Boyse. During this first period in Jerusalem, John wrote several books including two short works entitled *Jerusalem Prayers* and *The Stations of the Cross in Jerusalem*.[29] Both combined pilgrim devotion with some historical-critical questions.

As we have already seen, John's first stretch on the staff of the college was short. But it is clear from those early days that he had many skills, all held together by an amazing attention to detail. His later literary output shows that he was not only a keen biblical scholar and theologian but also had skills in cartography, calligraphy, and carving. During these years, he

28. John Wilkinson, in *St. George's Update* (Jan. 2012), 6, St. George's College archive.

29. See Wilkinson, *Jerusalem Prayers*; *Stations*. Both were printed by the Commercial Press in Jerusalem.

was busy working on the connections between biblical texts and archeological sites in the Holy Land, and exciting students with the unique adventure of pilgrimage and study. His life was colorful in other ways too. During the 1950s he had met Alexandra Helen MacFarlane, an archeologist digging at Jericho with Kathleen Kenyon for the British School of Archaeology in Jerusalem. In 1966, after he had returned to England, he married Alix (as she was always known) at St. Bride's Church, Fleet Street, in London. They became a well-known couple at home and in the Middle East. Alix later wrote books on Egyptian jewelry and gardens, and traveled extensively. In 1968 John edited *Catholic Anglicans Today*, a collection of essays written by leading Catholics in the Church of England at the time.[30] This and other works written during the 1960s reflect some of his wide interests and something of his good standing in the Church of England.

The letter to Bishop Appleton, quoted above, resulted in John and Alix moving to Jerusalem when the college reopened in 1969 following the war.[31] John was known as "dean of studies" (the new name of the job).[32] In the following years, he was assisted by the Rev. Edward (Ted) Todd (course director), the Rev. Edward Every and the Rev. Peter Schneider (lecturers), and the Rev. Ronald Metz (administrator). A tutor from Ceylon (Sri Lanka), the Rev. Canon Victor Satthianadhan, also helped.[33] In addition to responsibilities in the Holy Land itself, John traveled a great deal to find out what the college could offer the Anglican Communion. In Jerusalem, he immersed himself once again in the task of exploring the Holy Land in relation to biblical texts with students attending courses. By the time he got going, major developments in archeology were taking place all around him. John commented that he was glad he had missed the 1967 war as it enabled him to keep a neutral stance on local political issues. The reality was, of course, that when he got back to St. George's, the situation had changed radically and he soon became embroiled in the new political tensions. The college was now in a divided city with East Jerusalem under Israeli military occupation. The lives of local staff and visiting pilgrims were all inevitably affected.

John Wilkinson was a very productive man and the political unrest around him was no deterrent to his academic work. A closer look at his

30. See Wilkinson, *Catholic Anglicans*. He also wrote *No Apology*, *Interpretation and Community*, and *The Supper and the Eucharist* during this period.

31. See the announcement in *Bible Lands* 17:8 (Autumn 1969) 256.

32. Although Felix Boyse was the first principal, John's new title means that he is still often referred to as "the first dean."

33. Listed in the 1972–1973 course brochure in the college archive. See also *Bible Lands* 17:11 (Summer 1970) 337.

literary output shows not only what his own interests were but also how these formed the layers of the college's courses through his planning and teaching. By the time he returned to Jerusalem, John had written several more books, mostly reflecting teaching material he had used in St. George's courses before. His interests spread widely across church history, liturgy, biblical and other texts, and archeological sites. In 1971, when he had been back in Jerusalem about two years, he published the book for which he is mostly remembered today: *Egeria's Travels*.[34] As we have already noted, this text is the travel diary of a lady from Europe who visited the Holy Land and the holy places at the end of the fourth century. John's translation with an introduction and notes became widely known, and with it, St. George's College. Once published, the book gave John an academic credibility that helped launch the college into another phase of its development. The book was, of course, on St. George's reading lists and Egeria's own practice of traveling, visiting sites and holy places, reading Scripture, and praying has provided a model for St. George's pilgrims ever since.

Wilkinson's interest in pilgrims to the Holy Land continued beyond Egeria and the fourth century. Another book, published in 1977 but worked on during his time as dean in Jerusalem, was *Jerusalem Pilgrims Before the Crusades*.[35] This consisted of a collection of eighteen texts left behind by pilgrims who had visited Jerusalem and the Holy Land before the Crusades. The texts themselves are fascinating as, like Egeria, they tell us what the pilgrims saw in key places during their visits to the Holy Land. Included are writers such as Jerome, Procopius of Caesarea, the famous "Piacenza Pilgrim," Sophronius of Jerusalem, Adomnan, Epiphanius the Monk, and other pilgrims. In typical Wilkinson style, the book includes maps and plans as well as a gazetteer, or glossary, of the numerous place-names mentioned. The book draws its readers into the development of pilgrimage through introductory discussions of the sites and holy places across the Holy Land, Egypt, and beyond.

Wilkinson also considers realities on the ground, including travel. There are details about roads, illustrated by his own maps, as well as identifying the many locations. People traveled by road, on foot, horseback, carriage, and cart. John discusses conditions and hospices as well as the development of itineraries, guides, and guidebooks. Pilgrims encountered numerous animals along the way including lions, leopards, and gazelles. On the Nile and Red Sea, of course, pilgrims traveled by boat. But more important is John's work on pilgrims themselves, their motivations, their

34. See Wilkinson, *Egeria*.

35. Wilkinson, *Jerusalem Pilgrims*.

practices. They went to the Holy Land seeking perfection in their spiritual lives, offering devotion and penitence. They went not out of mere curiosity but wanting to see and touch the places that had played a part in their savior's life, death, and resurrection. They went to pray and to find healing. This heightened sense of devotion often resulted in pilgrims kissing holy places and holy things. The first millennium saw the development of relics in Christianity, and pilgrims often took offerings with them to leave in the holy places, as well as taking things away with them when they left.

Jerusalem Pilgrims Before the Crusades, therefore, continues the interests laid down in *Egeria's Travels*. Both books illustrate a great deal about the emergence and development of Christian pilgrimage to the Holy Land. John takes his interests further still in *Jerusalem Pilgrimage 1099–1185*, which deals with pilgrims during the new burst of Christian interest in the Holy Land during the Crusader period.[36] Published in 1988, this book was written after John left the college but again reflects work done previously during his time in Jerusalem. In this work, he includes the texts of Saewulf, Daniel the Abbot, Peter the Deacon, Theodoric, and John Phocas, among others.

The courses at St. George's were pilgrimage courses entailing prayer, study, and reflection. Like their forebears in previous centuries, pilgrims in the twentieth century were still traveling to the Holy Land to see and touch the holy places, along with performing rituals of devotion and penitence. However, the difference between ancient and modern pilgrims is that modern pilgrims have historical-critical minds which seek objective truth about places and yet also want to pray in them. The practice and study of pilgrimage—reading texts, visiting sites, as well as reflecting and praying—became fundamental to St. George's College courses as conceived by John Wilkinson.

But another development is important, too. We have seen in part 1 that archeology played its part in the British presence in the Middle East from the beginning. The story of Edward Robinson and Eli Smith was told in the opening chapter. Following their travels, many locations were identified and excavations carried out. Many Old and New Testament sites became well known. Following the 1948 war, Israeli archeologists continued excavating. After the 1967 war, however, archeology in the Holy Land took a dramatically new turn, especially in Jerusalem. Although there had been exploration of Jerusalem's Old City from the nineteenth century onward, there had not yet been systematic excavation. Now, with the occupation of East Jerusalem, Israeli archeologists turned to the Old City and Temple

36. Wilkinson, *Jerusalem Pilgrimage 1099–1185*.

Mount in particular. When the 1967 war ended, archeological excavation in the Old City grew apace with the eventual uncovering of the entire region around the Temple Mount. Of course, the Israelis had modern resources on their side as well as funding and political motivation.

With significant archeological developments taking place around him during this period, Wilkinson, as dean of studies at St. George's, was well placed to incorporate many of the new discoveries into his work as he traveled around Jerusalem with his students. It was an exciting time in archeology, and as the many layers of Jerusalem's history were uncovered, new dimensions of the world of Jesus and the early Christians started to appear.

Another important book by John Wilkinson is *Jerusalem as Jesus Knew It: Archaeology as Evidence*.[37] This contains further material used at St. George's during these years. The book eventually got onto all the St. George's College reading lists. It should be seen against the broader background of scholarly development at the time. The "quest for the historical Jesus" had started with Albert Schweitzer in the nineteenth century.[38] Further waves of the quest stretched across the twentieth century.[39] In the early 1960s, Joachim Jeremias had published *Jerusalem in the Time of Jesus*, focusing on the social world of Jesus in first-century Jerusalem.[40] In 1973, while Wilkinson was in Jerusalem, Geza Vermes, the famous Dead Sea Scrolls scholar, published *Jesus the Jew*, which is now acknowledged as a classic in Jesus studies.[41] These books focused on the world of Jesus and on the Judaism of his day, but key archeological developments in Jerusalem itself were only just unfolding. Source and form criticism in Europe had little interest in archeology. Wilkinson was in a prime position, living in Jerusalem, to begin to work on the background to the Gospels, incorporating the most recent archeological developments in the city. Encouraged by the Dominican fathers of the École Biblique, who were leaders in biblical archeology, John was a lone Anglican in the field.

Jerusalem as Jesus Knew It takes readers through the Gospel outline of Jesus' life, death, and resurrection, introducing key places mostly in and around Jerusalem. It begins with the lay of the land, introducing matters of climate, soil, history, and social setting. Readers are introduced to the various Herods of Jesus' time and developments following the death of Herod

37. Wilkinson, *Jerusalem as Jesus Knew It*. Published in the US in 1983 as *The Jerusalem Jesus Knew*.

38. See Schweitzer, *Quest*.

39. For a useful account of the various "quests" for the historical Jesus, see Bond, *Historical Jesus*.

40. Jeremias, *Jerusalem*.

41. Vermes, *Jesus the Jew*.

the Great. This sets the contextual and political scene for the study of Jesus in Jerusalem. The Jerusalem temple is, of course, central, and various New Testament narratives related to the temple are examined: the presentation in the temple, Jesus' teaching in the temple, the temptations of Jesus (with the devil taking him to the pinnacle of the temple), and Jesus going to Jerusalem for the Jewish festivals. Texts from the Gospels are linked with places in the land. Five further expositions take the reader through Bethesda, Siloam, the raising of Lazarus at Bethany, Jesus entering the city on Palm Sunday, and the so-called cleansing of the temple. All the related archeological sites and the work going on at them during the early 1970s are brought into the discussion.

Another chapter moves on in the same style to the last days of Jesus' life with the study of texts relating to the Last Supper, Gethsemane, the trials of Jesus, the way of the cross, the crucifixion, and the resurrection. Again, the places are key: Mount Zion, the Cenacle, and David's Tomb (thinking of the Last Supper and Pentecost); the Garden of Gethsemane (thinking of the arrest of Jesus); the Church of St. Peter in Gallicantu on Jerusalem's southern slope (the possible house of Caiaphas); and the Antonia Fortress, or Herod's Palace (with the debate about where Pilate tried Jesus). John was already aware of the continuing debate among pilgrims and scholars about the real route of the stations of the cross. Places relating to the resurrection appearances and the ascension are also discussed in relation to Gospel texts. The various Emmaus sites and the Imbomon, or Chapel of the Ascension, on the Mount of Olives are all treated.

Concerning Jesus' last days in Jerusalem, the grueling horrors of crucifixion, as well as the different types of tombs in which Jews were buried at the time, are discussed. The methods and politics of crucifixion are covered—for example, the *kokh* or "oven" niches and *arcosolium* shelves for burial are described, giving a vivid sense of the reality of these events, and the history of Golgotha and the different tomb types are discussed—all with examples and illustrations from Jerusalem's landscape. The final chapter introduces the Church of the Holy Sepulcher, showing how an original quarry area developed from containing tombs to becoming a glorious Byzantine church built by Constantine the Great in the fourth century. At the end of the book, crucial questions about the relation between science, history, and faith are raised. There are also maps, charts, and pictures of the places as they were in John's day. In the chapter on Christ's tomb there are pictures of John's own models of the Church of the Holy Sepulcher, showing how it began and developed.

All in all, *Jerusalem as Jesus Knew It* combines historical matters with the story of Jesus from the New Testament and archeological data as it was emerging from contemporary digs in John's own day. Whether reading the book or listening to John in St. George's courses, students would be drawn into an ethos of study that incorporates serious historical investigation as well as a sensitivity to issues of faith and belief. There is a real sense of the historical setting of the events of Jesus' life—absent from a reading of the Gospels themselves. But questions of authenticity also arise. Are the places identified by Christians over the centuries the actual places where things happened, and how do we know? Students reading the book or listening to John in courses would indeed follow in the "footsteps of Jesus," but they would do so with a serious eye on history and archeology. In college courses, students would visit a site in order to see the setting of a biblical text. They would read the text and hear an exposition as well as something of the history of the place. They would then pray at the site or near it, very much in the style of Egeria and the pilgrims who had visited the land through the centuries. John's academic work in the books mentioned reflects the course content and ethos of the college during the 1960s and 1970s. Course participants, led by John himself, were pilgrims with a sharp historical-critical awareness, and an eye on what was going on in the city and land around them as they traveled.

John Wilkinson's contribution to the growth and development of St. George's College stretched well beyond his literary output. The second area mentioned above is his creation of a college logo, which is still in use today. His interest in the Church of the Holy Sepulcher led him to investigate what the original fourth-century tomb looked like. It was probably destroyed entirely by the Caliph Hakim in 1009, so nothing remains today. But John was aware that pilgrims to the Holy Land from the fourth century onward were given small metal or glass flasks, or ampullae, containing oil and bearing small images of the holy places such as Jerusalem or Bethlehem. Pilgrims took these flasks home with them to Europe. In the early seventh century some such flasks arrived in Monza, Italy, where they are still in the cathedral. They bear varying images of Constantine's aedicula, or tomb, of Christ. Others, probably from the same period, were found in the twentieth century in nearby Bobbio.[42]

It is now clear that John chose one of these as the basis of his St. George's College logo. The image depicts a small hexagonal enclosure with pillars surrounding an area where the tomb would have stood. John took this aedicula and adopted it as the college's logo.[43] In the simple image, he

42. See Barag and Wilkinson, "Monza-Bobbio."

43. I am grateful to Rodney Aist for confirming that Monza ampulla 9 includes the image John used.

connected the college with the empty tomb of Christ and thus with the resurrection itself. The image brings together perfectly the college's focus on pilgrimage, archeology, history, liturgy, faith, and devotion. Contained within a circular border bearing the words "St. George's College Jerusalem," the logo appears on college notepaper and other merchandise, and was incorporated into the college gate during the 1990 "Comes of Age" campaign. It is also on the front of this book. The logo is a superb example of John's creative insight and originality.

We know from his letter to Bishop Appleton quoted earlier that John traveled a good deal on behalf of the college, and, indeed, such travel became a feature of the job description of all future deans. It was in the context of this travel that the idea of the regional committees of the college first came about. There was also a growing need during John's second period at the college to address questions about a constitution and a governing body, as well as legal and financial matters. John did a considerable amount in the early 1970s toward setting all this up. A discussion of this third area of John's expertise will appear in part 3, chapter 5, under "Committees."

John Wilkinson left Jerusalem in 1975 after six busy years at the college. He returned to London where he became the bishop of London's director of clergy training. He had been a canon of St. George's Cathedral, Jerusalem (1973–1975), and continued to support the college in numerous ways in the following years. He later returned to Jerusalem as director of the British School of Archaeology (1979–1984), and later still was awarded a PhD by the Courtauld Institute of Art and the University of London for his work on ancient synagogues and churches (1982).[44] Alix died in 2011, and John married Mzia Ebanoidze in the same year. His enthusiastic interest in Jerusalem, and especially St. George's College, continued throughout his retirement. He died in London in 2018, aged eighty-eight.[45]

While Wilkinson was dean of studies during the first half of the 1970s, a young graduate student called Clare Birch (later Amos) arrived in Jerusalem from England to do academic study at the École Biblique. She had been a theological student in Cambridge and went to Jerusalem to do postgraduate biblical study. She arrived just as the 1973 Yom Kippur War was breaking out, and stayed until the summer of 1975. During her time in Jerusalem, she was invited to dinner at St. George's College one evening by John and Alix Wilkinson. As a result, she soon got to know the college and its courses. After pursuing her studies at the École for two years she

44. This was published in 2002. See Wilkinson, *From Synagogue to Church.*

45. I officiated at his funeral service at Christ Church, Kensington, in London, on February 16, 2018. See his obituary in *Bible Lands* (Summer 2018) 17.

returned to England, though not before being offered a job at the college by the director of studies, the Rev. Edward (Ted) P. Todd. The position was secured in the summer of 1975, and Clare returned to Jerusalem to take it up in November that year.

Ted Todd was an Episcopal priest from the US who had trained at the General Theological Seminary in New York and served a curacy in Maine. While at the General Seminary in 1971, he attended a course at St. George's College and fell in love with the Holy Land. He was eager to get back to Jerusalem and was subsequently offered the job of course director. Traveling by boat from New York to Haifa, and accompanied by his wife Jane and their two children, Ted took up the position in 1972. He was a missioner of the Episcopal Church in the USA. While teaching a college course in 1973, the Yom Kippur War broke out. Ted recalls the panic of course participants and the cancelation of the course.[46] The program of courses resumed the following year. After John Wilkinson left the college in 1975, Ted became dean.

Ted and Clare worked well together in the mid-1970s. Clare was supported by CMS. She was twenty-three years old, and was to stay at the college until January 1978 when she married Alan Amos, then Anglican chaplain in Beirut. They moved to Beirut where Clare worked with the Middle East Council of Churches (MECC) and later with the Near East School of Theology (NEST). As dean of the college, Ted continued John Wilkinson's commitment to academic teaching and administration, and, with Clare's help, developed and expanded the college program. At this time, courses focusing on liturgy, especially the Holy Week and Easter liturgies of the Eastern Churches, held at the time of Eastern Easter, entered the college curriculum.

It was during this period that the ten-week course entitled The Bible and the Holy Land: Past and Present, started by John Wilkinson, was consolidated. Clare had expertise in both the Old and the New Testaments and also developed her interests in the book of Enoch. In addition, she encouraged college excursions to the desert. The ten-week course saw some of the earliest trips to the Sinai with the Israeli guide Ora Lipschitz. Another course called The Palestine of Jesus was already established and formed the staple diet of the college. As with all the courses, flexibility was key and meant that lectures and field trips of different types could be fitted in under the course title to suit different needs and changing lecturers. The absence of any syllabus or specific curriculum meant that courses could evolve and move in different directions at any time to suit changing needs and

46. In private conversation.

interests. This element could be both a strength and a weakness in college courses over the years but it always gave opportunity for creative teaching and varied group experience.

Reflecting on her years at the college, Clare recalls how she developed visits around a lecture entitled "Re-Acting to the Romans."[47] The lecture focused on possible reactions to Roman occupation of the land during the time of Jesus, including zealous support, radical opposition, and avoidance of both—which usually ended in death! This latter is what happened to Jesus. Visits using this theme were to places such as the Herodion near Bethlehem and Masada near the Dead Sea. It all helped fill out the political picture surrounding the life of Jesus. The courses usually went to Galilee for two or three nights and stayed in Nazareth with the Sisters of Nazareth, in Tiberias at the Scottish Hospice, or in a hotel in Safed farther east and home of Jewish mysticism. Courses also stayed on Mount Tabor on occasion with the Franciscans. Clare remembers using photographs taken by a British medical doctor who was living in Jerusalem at the time, Richard Cleave. He provided the college with visual aids for teaching. There were also some interesting visiting lecturers during this time including Kenneth Cragg, who continued his connections with Jerusalem, and John Robinson, the controversial New Testament scholar and bishop of Woolwich in London. Robinson was author of the controversial *Honest to God* and was known widely for his support of D. H. Lawrence's novel *Lady Chatterley's Lover*.[48] Robinson had taught Clare in Cambridge, and now took his expertise as a New Testament scholar and theologian to Jerusalem. Local academics in the Holy Land were also used to enhance college courses.

During this time, as always, students at the college came mostly from the US, although World Council of Churches grants enabled others, usually from the third world, to benefit from the experience of time in Jerusalem. There were seminarians from Virginia Theological Seminary (VTS)[49] and Nashotah House, both in the US.

These years formed the heyday of the college's life in its new building. But the accommodation was limited with just two floors. There was a small library in the Cathedral Close near St. George's Cathedral Guest House, or Hostel, where course members ate. The college's registrar and executive secretary, Helen Assad, served for many years,[50] as did the finance officer,

47. In private conversation.

48. See Robinson, *Honest to God*; Lawrence, *Lady Chatterley's Lover*.

49. The relationship with VTS grew in later years and became formalized following discussions during the first decade of the new millennium. The seminary has offered the college financial support and taken students to the college on an annual basis.

50. See her obituary in *Bible Lands* 21:8 (Winter 1985) 393–94. It relates that she

Albert Noursi, who moved from the cathedral to the college after the 1990 renovation, becoming one of the great Palestinian characters on the staff. Albert was a source of knowledge, experience, and wisdom and kept the college's finances on an even keel long before the appearance of the financial bureaucracy and computers that we know today.

Apart from Clare Birch and Ted Todd, there were few other course staff during the second half of the 1970s. There was no chaplain and none of the volunteer roles that made up the staff in later years. Two local Palestinian Christian ladies known as Sitt Abla and Um George did housework and laundry in the college. The dean of the cathedral during this time was the Very Rev. Clive Handford, later Anglican bishop in Cyprus and the Gulf. For most of Clare's time in Jerusalem, the bishop was the Rt. Rev. Faik Haddad, consecrated in 1974. In January 1976 the diocese of Jerusalem was restructured and the new province of Jerusalem and the Middle East established. This led to minor revisions in the life of the college, too, in that it now found itself part of a broader church context. When Clare left the college in 1978, she was replaced by a Lebanese priest called Joseph Haddad, an Eastern rite Catholic priest who had become an Anglican. He stayed only a year. Ted Todd left in 1982, moving later to St. John's College, Cambridge, England, and later still to Rome where he became rector of St. Paul's Within the Walls in 1985. Subsequently he became involved in the Camphill movement in Upstate New York, where he still lives.[51]

The 1970s were formative years for St. George's College. John Wilkinson provided important vision and expertise. Fundamental aspects of college life were consolidated by Ted Todd and Clare Birch. After they left, Todd was replaced as dean by the Rev. John Louis Peterson from the US. Another significant chapter in the college's history was about to begin.

Gilbert Sinden

Before John Peterson arrived, Brother Gilbert Sinden from Australia signed up for the ten-week course in the winter of 1978. Gilbert was a larger-than-life academic monk who later became course director for ten years from 1979 to 1989.[52] He belonged to the religious community known as the Society of the Sacred Mission (SSM), a monastery at Kelham near Newark in Nottinghamshire, England. His influence on St. George's cannot be

typed the manuscript for John Wilkinson's book *Jerusalem as Jesus Knew It*.

51. Camphill is an organization that helps people with special needs.

52. A plaque in St. George's College library has 1980 to 1990, but all the evidence points to a year earlier.

overestimated, and his monastic presence was legendary even in his own day. Gilbert's academic priest/monk image created a certain ethos at the college which helped cement the connection between academic study and pilgrimage in the courses. He contributed a visible Anglican spirituality, and his personality and enthusiasm sum up much of what St. George's became in the 1980s. A thoroughly "Renaissance" man with a commitment to learning, he was a wonderful teacher with a lively sense of humor. He was also an excellent cook, exuding hospitality and friendship in all directions. There was simply no one like Brother Gilbert, and he left his stamp on everything the college did while he was there and through later years.

Although SSM was not the only monastic influence on the college over the years, it was the main one, and to appreciate Gilbert Sinden fully it is worth looking at the background. SSM was founded in England in 1891 by a priest called Fr. Herbert Kelly.[53] Starting a community of men in Kennington, London, his original vision was for a mission in Korea. But Kelly's vision soon developed to include ordination training, and in 1903 he moved with his newly-founded religious community to Kelham Hall in the countryside between Nottingham and Newark. Kelham Hall is a staggering country house designed by Sir George Gilbert Scott and completed in 1863. A huge chapel with a magnificent dome was added in 1928. The chapel at Kelham, where the monastic offices were said daily, was dominated by a life-size rood designed by Charles Sargeant Jagger. The rood is a huge crucifix with the mother of Jesus on one side and the Beloved Disciple on the other. The Gilbert Scott house became home to SSM and was known in the Anglican Church simply as "Kelham," conjuring up a particular monastic ethos. In this location, Kelly provided theological training especially for non-graduate boys from working-class backgrounds in the days when there was little opportunity in the Church of England for such training outside Oxford and Cambridge.

SSM was an Anglo-Catholic monastic community within the Church of England, started in the nineteenth century (like some others including the Community of the Resurrection at Mirfield, West Yorkshire) in the wake of the Oxford Movement. Monasteries in England had been dissolved by Henry VIII during the Reformation in the sixteenth century. The Anglican revival of the religious life was slow and tentative but Kelly was a strong leader. The regime at Kelham was tough. Young men, aged sixteen, arrived for up to six years of training in theology and philosophy, and the monastic practice of prayer and spirituality. The monks each wore a black

53. For a history of SSM, see Mason, *Society*. The founder's original vision is laid out in Kelly, *Idea in the Working*. For an account of daily life at Kelham, see Holloway, *Leaving Alexandria*, 3–98.

cassock with a red girdle or rope around the waist with a large silver and black crucifix attached. SSM was involved in missionary work in South Africa, Australia, Korea, and Japan, as well as other places. Most of those in training at Kelham were eventually ordained and worked in parishes. Others joined the community as priests. But some joined as lay brothers, and Gilbert Sinden was one such.

SSM flourished in its glorious surroundings until the early 1970s when the Church of England was already experiencing shortages of ordination candidates. In the 1970s maintaining a house the size of Kelham was a financial strain on SSM and after many grueling years of struggle (Fr. Kelly died in 1950) Kelham Theological College closed. The community sold the house and moved to Willen Priory in Milton Keynes, Buckinghamshire, where they continued their monastic life and work. They also continued their missionary activity in other countries, including Australia. Several of the remaining brothers found other attachments where they could be useful. It was from this broad background that Gilbert Sinden emerged and eventually arrived at St. George's College.

Richard Albert Sinden (Gilbert was his religious name, taken when he became a monk) was born in south London on June 14, 1929, to Richard and Gladys Sinden (née Pritchard). He went to Kelham in 1949 and graduated with a BA degree in theology from the University of Nottingham. He then taught Old Testament studies at Kelham. For reasons now lost in the mists of time (probably because he was considered too academic), it was decided by those in authority at Kelham that Gilbert should not be ordained. He was professed as a lay brother on March 25, 1954, and, inspired by the possibility of moving to South Australia, he was transferred to St. Michael's House at Crafers, near Adelaide, in 1963. His status as a lay brother meant that he was always known simply as "Brother Gilbert," even after he was eventually ordained.[54] After a few years he took Australian citizenship and eventually became warden of St. Michael's. His academic interests were broad and, in addition to his Old Testament focus, he joined the Liturgical Commission of the Australian Church, playing a significant role in the preparation of *An Australian Prayer Book* (1978). He also authored two works connected to the prayer book: *When We Meet for Worship* and *Times and Seasons*.[55] In due course, Gilbert received an honorary doctorate from the Australian College of Theology (based in Sydney) in recognition of this

54. He is sometimes listed in St. George's College literature as "the Rev. Brother Gilbert."

55. Sinden, *When We Meet*; *Times*.

work. His influence spread far and wide and he became known as "the most powerful layman in the Australian church."[56]

After all his hard work at Kelham and Crafers, it was thought that Gilbert deserved a sabbatical year. This was granted and he decided to travel to India, Jerusalem, and Sweden to experience the church in contrasting locations. Things had moved on, however, and part of the sabbatical plan was that before setting off Gilbert would finally be ordained. And so he was made deacon in the chapel at Crafers by the then archbishop of Adelaide, the Rt. Rev. Keith Rayner, on April 30, 1978. Gilbert then left on his travels as a deacon, spending several months in India, and then joining the ten-week course at St. George's College. But he never made it to Sweden; the new deacon had been seduced by Jerusalem's enticing mystique.

The St. George's course was perfectly suited to Gilbert's interests. In addition to time in Jerusalem, it spent a week in Galilee and most of a week in the Sinai desert. It enabled a substantial encounter with the Bible and the land, incorporating all the dimensions of learning that were now central to St. George's courses. The roots of the ten-week course went back to John Wilkinson, and was effectively a full semester of study lasting nearly three months, sometimes more than once a year. In general, the ten-week course gave St. George's more of a "college" feel than the other courses, because of its length. There was plenty of time to get to know other students reasonably well and to share in a variety of life-changing experiences. Gilbert's interests and horizons were expanding as he fell in love with the land as well as the people.

When Gilbert arrived in Jerusalem as a participant in the ten-week course, he did not anticipate a longer stay. But during the ten weeks Dean Ted Todd offered him the course director's job and Gilbert accepted enthusiastically. Before taking it up, however, he returned to Crafers to be ordained priest (also by Bishop Rayner) on Ascension Day, May 23, 1979. His honorary doctorate was awarded on the same occasion. Later that year, Gilbert returned to Jerusalem to begin work at the college, supported by the Australian Board of Missions. He lived in the course director's apartment at St. George's College and later in St. George's School across the road from the cathedral. He played a key part in the life of the cathedral as well as in the college, and developed a sensitive empathy with the Palestinian people as he became intellectually embroiled in local politics.

In his new role, Gilbert embarked upon a journey of encounter with biblical geography. Through travel with college courses, he came to know the land extremely well. His Old Testament scholarship was transformed by

56. Mason, *Society*, 309.

his new physical context and he was soon in his element, discovering new levels of association between biblical texts and the land. Indeed, this combination was to become his great love, and his great skill, as he introduced others to its exciting challenges. Exuding knowledge and enthusiasm for teaching the biblical texts and the places associated with them, he breathed into the courses a living sense of God's mysterious ways with the world. As St. George's grew and expanded during the rest of the 1980s, Gilbert's style of teaching and his combination of scholarship and monastic spirituality came to play a significant role in the evolving identity of the college.

In an article entitled "The Jerusalem Experience," written in 1983 after he had been course director for four years, Gilbert draws attention to the growth of the college during those years.[57] He singles out four areas. The first is growth away from a concentration on ordination candidates to a wider intake of students. The early concentration on ministry both among local and expatriate candidates opened out to include laity as well. The second is the way in which courses themselves are expanding. The emphasis on the Bible and the land remained but course titles of the period reflect an interest in a wider range of subject matter, relating it to particular themes such as The Bible and Worship. There is also a concern to develop courses for pilgrimage leaders and missionaries.

The third area is ecumenical. The college had moved on from looking for local ordinands to a wider international and ecumenical perspective. At this stage Gilbert notes that there had been forty-seven different denominations and forty-nine different countries represented in courses. Gilbert's final area of growth is that there had been significant movement toward interdependence between the indigenous and the expatriate communities in Jerusalem. If there had been a sense of expatriates giving the indigenous Christians something through St. George's College, a greater sense of reciprocity had now grown up between the two. Indeed, these better relations extended to a sense of greater mutuality between the local Palestinian Christians and the international Anglican Communion.

For Gilbert, Jerusalem and the Holy Land themselves provided the setting for these developments. St. George's College was only the vehicle for the wider, fundamental experience. Gilbert wrote, "St. George's College exists to enable people from all over the world to make good use of their opportunity to enjoy the Jerusalem Experience."[58] Through the college, he played a crucial part in all this as he threw himself energetically into the

57. The original is held in the Society of the Sacred Mission Archive at the Borthwick Institute for Archives, University of York.

58. Sinden, "Jerusalem Experience," 364.

courses and into the overall life of the college. In subsequent years, Gilbert's vision and contribution have been unparalleled.

John Peterson

At the end of 1982, Dean Ted Todd left St. George's College.[59] There had already been discussion about a successor at St. Saint George's and a search had begun. Some thought Gilbert Sinden would be more than suitable. After two years as course director, he was very well known. But in the event, it was the Rev. Canon John L. Peterson from the US who was chosen.[60] In the Autumn of 1981, *Bible Lands* reported John's appointment as follows:

> The Foundation Committee have appointed the Revd. Dr. John Peterson to succeed the present Dean, Edward Todd when he leaves St. George's in December 1982. Dr. Peterson is a present Canon Theologian and Administrative Assistant to the Bishop of Western Michigan and Vicar of St. Stephen's Plainwell in that Diocese. He has been associated with St. George's College since 1976 and during his long and distinguished academic career has visited the Middle East many times. He studied at the Near East School of Theology in Beirut in 1963 and visited the Holy Land on archaeological expeditions in 1969, 71, 73 and '75. He and his wife Kirsten will be welcome additions to the life of the Close at St. George's.
>
> In the meantime St. George's College goes from strength to strength under the leadership of Dean Todd and the Director of Training, Brother Gilbert Sinden.[61]

John Peterson was born in Minnesota in 1942 and graduated from Concordia College in Moorhead, Minnesota, in 1965. Interested in biblical studies and archeology, he spent a junior year abroad at the Near East School of Theology and the American University in Beirut, Lebanon (1963–1964). This was followed by study at Harvard Divinity School (1965–1968) with George Ernest Wright, the famous "father of biblical archeology." In 1966 John married Kirsten Ruth Bratlie.

In the following years John's interest in archeology grew through digs at Tel Gezer (1969) and Tel el-Hesi (1971 and 1973). In 1975 he was in Jerusalem writing up his thesis at the Albright Institute. In 1977 he defended his ThD (doctor of theology) in biblical archeology in Chicago at

59. Reported in *Bible Lands* 21:3 (Spring 1983) 128.

60. Much of the material in this section comes from interviews with John Peterson.

61. *Bible Lands* 20:14 (Autumn 1981) 419.

the Seabury-Western Theological Seminary while functioning as a minister in a nearby Congregational church. The dissertation focused on the Levitical cities.[62] His doctoral supervisors were George Ernest Wright and later Edward F. Campbell, who wrote a commentary on the biblical book of Ruth. John also worked with Robert G. Boling who wrote commentaries on Joshua and Judges. This wide experience in biblical and archeological scholarship put John in a good position when he arrived at St. George's College. His experiences in the Middle East had changed his life.

Ordained into the American Episcopal Church in the cathedral in Kalamazoo, both as deacon and priest (1976 and 1977), John served in the parish of St. Stephen, Plainwell. He was also canon theologian at the cathedral where he worked with Bishop Charles E. Bennison Sr. It was Bishop Bennison who introduced John to the Episcopal Church in the USA and the wider Anglican Communion. Continuing his interest in the Holy Land, John returned to Jerusalem on several occasions and got to know the Anglican bishop Faik Haddad. As we have seen, Bishop Haddad was the first Palestinian Arab diocesan bishop in the Anglican diocese of Jerusalem, following the time of Archbishop Appleton and an interim period under Bishop Robert Stopford. John's connection with Bishop Haddad meant that he was known at St. George's, and this played a key part in his appointment as dean of the college in 1983.

When John and Kirsten arrived in Jerusalem, Ted Todd was still at the college and they overlapped for a month. Gilbert Sinden continued as course director. John attended a part of the ten-week course at the end of 1982 and then became dean on January 1, 1983. Courses were filling up and there was a general sense that the college was expanding and needed more room. Gilbert threw himself into the courses, while, in addition to teaching, John integrated the college with the diocese. By the end of 1983, a provincial clergy training course was being organized by the college for January 1984, in Larnaca, Cyprus.[63]

Looking back, much had happened at the new Anglican college in Jerusalem. Courses and summer schools had grown and developed. A building had appeared and enabled further possibilities. John Wilkinson and others had built a center for the courses and shaped course content. Early success was dashed by the 1967 war and closure. But more vision brought the college back, and John Wilkinson again played a key part. His serious academic work set a high standard for courses. By 1980 Gilbert Sinden's monastic profile and enthusiasm in teaching were bringing further layers

62. There is a copy in St. George's College library. Peterson, "Topographical Surface."

63. *Bible Lands* 21:4 (Christmas 1983) 151, 168.

of learning into college life, building upon much that had already been laid down. When John Peterson became dean, the college was growing rapidly and there was much work to be done. However, the building that had gone up in the time of Felix Boyse and John Wilkinson in 1962–1963 was already showing its age and needed serious improvement. Within a year or two of John Peterson's arrival, the foundation of the college gave John permission to raise the money needed to add another floor to the college building. And, indeed, the opportunity soon presented itself: the college's twenty-first birthday was on the horizon. A project that would stretch across the next decade was about to be born.

4

Coming of Age

THE YEARS 1983–1994 ARE among the most eventful in the history of St. George's College. The advice given to John Peterson following a structural survey of the 1962 building was that it needed serious updating. It will be recalled that the original building was quite simple, consisting of two floors and including accommodation for the dean and other staff, some downstairs offices, student accommodation with communal bathrooms, a common room, and a lecture room with a small library. Overall, it accommodated thirty-two students and there was now an obvious need for expansion. Courses were filling up and the college needed to move forward. A thorough renovation was the only way. A third floor could be added to the existing building to enable more accommodation and ultimately more teaching room and administrative space. The college could have a proper library. And there could be space for staff and visiting scholars. A whole range of things needed doing, including making all the student rooms en suite. John committed to raising three hundred fifty thousand dollars for a thorough, overall renovation to take the college into the future.[1]

As planning began, staff took up the idea that the existing building was twenty-one years old. Connections were made and the St. George's College "Comes of Age" project was launched. Of course, notions of extension and renovation of the 1962 building had been discussed since John Wilkinson's time. Now there was a determination to see it happen. The entire project would provide a thoroughly modern facility as a comfortable base for study and travel in the Holy Land. From this moment onward, a new rhythm was set. Fundraising was needed, and John would be away from the college for long periods of time doing it. While the new dean carried on teaching in

1. About $1.35 million today.

most courses, Gilbert Sinden remained at the helm as course director. The college secretary, Helen Assad, was an enormous help, keeping on top of secretarial work long before computers or even fax machines. John traveled mostly in the countries that provided students in courses: the US and Canada, the UK, Australia, and New Zealand. The regional committees in those countries were enormously supportive, especially the Americans.

THE PROJECT

The St. George's College "Comes of Age" idea was a perfect marketing tool for spurring the college's growth and development into its next phase. Two elements were identified and featured strongly in the campaign: physical extension and academic strengthening. Needless to say, there was a lot of support. The dominating idea was to add a third floor onto the 1962 building, as well as renovating the west end of the first, or ground, floor and the existing top floor. For the new third floor, the idea was of an "Academic Center" which would consist of: (a) a library, bringing together all the books from four scattered locations in the Cathedral Close; (b) a lecture hall, capable of seating up to a hundred people; (c) a common room, in which students could relax together and continue conversation and reflection following study and field trips; (d) visiting scholars' accommodation, for the academic work of visitors; and (e) visiting lecturers' accommodation, to house academic staff who would help raise the academic profile of courses.

The renovations to the existing two floors would allow for a meditation and seminar room, a dean's office, and student rooms on the middle floor, and renovated reception and seminar rooms, registrar's office, kitchen and housekeeper's quarters, and student rooms on the ground floor. The "Academic Center" and the renovated office and student accommodation space would strengthen the academic profile, the capacity, and the credibility of what was already an internationally-known institution. As ideas proliferated and the project grew, however, staff soon realized that the cost would be something more like seven hundred fifty thousand.[2]

John Peterson's introductory letter in the brochure produced for the campaign and sent to all friends of the college, captures the overall vision:

> Dear Friend:
>
> After twenty-one years of growing and developing a mature and viable program, Saint George's College is now embarked

2. Nearly $3 million today.

upon the first expansion activity in its history. I am very excited to share our plans with you.

Through the efforts of the Most Rev. A. C. MacInnes, then Anglican Archbishop in Jerusalem, who founded the College in 1962, and those of my three predecessors, Canon F. V. A. Boyse, Canon John Wilkinson, and Canon Edward P. Todd, Saint George's College has become established as the premiere "experience of the land" for English-speaking students of all ages, worldwide. With academic respectability, archaeological expertise, and pastoral sensitivity, the College has provided its students with growth and understanding of their faith as they encounter the place where that faith began. As a result, they have returned home enriched and eager to share this experience—what has come to be known at St. George's as "The Jerusalem Experience".

Now, based on the strength of that substantial foundation, built over the course of these first twenty-one years, St. George's College has come of age. The college is about to begin the next phase of its life:

. . . the further strengthening of the quality of its academic program and activity.

Because St. George's College offerings are uniquely open and available to all applicants it is vital that the academic nature of its highly valued program be maintained and even strengthened. In the recent years of enrollment increase, priority consideration has been given to housing more students. Now it is time to expand the College building so that essential space is provided for appropriate improvements in the academic program. Furthermore, if St. George's College is to maintain and expand its appropriate scholarly contribution among other academic and religious institutions in Jerusalem, it must continue to enrich its academic offerings and facility.

To make all this possible, it is essential that a new third floor be added to the building to constitute a major Academic Center. Central to that will be the integration of the college library in one location and a new properly equipped lecture room complete with much needed audio and visual presentation equipment. In addition, and essential to the Academic Center, will be quarters for distinguished visiting scholars and professors and the all-important Common Room for the valued informal learning-outside-the-classroom. Construction of this new center will be accompanied by carefully executed space conservation planning and renovations to the first and second floors with resulting increased student housing. It is the successful growth of the program and high enrollments achieved by my predecessors that make this project not only appropriate but necessary.

For the past several years, the governing body of the college, the St. George's College Foundation, has been studying and exploring this expansion program. With this document, we embark on the effort to make that program a reality. The College's increasing demand for enrollment and its established fiscal viability requires that we now exercise responsibly our fundamental mission:

. . . to provide a reliable and academically respectable course of study and devotion on the Bible and the Holy Land for students of all ages, countries and convictions.

Never before has the College been so healthy, so mature, so ready to take this kind of significant step. Never before has the College dared to move so courageously. The time is right because St. George's College has COME OF AGE. As you read these pages and review our plans for academic strengthening, I invite you to participate with us in this bold program. With your help, we will be successful.

Faithfully yours,
John L. Peterson
Dean[3]

The large part of the advertising brochure for the campaign then spells out detail that we have already mentioned, along with a breakdown of costs. Members of the college staff, regional committees, and the foundation are listed. It is an inspiring document and clearly reflects the faith, hope, and optimism of the people involved. It was a thoroughly exciting and all-encompassing project. The Christmas 1983 *Bible Lands* reports, "The college has launched an appeal in the USA toward the building of an extension third floor. Responses to the appeal seem quite encouraging."[4] Later, Michael Benton of the British Regional Committee of the college writes,

In 1983 after some years of discussion, twenty-one years after the present College building was erected, the governing body

3. From the "Comes of Age" brochure in the St. George's College archive.
4. *Bible Lands* 21:4 (Christmas 1983) 168.

> of the College (the College Foundation) decided to step out in faith and appeal for funds to improve and extend the building facilities. The intention is to build on a third-storey to increase the student capacity from 32 to 45, to provide improved library, lecture and office space and to include much needed study and living quarters for visiting scholars and professors. At the same time the opportunity will be taken to modernise the bathrooms and heating systems to enable better and more flexible use to be made of the existing building.[5]

Work on the project began immediately, and subsequently stretched out across a decade. Inevitably, progress waxed and waned with numerous long delays as well as lurches forward.

By the middle of 1985, however, the momentum and confidence were enough to justify a special ceremony to mark progress.[6] This was held on June 6, and is reported in *Bible Lands* as follows:

> To commemorate the costly extensions to St. George's College by the addition of a 3rd storey, a "Roof Breaking" ceremony took place in June in the presence of the Most Reverend George Browne, Archbishop of West Africa, representing the Anglican Consultative Council, the Rt. Rev. Charles [Vaché], Chairman of the North American Regional Committee and Sir Archibald Ross, KCMG, Chairman of the British Regional Committee, with all the staff of St. George's College and the Clergy of the Diocese. The Bishop in Jerusalem, armed with an Ecclesiastical pick axe and the Prayers of the faithful, managed to break the roof without knocking the College down. "The Coming-of-Age" Appeal to pay for the extension is now within sight of its nearly $1,000,000 target. All credit to Dr. John Peterson whose energy and enthusiasm is beyond praise.[7]

This "Roof Breaking" ceremony marked the official beginning of work on the building—a liturgical acknowledgment that the college was moving ahead with its new project. Clearly the cost had gone up, but things were now moving forward at an exciting, if steady, pace.

One of the main people needed for the project was a good architect, and John Peterson recalls that it was the Very Rev. Richard Coombs who, well on in the process, suggested a man called Don Neraas as key architect.

5. *Bible Lands* 21:6 (Winter 1984) 268–72, 271.

6. The order of service is in the college archive.

7. *Bible Lands* 21:8 (Winter 1985) 378. A million US dollars in 1985 would be nearly three million today.

During the decade leading up to the completion of the project, Richard and Barbara Coombs from Spokane, Washington, took increasing interest in the project and in 1988–1989 spent a year at the college as volunteers. Dick was dean emeritus of the cathedral in Spokane and Barbara, his wife, had been a third grade teacher. During their stay in Jerusalem, Dick wrote reports and Barbara kept a journal. After they left, they published their joint accounts as *Our Year in the Holy Land: A Chronicle of Service at St. George's College, Jerusalem, in the Time of the Intifada*. Concerning Don Neraas, Dick Coombs writes,

> I must say that Spokane's Donald Neraas is the hero of the "new" St. George's College. If Barbara and I have contributed anything to the college expansion program during our involvement, it has been suggesting his name when, a year and a half ago, it became evident that the building project was floundering. He took the challenge, as he has taken so many others, and pushed the project forward. He designed the expanded college building, drew the plans, redesigned where necessary, contributed creative ideas no one had thought of before, bewitched the tough Israeli bureaucrats, and taught those, whose inclination is to sit back and wait, to move forward instead. He never lost patience. And he has steadily kept his eye on the large picture. He is the one person in the several dozen who have been a part of this project without whom it would not have happened. And he has done it all without earning himself an enemy anywhere that we know about. In the beginning I thought it was a good idea to suggest his name. Now I think it was sheer genius.[8]

Don Neraas was to remain architect throughout the project and for the rest of his life. He would visit the college regularly from his home in Washington State, still attending to the condition and upkeep of the building in his final years.

From the beginning, John had appointed a Palestinian, Samir Khayo, whom he had met at an archeological dig at Tel el-Hesi years before, and whose logistical skills John admired, to oversee the new building project. Samir became "clerk of works" and contributed an enormous amount to the process of getting the project moving, traveling daily from his home in Ramallah through the military checkpoint. Samir was known later as "buildings and grounds manager," and remained in post well into the new millennium, working in the college every day from an office at the back of the library and attending in fine detail to the upkeep of the building. With

8. Coombs and Coombs, *Our Year*, 154.

his wife Nahida, Samir was at the heart of the St. George's College family. His contribution to the physical well-being of the college's building and to staff and student practical needs was unmatched.

Another development at this time was within the Peterson family itself: the arrival of Emily and Carrie. John writes, "Shortly after I became the dean of St. George's College on January 1st, 1983, Kirsten and I adopted two Palestinian babies from the Israeli Social Services. Emily was born in 1983 and Carrie in 1985. Both girls attended the Anglican International School in Jerusalem and they frequently joined welcoming parties for the new course members at St. George's College."[9] The girls played an important part in the life of the close and still think of St. George's as their home today.

Following the launch of the campaign, John Peterson traveled frequently on fundraising trips in addition to keeping a firm hand in teaching and research.[10] Course members themselves made donations once they became familiar with the college and its work. Gilbert continued to manage and teach in courses, consolidating and refining the academic input as student numbers strengthened and grew. As funds came in and possibilities expanded, of course, the original plan changed and the vision reflected in the original brochure was tweaked. A construction worker from Bethlehem was appointed to carry out a structural survey and it was concluded that the building would not carry the weight of the library on the new top floor. This limitation was unfortunate but gave birth to a new idea: the library would be on the ground floor, marking the centrality of study in the college's life. Unfortunately, the replanning resulted in the loss of accommodation for visiting lecturers and visiting scholars, and of some student rooms.[11] As the work continued, however, the Roman cistern, discovered when the first building was constructed, was incorporated as the Benshoof Cistern Museum, housing archeological artifacts from Tel Dothan. Additional space was dug out later in the process to put a dining room in the college basement.

As the project progressed through the decade, life in the college moved forward. Bishop Samir Kafity (Anglican bishop from 1984 to 1998) was always very supportive of the development and played a key role in encouraging staff and meeting students. He saw the value of the college not only for the students and local Christians but also for the wider Anglican Communion. For him, St. George's College and the cathedral were "the

9. In an email, June 12, 2024.

10. John later (1992) contributed several entries to *The Anchor Bible Dictionary*. See Freedman, *Anchor*.

11. The present-day student capacity is thirty-six.

Diocese's windows on the world."[12] Student numbers were growing during these years and it soon became clear that more staff were needed. For some years in the early 1980s an Australian called Paul Wilson, who had been a teacher at St. George's School, joined the college staff, assisting the dean and relieving Gilbert, who traveled a great deal on library business. Paul did an outstanding job but sadly drowned while swimming at Tel Aviv in 1984.[13]

In the mid-1980s, a new course tutor arrived in the person of David Praill, a British priest who had originally studied mathematics at York University in England, and then trained for ordination at Cranmer Hall, Durham. He was a curate in Welwyn Garden City for two years and went to St. George's College in 1985, accompanied by his wife, Sarah.[14] Sponsored by CMS, David loved the desert and this became his key interest. Later (1993), after leaving St. George's, he led a forty-day sponsored walk in the Holy Land and wrote up an account of the experience in *Return to the Desert: A Journey from Mount Hermon to Mount Sinai*.[15] The book captures David's love of the desert and much of the ethos of the college's desert courses during his time. By now the college was attracting other, adjunct staff including Vicki Balabanski, a New Testament scholar from Australia working at the École Biblique. Vicki and her husband, Peter, helped at St. George's College and at the cathedral.

One of the great characters on the college staff during this period was Miss Eileen Fenton, sister of the well-known Oxford New Testament scholar John Fenton.[16] Eileen had studied theology at Oxford and brought a wealth of knowledge and learning to the St. George's courses. She had been headmistress of a girls' school in England for some years and was later involved with teacher training in Norfolk. She also held the Lambeth diploma in theology. By the time she joined the college staff, she had already taught at St. George's Boys' School in Jerusalem. Then, she became increasingly involved with the college, and in later years, following retirement, she would still return to Jerusalem for several courses a year, traveling from her cottage in Wales.

Gold dust for the college, the students loved Eileen. She was a committed teacher who was keen on the Constantinian period. In the days long before PowerPoint presentations she prepared visual aids, displaying

12. *Bible Lands* 21:8 (Winter 1985) 378.

13. See his obituary in *Bible Lands* 21:6 (Winter 1984) 298–99.

14. Reported in *Bible Lands* 21:7 (Summer 1985) 324.

15. Praill, *Return*.

16. John's son, James Fenton, was professor of poetry at Oxford University, 1994–1999.

postcards on large pieces of card. She gave lectures in the college building and accompanied courses out in the field where she proved to be an excellent companion, continuing conversations with course members, and extending and enriching their entire learning experience. She had a teacher's clarity and patience and a professor's inquiring mind. She could also be a quiet, sensitive, and reassuring presence in the group—a wonderfully eccentric, old-fashioned English lady with a warmth of welcome and a typical Oxford accent. They don't make 'em like that anymore!

The 1987 St. George's College course brochure details the following staff: John, Gilbert, David, and Eileen. From this firm base, new ideas for courses and new ways of developing the college's "reach" were emerging. In the same year, John Peterson invited a number of British clergy with responsibility for continuing ministerial education in the Church of England to the August course, The Bible and Its Setting. The course visited Galilee and the Sinai as well as the usual sites in and around Jerusalem and Bethlehem. Hugh Williamson (later Regius Professor of Hebrew at Oxford University) was the visiting lecturer. Stephen Platten (a residentiary canon at Portsmouth Cathedral at the time and later bishop of Wakefield) recalls how formative this international and ecumenical course was, and how John Peterson's initiative helped spread the word about the college to the wider church.[17]

In 1989 Marcus Losack joined the college as course director.[18] Marcus hailed from Ireland and had studied at Trinity College, Dublin, as well as Corpus Christi College, Cambridge. He held a degree in theology and a master's degree in philosophy and ecumenical studies. He trained for ordination at Salisbury and Wells Theological College and was a curate in the diocese of Chester. He was married to Noeleen. By the time he arrived at St. George's, he had lived in Libya for a period and, like David Praill, was keen on the desert. As these remarkable and able individuals strengthened the academic content of the courses, the building project progressed around them.

During the first couple of weeks of December 1988, the new project started to gather momentum. Dick Coombs wrote, "At last, at long last, the contract for the new building was signed this morning. Construction will begin next week. We are already moving offices into temporary quarters, and the next course which arrives several days after Christmas will be housed at the cathedral hostel or at the YMCA across the street."[19] He

17. In private conversation.

18. Announced in *Bible Lands* 22:1 (Summer 1990) 36.

19. Coombs and Coombs, *Our Year*, 153.

added, "While construction is under way the college will continue to operate its full program. Students will sleep at the Y, take meals in the hostel, as usual, and hear lectures and have social events in the public rooms at the Y. This all seems reasonable, and there is no reason it cannot work that way. But there is often a slip between plans and reality. So we are all a bit anxious to learn how well it works."[20]

The "Y" was the East Jerusalem YMCA just near St. George's Cathedral. It served as an appropriate "home from home" while renovations at the college were in their final stages. *Bible Lands* for Summer, 1990, reports,

> All through this year, the College has been working out of three scattered locations while its building is being extended and refurbished. The offices have been located in St. George's School, the Library in St. Mary's (the junior department of St. George's School), and the course members and the lecture room in the East Jerusalem YMCA. It has not been easy, but the cheerful helpfulness of everyone at the 'Y' and the School have contributed greatly to a year which has run much more smoothly than anyone could have hoped. Meanwhile, the vision of the "Comes of Age" extension programme is taking shape as the builders transform the old College building. Already we can see the setting of the new academic center (Library, Audio-visual-lecture Room and study facilities) and the upgraded student accommodation taking shape.
>
> We are now looking forward eagerly to the week of Celebration in late April when we hope most of those who have contributed significantly to the realisation of the "Comes of Age" vision will join us in Jerusalem to give thanks and to offer these magnificent facilities to God.[21]

So it was that students lived at the "Y" for a season and the college continued to function. As time passed, the project neared completion. There was a great deal of financial and practical support from individuals and churches throughout the world. Quite a lot of "named gifts" came in and were eventually acknowledged around the college building on plaques or tiles made by Stefan Karakashian of "Jerusalem Pottery" on the Via Dolorosa, providing the college with one of its many striking characteristics. Every student room in the college has a "Holy Land name" such as "Bethsaida," "The Annunciation," or "Caesarea Philippi" marked on the door by a similar tile. Sometimes a donor would give a specific amount for a room

20. Coombs and Coombs, *Our Year*, 154.

21. *Bible Lands* 22:1 (Summer 1990) 36.

or section of the library and these were then given a tile to acknowledge the donation.

St. George's College staff, Palestinians and expatriates, worked extremely hard during this period contributing enormously to enabling the project to progress on a day-to-day basis. In the final stages Sally Thomas from the United States was appointed to oversee the interior decoration. The striking Palestinian decor, which still enhances the college building today, was agreed upon, and the result was homely and warm, with a very smart look. The renovation was a staggering achievement and on April 25, 1990, a ceremony marked its completion.[22] Amid great excitement and after a decade of planning and fundraising, a whole week of events took place at Eastertide that year. Services in the cathedral, lectures at the college, and gatherings on the grounds all added to the swell of enthusiasm for St. George's. People from all over the world attended and a new phase of the college's life was launched. Summing up a good deal of the history of the college, *Bible Lands* later reported as follows:

> In 1984 an appeal was launched for funds to enlarge the building by adding a third storey to increase the student capacity to 45, to enable the library (for the first time) to be housed within the College building, to provide improved lecture and office space and study and living quarters for visiting scholars, and to modernise the plumbing and heating. This work was completed and the newly enlarged building was blessed during a splendidly International Week of Celebration in Eastertide 1990.[23]

St. George's College had finally "come of age" and was now ready to turn a new corner into a new chapter of its life.

Alongside the work on the physical building, there was also the "academic strengthening" that had been identified in the campaign brochure. We have met some of the staff during the years of the project. Something of what was happening in courses can be seen from the 1988 "Aims and Objectives of College Courses."[24] A sense of the college's purpose and course content can be seen there, showing the emphasis on different ways of learning as well as underlining the combination of learning and devotion. In part 3 we shall meet numerous visiting academics and see how courses grew and developed.

22. The order of service is in the college archive.

23. *Bible Lands* 22:5 (Summer 1992) 214–17, 216. The whole article gives a good general sense of the overall work of the college.

24. See appendix D at the back of this book. Appendix E shows lists of courses.

Even after the opening ceremony at St. George's, and the new building having been launched, there were still elements in the project that continued to progress. Three characteristic features at the college come to mind here in particular, and form a significant part of St. George's College physical identity. They are: the Bible garden, the library, and the Benshoof Cistern Museum. We shall now look at these in turn.

THE BIBLE GARDEN

The first characteristic feature at the college is the "Bible garden," or "biblical garden."[25] Once the new floor had been added to the college building and the overall renovation was complete, attention fell to another idea. From about 1985 onward, Gilbert Sinden had been putting about the idea of a Bible garden in the college grounds. A Bible garden is a themed garden using plants mentioned in the Bible. Bible gardens are not unknown elsewhere in the area: there is one at Hebrew University on Mount Scopus in Jerusalem and another at the biblical nature reserve known as Neot Kedumim between Jerusalem and Tel Aviv.[26] There are several in the US and one in Japan. Everyone agreed that a Bible garden at St. George's College would be another exciting educational attraction. John Peterson had been responsible for fundraising for the whole "Comes of Age" project so far, and so it now also fell to him to take responsibility for the Bible garden.

John appointed Mr. F. Nigel Hepper, a research botanist at the Royal Botanical Gardens at Kew Gardens in London, to design the Bible garden. On the practical level, it was a matter of landscaping the whole area around the college building. The idea was that the garden would contain some of the many plants mentioned in the Bible. It would have an educational dimension, and in later years there was more than one course at St. George's on the plants of the Bible. But it would also provide an attractive and peaceful location where course participants might sit and reflect spiritually on their pilgrimage experience.

In due course, the area outside the college building, including the garden and the car park, was prepared. Fifteen tons of soil were brought in and small walls were installed over the area of the cistern which would later become the Benshoof Museum. Pathways were created, beds of soil were laid, and a steel frame for a grapevine was erected. Water pipes and electric

25. I have used "Bible garden" here, although usage varies generally. Nigel Hepper uses "Bible Garden" in the title of his short book on the St. George's College garden. See Hepper, *Bible Garden*. See also *Bible Lands* 22:4 (Winter 1991) 194.

26. *Neot Kedumim* is Hebrew for "pleasant pastures of old."

cables were put in, enabling irrigation and lighting at night. The car park area was resurfaced and provided an ideal place for the course bus to enter and turn around. A man called Adam Toft came to be the resident horticulturalist from 1990 to 1992. He and Samir Khayo oversaw the creation of the garden following Nigel Hepper's design.

The garden stretches all around the building with smaller and larger beds scattered about and winding around, especially on the front and sides of the building and over to the cathedral and King Edward VII tower. The general layout with its various themes was originally roughly as follows: on the south side (outside the library) was a lawn with trees and shrubs, and also chairs and tables; on the north side were fragrant and flowering plants; on the west were fruits; and on the east, an area of recreation. There are eight gardens as follows: the Olive Tree Garden, the Aqueduct Garden, the Cedar Garden, the Conifer Garden, the Fruit Garden, the Tower Garden, the Well Garden, and the Rose Avenue.

In the Bible there are numerous references to gardens, some of them very important. There is the garden of Eden, of course, at the very beginning (Gen 2:8; Ezek 28:13) and the garden of the end of time (Rev 22:1–2). There are gardens mentioned in all sorts of contexts in the Old Testament (e.g., Isa 1:29, 61:11, 66:17), and in some particular locations relating to Jesus' death and resurrection in the New Testament: the garden of Gethsemane (a combination of Matt 26:36, Mark 14:32, and John 18:1) and the garden in which Jesus is crucified and rises from the dead in John's Gospel (John 19:41, 20:15). The theme of the garden is important in Christian biblical theology, and the garden of Eden comes to symbolize original innocence or perfection. Gardens in the New Testament symbolize resurrection and new creation.

A wide variety of plants and trees is mentioned in the Old and New Testaments. Some key examples included in the St. George's College garden are as follows:

- Olive (the dove comes back with an olive branch in Gen 8:11).
- Tamarisk (Abraham plants one in Beersheba in Gen 21:33).
- Pomegranate (one of the seven fruits of the promised land in Deut 8:8).
- Cedar (supplied by Hiram, King of Tyre, to Solomon for the temple in Jerusalem in 1 Kgs 5:10).
- Apricot (the fruit in Song 2:5 is probably apricots).
- Broom (Elijah knows this tree in 1 Kgs 19:4).

- Hyssop (used in the Passover at Exod 12:22).
- Almond (Aaron's rod produced ripe almonds in Num 17:8).
- Myrtle (one of the trees for making booths in Neh 8:15).
- Date palm (disciples wave branches thought to be palm leaves as Jesus enters Jerusalem in Mark 11:8; see also Ps 92:12).
- Fig tree (Jesus curses a fig tree in Mark 11:13, 21).
- Grapevine (used in John 15).
- Christ thorn (Christ's crown of thorns is made of this in John 19:1–2).
- Judas tree (Judas hangs himself on a tree in Matt 27:5; this is the traditional tree upon which he did that).
- Aloes (Nicodemus brings them with myrrh in John 19:39).
- Sycamore (Zacchaeus climbs one in Luke 19:4).

Each different type of plant or tree in the Bible garden was marked by a plaque bearing the name of the species in Latin, English, and Arabic, and bearing a relevant biblical quote or paraphrase and the name of the donor. Plaques bearing donors' names had been used in the college building on the doors of rooms and in the library. The same style, created by Mr. Stefan Karakashian of "Jerusalem Pottery," was now used in the Bible garden. In the garden, the plaques were raised on steel poles to make them easier to read. The whole project provided a glorious educational opportunity, inviting course participants through yet another doorway into understanding the Bible and the Holy Land.

In 1992 *Bible Lands* published the report of a Mrs. Frances Johnson who visited the college in March of that year. She much appreciated all the recent developments at the college and especially the Bible garden. She relates that she arrived at St. George's Cathedral Close late one night and stayed at the guest house. She continues,

> After a comfortable night, I breakfasted at 7:30am and set off with my camera at 8am to see the College, now with its additional floor and transformed grounds. It was indeed a pleasing sight, and as I followed the well laid out paths between low stone walls, I kept looking ahead to discover the Biblical Gardens. As I walked along the Rose Avenue, I caught site of yellow crocuses and tall white narcissi. The little stone walls surrounded the Cedar Garden, the Olive Garden, the Conifer Garden, the Fruit Garden and gardens near the Tower. Memorial plaques in "Jerusalem Pottery" are in place, and labels give plant names in Latin,

> Arabic and English with Biblical References. Seats are provided to enable pilgrims to rest and pray in this peaceful enclosure.
>
> On my last evening I had the pleasure of meeting Mr. Nigel Hepper from Kew gardens who had supervised the original planting, and was out for a few days to arrange the Spring planting after heavy snowfalls and winter rains.
>
> Having attended the roof breaking ceremony many years earlier in anticipation of adding a third floor to the College, I was specially pleased to see the completed building both outside and inside.
>
> Now that the College has "Come of Age" may I wish it well, and pray that pilgrims, pastors and students attending the well planned courses, may take advantage of the things which the Holy Land has to offer, and under well qualified staff receive inspiration for their future lives and ministries.[27]

A special dedication ceremony for the Bible garden took place on May 6, 1993, led by the Palestinian Anglican/Episcopal bishop in Jerusalem, the Rt. Rev. Samir H. Kafity.[28] With its tables, chairs, and quiet corners, the garden has proved to be a wonderful part of the Jerusalem experience for all who attend the college.[29] Under Dean Richard Sewell (in 2025), there are plans to renew and refresh the Bible garden (and its plaques) for continuing educational and spiritual use.

THE LIBRARY

The second characteristic feature at the college is the library. By the end of 1990, the newly renovated and expanded St. George's College had an impressive library on the ground floor, just inside the main entrance to the college. As we have seen, the original plan was a for a library on the new third floor, but the building would not have taken the weight. It was thus decided to house the library on the ground floor. This change was appropriate in the end, as John Peterson wanted to see learning symbolized at the physical center of the college. The funding for the library came through the presiding bishop of the Episcopal Church in the USA, the Rt. Rev. Edmond Browning, and his wife Patricia. Their generosity is marked by a plaque on the main door of the library: "The Edmond and Patricia Browning Library."

27. *Bible Lands* 22:5 (Summer 1992) 218–19.

28. The order of service is in the college archive.

29. The roof garden with tables, chairs, and a cover was given by NARC in 2007, and a garden fountain in memory of Nancy J. Peterson (John's sister) was given by Emily and Carrie Peterson in the same period.

The new library was a transformation, to say the least. Spacious, light, open, and inviting, it looked truly modern and provided a place where students and pilgrims could sit, study, and reflect.

There are roughly twenty-one thousand volumes in the library, including material on biblical studies, church history, liturgy, Judaism, and Islam, and a good deal on archeology and the history of the Holy Land. There is also the Gilbert Sinden Archive containing material relating to the diocese and the college, and a wide range of periodicals and magazines. On the ground floor, a glass case holds items from the Dothan collection and is effectively an extension to the Benshoof Cistern Museum.[30] Originally there were two floors to the library with stacks and sitting space on each. On the ground floor there was a sizable area providing space for the librarian to catalog books. The card index for books was eventually turned into an online catalog. By the end of 2024 there were plans to turn the upper floor of the library into two rooms for visiting scholars on sabbatical. Books from there would be moved downstairs to take the place of the cataloging area.

In 1990 the new library was in stark contrast to anything the college had previously known. Before the "Comes of Age" project, most of the library had been housed in what is now the cathedral's parish hall, which runs opposite the entrance to the cathedral offices. It was dark, dusty, and uninviting. Other books were in the tea room in the college, others in the room over the main gate into the cathedral from Nablus Road, and others still in the cathedral guest house. The books themselves came from several places, including the Newman School of Missions and other institutions in Jerusalem. Some books were bought locally and others were donated by staff and course members. The library had evolved considerably over the middle years of the twentieth century. When Gilbert Sinden joined the staff in 1979, he soon became librarian, bearing responsibility for upgrading and cataloging in preparation for the move into the new building.

Two people in particular played a part in the development of the library at St. George's College. First, Newland Smith, one of the leading librarians at Seabury Western Theological Seminary in Chicago, who John Peterson knew and appointed as consultant. Newland visited Jerusalem regularly, helping in the long process of revitalizing and updating the library and moving it into its new location. The other person was Margaret Dewey, who was known to Gilbert Sinden through SSM. Margaret was originally from the US but had taken British citizenship and had become attached to SSM in England and then in Australia (though not then a member). Significantly,

30. Dothan is an archeological site north of Nablus in the West Bank. It is associated with Gen 37 and the figure of Joseph. See the next section here for more details.

she was from the great Dewey family which gave its name to the "Dewey decimal system" of library cataloging. Margaret already had a long history of teaching and writing in theology, and had lectured at Kelham in the 1970s as well as in other theological colleges. She had run a retreat house in Gloucestershire at one stage and had an interest in spirituality. She edited the Kelham newsletter for twenty-eight years, and also wrote a short history of USPG.

Gilbert was keen to attract SSM people to Jerusalem and to build up a prayer group at St. George's. Margaret's association with SSM made her an ideal person, and she would often appear in Jerusalem and elsewhere at St. George's events. Along with an SSM brother and priest, the Rev. Tom Brown, and an SSM associate, Norma Kent, Margaret Dewey helped provide a spiritual presence at St. George's and was herself librarian for a while. Later, when women were allowed, she joined SSM. Margaret contributed a good deal to the library at the college and to the ethos of prayer and study. She died in Melbourne, Australia, in 2017. Once the library was up and running it was put into the Dewey system (more suitable than Library of Congress for what is quite a small theological library). Gradually it expanded through donations, and through John Peterson and other staff bringing books from the US and elsewhere. By comparison with other libraries in Jerusalem, especially the École Biblique, Tantur, and Hebrew University, St. George's library is limited. But it holds interesting archival material on the Anglican diocese of Jerusalem and for this reason is unique.

In the early days of the new library, a room at the back was devoted to course handouts that had been created by John Wilkinson and others. In later years, the handout system disappeared as lecturers developed their own teaching materials, and especially as computers became more available. In fact, the room housing the handouts was eventually used as a "computer room" for course members. This provision was eventually superseded by the availability of Wi-Fi in all rooms. Later the room became something of a general storeroom for unused items, and has been used for several different purposes since.

The new library was finally dedicated on the afternoon of Easter Day, April 3, 1994, with Bishop Ed and Patricia Browning present.[31] Margaret Dewey wrote in *Bible Lands*, "The service of dedication began in St. George's Cathedral, and the clergy and congregation then processed through the Biblical Garden to the College, where the actual dedication took place, and the names of all who had contributed to the appeal were read out. There followed a reception (with Palestinian Easter sweets!) and an opportunity

31. The order of service is in the college archive.

for all those present to look around the library. Today, the library is at the heart of the college."[32]

Since everything has now gone digital, and with the added increasing expense of keeping everything up to date, St. George's College library must play a different role in the future. The college staff and foundation are now involved in ongoing conversations about new ways of using this important resource.

THE BENSHOOF CISTERN MUSEUM

The third characteristic feature at the college is the Benshoof Cistern Museum.[33] This is a small archeological museum located underground in a Roman cistern not far from the college's front door. Its name derives from the donors, Edward and Barbara Benshoof of the US, whose generosity made it possible. From a glass door in the college garden, visitors descend steps to find two floors of material from the archeological site at Dothan, north of Nablus, in the West Bank.

The museum came about through John Peterson's acquaintance with Robert E. Cooley, who was associated with the archeological dig at Dothan. The cistern was discovered when the college was built, but had never been used. It is usually thought to be from the Roman/Byzantine period and it is often surmised that the Tenth Legion led by Titus resided in this area north of the city, near a cistern, in AD 70 when the Romans took Jerusalem. The Benshoof Museum puts the cistern to good use, and frequently attracts archeologists and others to see the collection. It is also an educational, teaching aid for the college. Students can see for themselves a small, manageable exhibition of biblical archeology close at hand. As we have seen, some of the artifacts are also located in the library in an attractive glass cupboard that can also be seen from the sitting room on the ground floor.

Dothan is not widely known but its main biblical connection is with Gen 37 and the story of Joseph and his brothers. Joseph is the youngest of Jacob's twelve sons. He has dreams that the sheaves out in the fields rise up and his brothers' sheaves turn to worship him. He also has a dream that the sun, moon, and stars are bowing down to him. Joseph alienates his brothers who are jealous of him. His father sends him to find his brothers near Shechem (modern Nablus). He has heard that they have gone to nearby Dothan, and so he goes there to find them. When they see him, they throw

32. *Bible Lands* 22:10 (Winter 1994) 478–79.

33. A short brochure produced by the college and held in the college archive describes some of the content of the museum.

him into a pit without water, and eventually sell him to passing Ishmaelites who take him to Egypt. The brothers smear his special robe with animal blood and tell his father he is dead.

The geographical focus of Gen 37 is Dothan, which was excavated by Joseph P. Free of Wheaton College, Illinois, between 1953–1964. The archeological tel revealed that Dothan had probably been occupied from the middle of the fourth century BC until about AD 1400. During several seasons of excavations, a multitude of items was recovered from the late Bronze/early Iron Age period (the early biblical period). The material includes pottery vessels, religious items, amulets, ornaments, weapons, and skeletal remains. The collection at the Benshoof Museum at St. George's College comes from three tombs found at Dothan, and mostly from Tomb 1 which had Canaanite remains dating to the fourteenth to thirteenth centuries BC, the period which might well be that of the Joseph of the Genesis narrative. There is nothing thought to relate to Joseph himself but the location is shown to be strategic and rich, a major junction of roads and trade routes. Another biblical reference to Dothan is 2 Kgs 6:13–14, where the Aramaean king sends men in search of the prophet Elisha who is in Dothan. And in the apocryphal book of Judith, Dothan is mentioned in the accounts of attacks by Holophernes on Judea (3:9, 4:6, 7:3–18).

It has been significant that St. George's College has been able to house part of the Dothan collection. Robert Cooley is still involved with the publication of data from Dothan and visits the collection occasionally. But there has been no excavation at Dothan for many years now because of the political situation in the country. Students in courses at the college are always shown the collection near the beginning of a course and this often triggers important discussions about the relation between the Bible and archeology, which come up frequently as courses travel the land. The collection is a huge asset to St. George's College and in many ways symbolizes its continuing interest in biblical archeology. A note in *Bible Lands* records an "Act of Thanksgiving" for the museum led by Bishop Samir Kafity on Sunday, December 18, 1994.[34]

Gradually over the early years of the 1990s, the building project at St. George's College came to completion. Writing in *Bible Lands* in 1994, Margaret Pawley, a member of the British Regional Committee of the college (and well known with her husband Bernard in the ecumenical life and work of the Church of England), has the following to say about what was happening:

34. *Bible Lands* 23:1 (Easter 1995) 25.

> The "Coming of Age" celebrations at St. George's College, Jerusalem, in April 1990, marked the culmination of years of steady expansion and development of this Anglican institution for Biblical Studies since its inception in the 1960's, and the beginning of a new era.
>
> A building programme had been completed which not only extended and beautified the existing facilities, both for the accommodation of students and for educational purposes, but greatly enhanced the look of the College. A carefully laid-out garden of flowers and shrubs mentioned in the Bible, greets the current visitor to St. George's. With the Anglican Cathedral within the same compound as a backdrop, the newly-faced stone facade of the College has a marvellous setting and an enticing aspect.
>
> Inside there are more new attractions for the 400 odd students who are able to choose to come each year. The space within the College building has been re-allocated so as to provide areas of light, easy circulation, community living and a library. Everywhere signs and symbols are reminders that St. George's lies in East Jerusalem and is part of the land of Israel. Architectural features pronounce this clearly, as do various artefacts attached to the walls, which have their origins in local workmanship.[35]

Pawley notes the attractive "indigenous atmosphere" of the renovated building, drawing attention to some of the courses offered, and to an increased interest in the desert, and desert spirituality. The staff is international, she says, and students attend from all over the world, and from all the different churches. She refers to the financial struggle in providing all the improvements but notes the usefulness of the British Regional Committee (BRC)[36] in providing assistance, especially for less well-off students.

MISSION ACCOMPLISHED?

The completion of the "Comes of Age" project at St. George's College brought with it a sense of moving forward. Even if some elements of the project stretched on after the opening of the new building, there was a sense of "mission accomplished." St. George's now had a bright, modern facility that enabled a high standard of educational activity. Courses were strong and full, and there was a well-educated and experienced staff to lead them. The

35. *Bible Lands* 22:9 (Easter 1994) 420–22, 420–21.

36. The committee which supports St. George's College in Britain. For more on the supporting committees, see part 3, chapter 5.

college was becoming very well known; it had joined the various schools and universities in the Middle East as a credible institution, and was well known among the seminaries and universities in the English-speaking world, both throughout the Anglican Communion and increasingly among the other churches worldwide. It did not yet have financial stability in the form of an endowment, however, and this was a source of regret to John Peterson and others for years to come. The business of paying staff, even deans and course directors, was always precarious and challenging, especially through tough political periods. Staff salaries continued to be supported through CMS and other such donors. But, in any case, the college was now well poised for a bright future. A great deal of work had been done—a great deal of energy had been exerted—and an enormous amount had been achieved overall.

However, there was also a sense of the need to let the college turn a new corner. Early on in the "new building," Gilbert realized he couldn't stay for ever, and John had been there nearly a decade. Both would leave in the next couple of years. In September 1989 the Rev. Ray Barraclough arrived with his wife, Dorothy, from Australia.[37] They were supported by the Australian Board of Missions (ABM). Ray was appointed senior lecturer at the college and, after being "Gilbert's apprentice"[38] for the period of the ten-week course, he took on a good deal of the course teaching. Dorothy was a registered nurse and provided much-needed care of course members out in the field as well as volunteering in some of the local hospitals such as St. John's Ophthalmic Hospital.

Ray Barraclough had trained for the ministry at Moore College in Sydney and had been ordained in 1973 and 1974. Having served in parishes in Queensland, been chaplain at the University of Queensland and a lecturer at St. Francis Theological College in Brisbane, he was already a popular writer and a spokesman for human rights and social issues in Australia. He had been awarded a doctorate in New Testament studies from Macquarie University in Sydney for a thesis entitled "The Political Ideas of the New Testament Writers and Their Attitudes to Roman Rule." Ray had a New Testament focus in his teaching and was keen to bring serious academic biblical study into the courses. However, he also appreciated the wider pilgrimage emphasis and provided groups with manageable, "bite-size" material that fitted easily into the programs. His solid biblical training gave courses considerable academic stability after Gilbert left, and his

37. Reported in *Bible Lands* 22:1 (Summer 1990) 36.

38. From private conversation.

poems relating to sites in the Holy Land inspired pilgrims.[39] During this period, Marcus Losack continued as course director.

The political landscapes of the Middle East were again shifting during the late 1980s. Not only was the first intifada (or Palestinian uprising against Israeli occupation, 1987–1993) in full stride but August 2, 1990, saw the beginning of the first Gulf War with the invasion of Kuwait by Saddam Hussein of Iraq. It was known that Saddam's rockets could reach Tel Aviv, and residents in Israel and the West Bank were encouraged to wear gas masks at times of high alert. The college staff did this on more than one occasion and hid in the college basement. Amazingly, college courses did not cease completely during this time but there were very few participants in some. The college pulled through and weathered the storm. But change was inevitable.[40]

Gilbert's feelings that he could not stay in Jerusalem forever came to a head and he decided he should move back to Australia, to his brothers in SSM. As his time at St. George's College drew to a close, he could frequently be heard commenting that he had gone to Jerusalem for ten weeks and stayed ten years! He left the college in 1989. He was careful, however, to get written into his contract a month every year back in Jerusalem. He had had an amazing decade and had grown exponentially in his teaching and administrative capacities. In a piece entitled "Ten Years in Jerusalem," written after he got back to Australia, Gilbert drew attention to two important areas that had taken him by surprise during his ten years at the college: first, the way his understanding of the geographical setting of the Bible had changed. He writes, "I went on looking for a 'top dressing' on what I already knew; I leave ashamed that I had presumed to teach for so long out of so much ignorance."[41] Those who have gained some familiarity with the land will know what he meant. The other area that touched Gilbert was the spiritual effect of the land and its people, and the challenge this brought to him through the surrounding conflict.

In his new life back in Australia, Gilbert was to become "theological advisor" to Archbishop David Penman in Melbourne, and he moved there in early 1990 to the nearby SSM house at Digger's Rest. However, things were not to work out as planned. Soon after Gilbert took up the job, Archbishop Penman died suddenly and was replaced by Archbishop Keith Rayner of Adelaide. It had been Archbishop Rayner who had ordained Gilbert before

39. A small volume of poems entitled *Poems for Pilgrims* was printed at the college.

40. *Bible Lands* 22:3 (Summer 1991) 128–29. A report says that the college "is still in business."

41. Sinden, "Ten Years," 411.

he left Australia for Jerusalem in 1979. Gilbert was ready to transfer to the new archbishop but only a few days after Penman's funeral, which Gilbert played a significant role in organizing, Gilbert himself was taken ill while celebrating the Eucharist on November 21, 1990, and died suddenly, later in the day, following a series of heart attacks. He was sixty-one. The Rev. Tom Brown of SSM, who had been with Gilbert for several weeks in Jerusalem in 1981, officiated at the funeral which took place in St. Paul's Cathedral, Melbourne, on November 27. Archbishop Rayner presided. The director of SSM, Fr. Dunstan McKee, delivered the sermon. The service was followed by cremation at the Fawkner Crematorium in Melbourne. Gilbert's ashes were buried at St. Michael's Priory, Digger's Rest, alongside other SSM brothers.

In his sermon at the funeral, Fr. Dunstan McKee said of Gilbert, "He had an ability to expound the scriptures and to help people understand the teaching of the church that opened your eyes: you suddenly understood; he made you see what you hadn't seen before. Goodness knows how many people he helped through difficulties, how many were strengthened in their faith, how many learned a new respect for themselves, because of his immense and costly care for them. He would battle tenaciously for the underdog, for the rejected, for the devalued." McKee continued about Gilbert's time in Jerusalem, "He threw himself into teaching again, into more study of the archaeology of Palestine and the background to the New Testament. His interest in liturgy was rewarded by the various rites represented in the Holy Places. His flat in Jerusalem became a home away from home for countless visitors, especially from Australia, and also for his SSM brothers. His concern for the rejected, for the devalued, now became a passionate concern for peace and justice, especially justice, in Israel and the Middle East. He flourished." Finally, McKee added,

> But there is something more, which is the heart of it all. And that is a faith at once simple and profound, a fundamental trust in the goodness, the power, the love of God which Gilbert spent so many years helping others to see. Without that complete trust, tested often by events, undermined at times by feelings of unworthiness and loneliness communicated to others, a trust which was the source of his energy and his work; without that, Gilbert would not have been the Gilbert we knew. With it, with that almost childlike trust in God, I can say along with many others, "I thank God for the gift of Gilbert. I am so glad he was my brother."[42]

42. McKee, "Gilbert Sinden R.I.P.," 419–20. The complete sermon is 418–20.

It was the end of an era. Gilbert had played a tremendously important role in the growth and development of St. George's College. He had thrown himself headlong into its mission and had contributed to its courses with learning and love, for a decade. He had left his stamp upon the college's life and memory. Now, he had been laid to rest. But Gilbert would live on in the minds and hearts of the many people he had touched so deeply, both through SSM and through his years at St. George's College.[43]

For the college itself, another new day was dawning. Following the completion of the "Comes of Age" project, staff settled into the newly renovated building, and courses continued to fill up. In 1992 the Rev. Richard LeSueur from Canada was appointed course director. Richard had trained for ordination at Wycliffe College in the Toronto School of Theology and had spent thirteen years in parish ministry. He was already experienced in desert programs and spirituality, and brought a great deal of wisdom to college courses. He moved with his wife, Rhonde, to live in St. George's School opposite the cathedral on Nablus Road. Starting with the ten-week course, Richard was responsible for teaching at the college for the next three years. Under his leadership, programs flourished and interest broadened.

But there were changes on the horizon. In 1994 John Peterson announced his appointment as secretary general of the Anglican Communion.[44] Like Gilbert, John had been in Jerusalem ten years and had seen the "Comes of Age" project through to completion. He had achieved and contributed an enormous amount—but it was time to move on. His next ten years were spent in London, and his support for the college continued from there. Before John left Jerusalem, the search for a new dean was launched. In due course someone was appointed and hopes for the future were high. But the appointment didn't work out and the new dean soon left. The college was in a mess and the searching began again.

In part 3, we pick up the story of the deans and staff after looking at some matters of structure and management.

43. Following Gilbert's death, an archive was named in his honor at St. George's College. SSM gave a grant to support the "Gilbert Sinden Archives." Seventy-five boxes of material relating to the diocese and the college are kept in the library. See *Bible Lands* 22:4 (Winter 1991) 194.

44. See the announcement in *Bible Lands* 22:10 (Winter 1994) 479, and further news in *Bible Lands* 23:1 (Easter 1995) 30–32.

Maps and Photographs

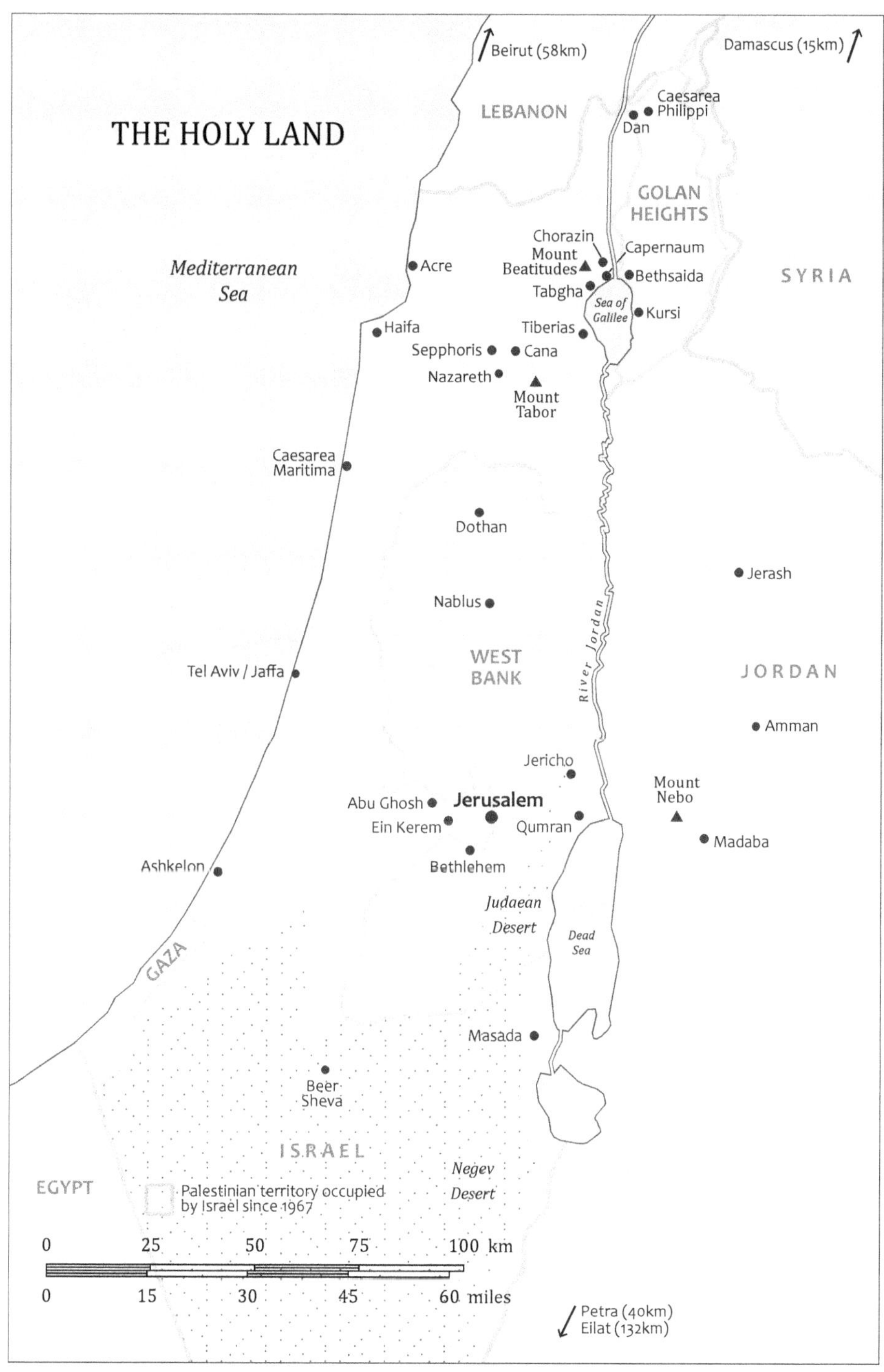
THE HOLY LAND
Beirut (58km)
Damascus (15km)
LEBANON
Caesarea Philippi
Dan
GOLAN HEIGHTS
Mediterranean Sea
Acre
Chorazin
Mount Beatitudes
Capernaum
Bethsaida
SYRIA
Tabgha
Sea of Galilee
Kursi
Haifa
Tiberias
Sepphoris
Cana
Nazareth
Mount Tabor
Caesarea Maritima
Dothan
Jerash
Nablus
River Jordan
WEST BANK
Tel Aviv / Jaffa
JORDAN
Amman
Jericho
Mount Nebo
Abu Ghosh
Jerusalem
Ein Kerem
Qumran
Madaba
Ashkelon
Bethlehem
Judaean Desert
Dead Sea
GAZA
Masada
Beer Sheva
ISRAEL
Negev Desert
EGYPT
Palestinian territory occupied by Israel since 1967
0 25 50 75 100 km
0 15 30 45 60 miles
Petra (40km)
Eilat (132km)

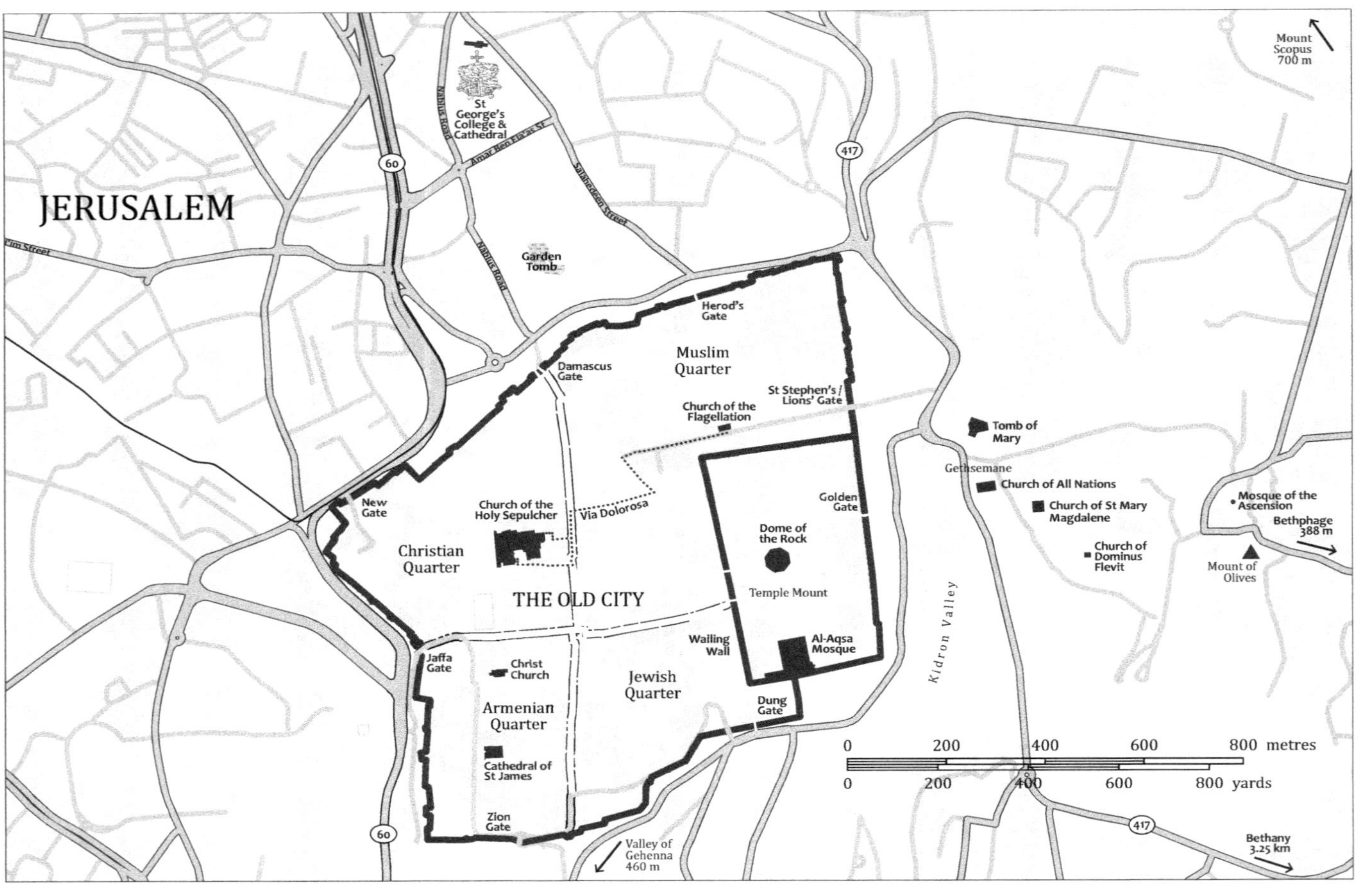
JERUSALEM
Mount Scopus 700 m
St George's College & Cathedral
Nablus Road
Amar Ben Fla'as St
Salaheddeen Street
Garden Tomb
60
417
Herod's Gate
Muslim Quarter
Damascus Gate
St Stephen's / Lions' Gate
Church of the Flagellation
Tomb of Mary
Gethsemane
Church of All Nations
Church of St Mary Magdalene
Church of Dominus Flevit
Mosque of the Ascension
Bethphage 388 m
Mount of Olives
New Gate
Church of the Holy Sepulcher
Via Dolorosa
Golden Gate
Dome of the Rock
Christian Quarter
THE OLD CITY
Temple Mount
Wailing Wall
Al-Aqsa Mosque
Kidron Valley
Jaffa Gate
Christ Church
Jewish Quarter
Armenian Quarter
Dung Gate
Cathedral of St James
Zion Gate
Valley of Gehenna 460 m
0 200 400 600 800 metres
0 200 400 600 800 yards
Bethany 3.25 km

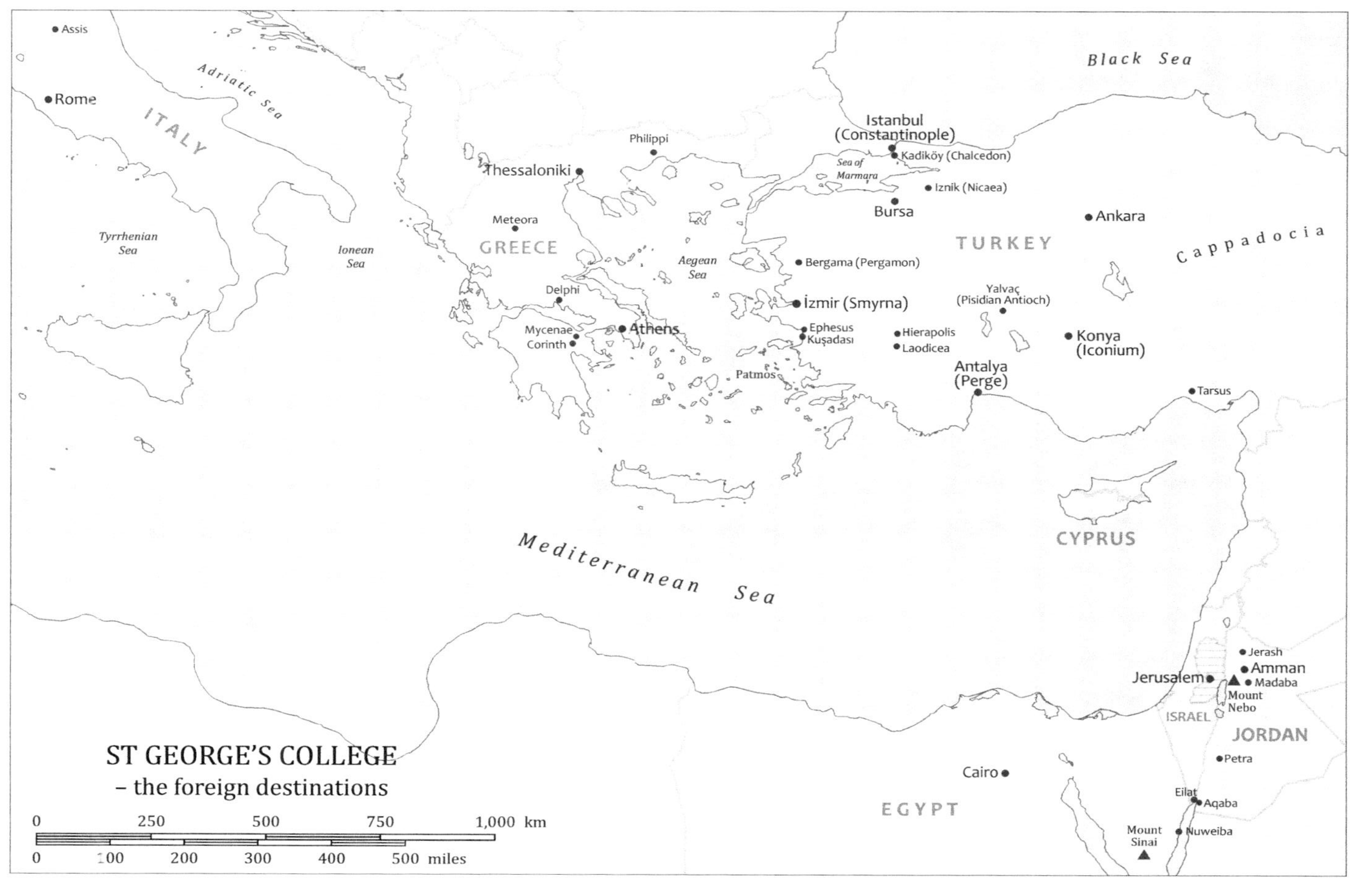
ST GEORGE'S COLLEGE
– the foreign destinations
Assis
Rome
ITALY
Adriatic Sea
Tyrrhenian Sea
Ionean Sea
GREECE
Thessaloniki
Philippi
Meteora
Delphi
Mycenae
Corinth
Athens
Aegean Sea
Patmos
Istanbul (Constantinople)
Kadiköy (Chalcedon)
Sea of Marmara
Iznik (Nicaea)
Bursa
Black Sea
Ankara
TURKEY
Cappadocia
Bergama (Pergamon)
İzmir (Smyrna)
Ephesus
Kuşadası
Hierapolis
Laodicea
Yalvaç (Pisidian Antioch)
Konya (Iconium)
Antalya (Perge)
Tarsus
CYPRUS
Mediterranean Sea
Jerash
Amman
Jerusalem
Madaba
Mount Nebo
ISRAEL
JORDAN
Petra
Cairo
EGYPT
Eilat
Aqaba
Mount Sinai
Nuweiba
0 250 500 750 1,000 km
0 100 200 300 400 500 miles

4. Jerusalem—view of the Old City from the Mount of Olives

5. Michael Solomon Alexander's grave in the Protestant Cemetery on Mount Zion

6. Christ Church, Jerusalem

7. St. George's Cathedral, Jerusalem

8. Archbishop Campbell MacInnes

9. John Wilkinson

10. John Wilkinson carving the cornerstone

11. The cornerstone

12. Building St. George's College

13. The completed 1962 building

14. A college group in the early 1960s

15. Gilbert Sinden

16. John Peterson

17. The "Comes of Age" booklet

18. The "roof-breaking" ceremony, 1985

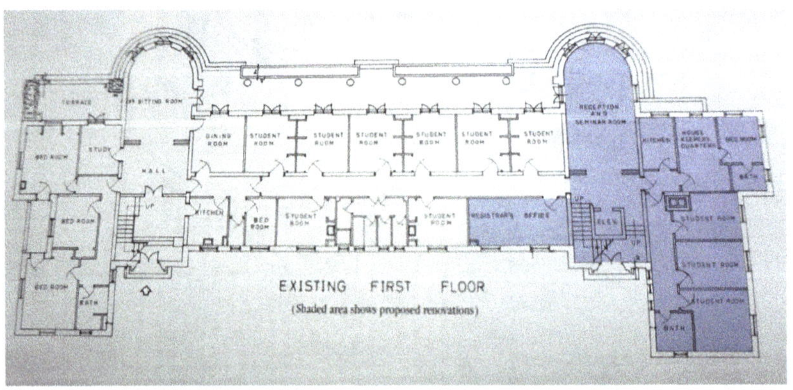

19. Plan of the original first floor

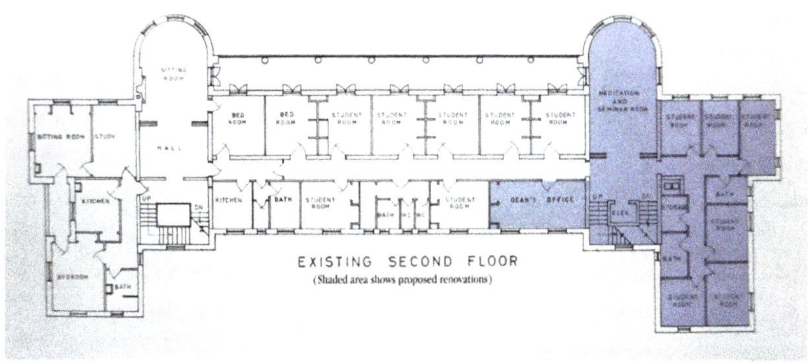

20. Plan of the original second floor

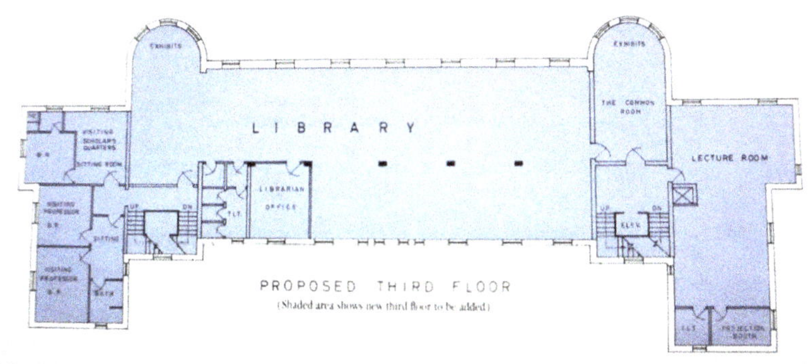

21. Proposed third floor

22. Proposed north and south elevations

23. St. George's College today

24. Olive tree in the Bible garden

25. The Edmond and Patricia Browning Library

26. The Benshoof Cistern Museum

27. The lecture room

28. The common room

29. The second floor landing

30. The chapel

31. A student room

32. The roof garden

33. Stephen Need when course director

34. A college group, 2010

35. Centenary celebrations, 2020

36. Dean Richard Sewell

37. College and cathedral staff, 2023

PART 3

Staff and Courses

5

Staff: Basic Framework

Following the "Comes of Age" project in the 1980s and the departure of Gilbert Sinden in 1989 and then John Peterson in 1994, life at St. George's College continued, vibrant and busy. As this unique institution became even more well known, student numbers grew and academic standards strengthened—all now in the context of the renovated building. Back-to-back courses and widespread interest kept staff well occupied.

Before picking up the continuing story of the college deans and staff, however, we turn first in part 3 to some aspects of overall structure and management. In addition to seeing how the college operates "on the ground," we shall encounter some of the many colorful personalities that contributed to its life at various stages over several decades. Then, in later chapters, we follow some of the college courses out into the field.

From the early 1960s and through the following years, a basic management framework emerged at the college which still operates today. In the present chapter, we look at the main facets of that framework and see how they all fit together, including: staffing, the college foundation and regional committees, visiting scholars, and some educational matters. First, the underlying structure.

UNDERLYING STRUCTURE

When it comes to staffing at St. George's College, there are two basic tiers: first, the on-site staff working in the building in Jerusalem; and, second, the foreign support, largely the regional committees in the feeder countries, and the college foundation, or governing body. The on-site staff always consists of two elements: the local Palestinian staff and the expatriate staff. Usually, though not always, this breakdown involves local Palestinian office and buildings staff, on the one hand, and an expatriate dean and course staff, on the other. The Palestinian staff mostly have oversight of such matters as course bookings and management, library, finance, security, buildings, and grounds. The expatriates usually, though not always, run the courses and do the teaching. The dean oversees everything.

The local Palestinian staff cover a great deal of management. So, for example, after 1990 Albert Noursi, who had overseen finance in the diocese for many years and operated from a room in the cathedral gate area, moved into the college building and looked after college finances from there. He was succeeded by Mrs. Rana Khoury, a tower of knowledge and stability in the college. For many years Mrs. Genia Stephan has been registrar, looking after course bookings and a good deal of outside communication as well. In the buildings and grounds, Samir Khayo was active over a long period and was assisted by Daoud Abdo. In the security room, watching the building and gate, there is always someone in charge on a twenty-four-hour basis, including, for example, Tamer Razzouk, Michael Kort, and a string of others. Khalil Bassa was housekeeper, and for a long time was assisted by Azzam Bassa and other members of their family from Bethany. For over thirty-five years Samer Bassa has been the gardener, working more recently in the grounds of St. George's Cathedral as well. It is very noticeable that, throughout the college's history, with a great deal of transience and expatriate staff arriving and leaving, the Palestinian staff (Christians of different kinds, and Muslims) have always provided much-valued stability and continuity.

Looking at the on-site staff at the college brings us to consider the expatriate staff. First, the dean. The dean of St. George's College is the leader of the college, with responsibility for everything that happens. He is appointed by the college foundation, but in practice he is "where the buck stops." Different deans have had different skills and interests, and, although there are specific responsibilities, the role, like some of the others, is flexible in terms of emphasis. The dean is responsible for the oversight and management of the whole institution, its courses, staff, and finances, as well as relations with the bishop and the cathedral, and with the wider government of the college through its foundation. Some deans have played a key role in teaching and leading courses. Others have focused more on administration and renovation, contributing only perhaps a couple of lectures on a chosen subject in any given course. So far, the college deans have always been British, American, Canadian, or Australian.

Under the dean are the course staff, who have usually also been expatriates. The course director is the most important person, and is usually the main teacher although on occasions in the "fat years" there might also be a “senior lecturer” providing focused lectures in the college and out in the field. There are also volunteer positions designed to help with courses, and there might be several occupants of such roles in any given year. Sometimes volunteer staff stay for a whole year, while others might do a short stint and return later. One volunteer role, helping the course director, is the course volunteer or assistant, very often a seminarian or someone considering ordination, a “gofer,” who holds the group together, especially when traveling, counts the group numerous times a day, pays entrance fees at sites, and does many practical jobs that need doing in order to keep the course running smoothly.

Another volunteer role is the chaplain, who is responsible for the spiritual care of course members and for providing liturgy both in the college and out in the field. Chaplains can be asked to say prayers at any time and in any location, for example graces at meals or worship at holy places. They celebrate the Eucharist, draw up rotas for Eucharists and prayers, sometimes lead the stations of the cross in the Old City toward the end of a course, and offer pastoral counseling and support to course participants throughout. The chaplains usually stay for short periods, perhaps a course or two, although some have stayed for a year or more. Other chaplains might come with their own group or serve in one of the college’s scheduled courses. Others might serve in whatever courses are running during their time.

Among other roles, the volunteer position of warden is important to the smooth running of the college. The warden looks after the domestic needs of course participants and liaises with the Palestinian housekeeping staff. Usually an expatriate, the warden is responsible for welcoming and saying goodbye to all course participants at whatever time of day or night they arrive or leave! Chaplains’ wives are often wardens. They provide domestic care, warmth, and hospitality—a crucial part of the college’s ethos and ministry. The first warden was Judith Lidberg from the US (1988–1993). These various volunteers are essential to operating the college and its courses, and, although the jobs might have had different titles at different times, if any one of them is absent, course quality and even viability can suffer.

Sometimes a person in one role might be able to contribute in others as well. If a chaplain is also a teacher, for example, then he or she can provide some lectures in addition to the basic chaplaincy work. The best-known case of this was when the Australian bishop John Bayton joined the staff for two years in the mid-1990s. Bishop John was an experienced parish priest and had been bishop of Geelong, an assistant bishop in the diocese of Melbourne. John had founded an icon school in Melbourne, the St. Peter’s School of Icons, and brought with him wide and lively theological interests. His fascination with icons was not only theological. He also “wrote” many icons himself and some were reproduced as note cards which were sold at the college shop. Bishop John's wife, Anne, was warden for two years, and together they provided a great deal of life and stability in the college.

Other Episcopal chaplains from the 1990s also come to mind. Bishop Charles Vaché, who had been bishop of Southern Virginia and had served on the college's North American Regional Committee, was one. He went to the college in 1992, and his support was appreciated by many throughout the Anglican Communion as the college became more widely known internationally. Another well-known couple who served as chaplain and warden were Bishop Alf and Joy Holland from Australia. Alf had been bishop of Newcastle and went to the college after he retired. Joy was an outstanding warden. They arrived in 1993 and threw themselves into the life of the college, providing teaching, pastoral care, and practical management skills all around. Joy's hospitality and Alf's wisdom, embodied in his reflections out in the field, were a great support to Dean John Peterson. The Hollands provided a significant amount of help in many aspects of college life during the period following the building renovation.

Other elements of staffing are worth mentioning. The question of gender has long been a controversial element in the appointment of chaplains at the college. Although the Palestinian Anglican Church in the Middle East has so far not ordained women, the Anglican Church in the college's main feeder countries has. Women priests have often arrived at the college with their own people and celebrated the Eucharist for them, though not in the cathedral or in church buildings around the country. Women might celebrate out of doors, out in the field, especially in Galilee at places like Tabgha. Male Anglican priests have sometimes been allowed to celebrate in Catholic churches, such as at Abu Ghosh. But women are not allowed.

However, because of the difference between St. George's College building and St. George's Cathedral and diocese (the college is not a church), the situation has been that visiting women priests have celebrated in the college building. Indeed, there were two occasions (at least) when a woman served as chaplain to the college for a longer period: one American, the Rev. Jodene Hawkins (for a year), and one New Zealander, the Rev. Lois Symes (for two years). They were welcomed by course members but found their ministries in the Cathedral Close and in the land generally a challenge, since a woman in a clerical collar is a rare and often threatening sight to locals, especially the Catholic and Orthodox.

Another dimension of chaplaincy must also be mentioned here: connections with religious orders. We have seen that Gilbert Sinden, SSM, provided a visible spirituality by his presence on the college staff and through his desire to see a small group of "religious" (members of religious communities) in the college. The presence of some who were living with a particular religious commitment and under specific religious vows gave the college an unofficial religious ethos. The connection with Kelham left its mark. In later years, another religious community became part of St. George's courses though not resident. For the years 2005–2011, the American Episcopal religious order, the Society of Saint John the Evangelist (SSJE), from Cambridge, Massachusetts, served the college as chaplains.

The Society of St. John the Evangelist was founded in Oxford by Richard Meux Benson in 1865 at Cowley in Oxford, England.[1] Benson was vicar of Cowley, and the community were known as the "Cowley Fathers." They were an Anglican religious order like SSM, with both clerical and lay brothers dedicated to mission and education. In the twentieth century, the society expanded to the US, among other places, and set up a house in Cambridge, Massachusetts, close to Harvard Square. Over the years they grew more in the US than in England. For six years they sent at least one and usually two brothers for several courses a year at St. George's College. At one stage they were considering setting up a house in Jerusalem but this idea never bore fruit. In any case, they served the college extremely well, providing an ethos of teaching, spirituality, and pastoral care whenever they were there. Sadly, they withdrew in 2011 because of other pressures and responsibilities in their community.

One of the challenging elements in the St. George's College staff dynamic has always been a complex intercultural element. There can be up to five nationalities operating on the staff at any one time, and sometimes more. The usual ones are: Palestinian, British, American, Australian, and New Zealander. The Palestinians' first language is Arabic, with English as well. The expatriate first language has mostly been English, usually with little or no Arabic! In addition, within the expatriate English there have been numerous usages and accents. The result? A good deal of fun as well as plentiful misunderstanding!

Another difficult aspect of staffing at the college has been the transience and rapid turnover of staff. Some of the roles are filled by volunteers while others are salaried. On both sides, people arrive for shorter or longer periods. This results in there always being someone arriving or leaving, creating a stressful dynamic in terms of managing the institution. Stability and continuity can be in short supply. Another thing contributing to this is the business of staff getting Israeli visas to stay in the country. There are often uncertainties and refusals resulting in a planned staff person not arriving or even disappearing! In the resulting turbulent dynamic, job titles

1. For an account of the origins of SSJE, see James, *Cowley Fathers*.

can change: "course volunteer" might be "course assistant" and eventually "Porter scholar." Warden has sometimes been "minister of hospitality." And "course director" has often been "director of studies."

And finally, the staff meeting—a crucial feature of college life though it can be difficult to arrange. Ideally, and outside of course time, the staff of the college (both local Palestinian and expatriate) meet at the beginning of every week to discuss matters of business and procedure. The meetings are essential in terms of management but are also important community- and morale-building events. The problem is that when a course is in session, it is difficult for course staff to attend. When the dean is away, which can be quite often, he cannot attend either. In practice, therefore, staff meetings can drift and business can be neglected. In good times, the staff meets immediately when everyone is back, or perhaps there is a meeting of whoever can attend. Sometimes, an away-day at a local institution in or near Jerusalem enables staff to get together again. During times when there has been no dean, the staff has not met regularly and this could be problematic, resulting in lapses of communication and waves of misunderstanding. In any institution, staff meetings are the glue that holds things together, and they are particularly important in a busy and fast-moving institution like St. George's College.

COMMITTEES

We turn now to the off-site or "foreign support" part of the structure at St. George's College, namely, the foundation and the regional committees. During the 1960s, including John Wilkinson's first years as well as the period from 1963 to 1969, there was very little structure at the college. The concentration, as we have seen, was on getting the first building into place. When Wilkinson left there was no head of the college until he returned in 1969. In the meantime, the college was staffed by academics at St. George's Cathedral. Following the 1967 war Archbishop MacInnes retired and Archbishop Appleton arrived. It was Appleton who reignited the college and brought Wilkinson back. From that time and into the first half of the 1970s a solid structure began to appear.

Of course, management and legal issues had been discussed before, but by 1973 a college constitution had been drawn up under John Wilkinson.[2] George Appleton's plan was to initiate a three-year experimental period (1969–1972) followed by a second three-year period of consolidation (1973–1975).[3] The constitution shows that the college was to be governed

2. See appendix B.

3. Feasibility study booklets were drawn up to support this.

by two groups: an International Governing Council and a Management Committee. We have seen that there had been an international group in the 1960s but this had weakened as a result of the war. John Wilkinson clearly now wanted to get management into place and an international group would cement wider Anglican Communion and other support. This international group would appoint a management group based in Jerusalem consisting of Jerusalem staff and others. The Governing Council would determine matters of policy while the Management Committee would implement them. In the constitution, the Management Committee is also called the St. George's College Foundation.[4] The structure thus laid down was given legal status and St. George's College was registered in Israel under the 1909 Ottoman "Law of Societies." Under this, groups could secure legal status as a "society." This overall structure prevailed until the mid-1970s when John Wilkinson left.[5] However, over the years the terminology changed so that today the international group is known as "the Foundation," and there is no separate management group in Jerusalem other than the staff at the college and cathedral.

With this structure in place but with the need also to encourage a wider pool of financial and other support, the regional committees were gradually established in the US (and later Canada), Britain, and Australia and New Zealand (together). From the early days it was inevitable that participants in college courses would return home to their countries with considerable enthusiasm and zeal, to tell others about their experiences. The life-changing magic worked its way into people's experience and they wanted to spread the word back home. It was thus that quite independently of the college's doings, Friends' groups were formed back home, and gradually committees were formed in different countries.

As the supporting committees became formalized, they received the names "British Regional Committee" (BRC), "North American Regional Committee" (NARC), and "Australia/New Zealand Regional Committee" (ANZRC). In later years the titles were sometimes simplified to "British Committee," "American Committee," and "Australia/New Zealand Committee." Across many years, these committees had numerous different people on them and a variety of different leaders at their helms. The purpose of these independent committees has varied and the emphases have been different in the three different continents. Basically, the idea was that the committees would spread the word about the college (advertising and marketing)

4. See appendix B.

5. It is also clear that in 1975 an arrangement with the Jerusalem and the East Mission Trust (J&EMT) provided the college with a measure of independence: a "license" was established which leased the college property to the foundation.

and raise money to help people to attend college courses (funding). Each committee has usually consisted of something like a dozen members, often headed up by a bishop in the country concerned. Frequency of meetings and related events has varied according to local needs and custom.

A 1985 paper entitled "Concerning the Regional Committees,"[6] written during the decade of the renovation, outlines the responsibilities of the committees, emphasizing that they will work with the dean and staff at all times as follows: supporting the college, its staff, and courses; informing the college of the needs of the various regions; recruiting students; finding funds for scholarships for potential students from their own countries as well as students from less affluent countries; helping find visiting professors and permanent staff when needed; and liaising with former students of the college back in their countries.

Today, the chairman of each of the committees is a member of the St. George's College Foundation, which is itself chaired by the reigning Palestinian Anglican bishop in Jerusalem. These four constitute, along with the dean of the college, the "executive committee" of the foundation. There are usually a dozen or so members of the foundation consisting of the five mentioned, as well as local Palestinian clergy and laity, and usually representatives of the Anglican Communion and other bodies. The foundation is thus the official governing body of the college and works with the dean to oversee the management of the college, dealing with finance, general policy, and direction—and, of course, with staff appointments to the major positions. It meets annually at the college.

The North American Committee eventually gained 501(c)(3) charitable status in the US, and has supported the college financially through thick and thin.[7] Most course participants in college courses are American, and the college is known and respected more widely in the US and Canada than in the other countries. The other committees have given specific support over the years as and when they have been able. In recent years the British have supported a significant number of participants in an "ordinands," or "seminarians," course. The Australia/New Zealand Committee has supported the college particularly by taking large numbers of participants to courses. Bishop Keith Slater of Grafton, Australia, played a strong role in this respect in the early years of the new millennium.

The overall structure of management at St. George's College, therefore, is as follows: the college foundation, chaired by the Anglican bishop in Jerusalem, under which operates the dean of the college and the various layers

6. See appendix C.

7. The trust of the BRC has charitable status. ANZRC has no charitable status.

of management and course staff. Alongside these, the regional committees, represented on the foundation, support the college in the feeder countries. It is a system that has served the college very well over the years and has helped it survive through some difficult periods. In 2003 the archbishop of Canterbury (then Rowan Williams) became patron of St. George's College and this has continued with Archbishop Justin Welby.

VISITING SCHOLARS

Another element in the staffing structure at the college, introduced by John Wilkinson and reinforced by John Peterson during the renovation project, was academic: the "visiting scholar" and "visiting lecturer" positions. From early in the "Comes of Age" project, it was envisaged that the "visiting scholar" would be someone working on a project in the college who might give a lecture or two in a course. The "visiting lecturer" was someone who would provide a series of lectures for a course, as well as travel with the group throughout its time in Jerusalem and the Holy Land, and be available for conversation and discussion. Such a person meant that a course could have a specific focus or theme (e.g., Old Testament or New Testament). However, the ideas were flexible and the two roles often overlapped and merged. Also, as the college became more widely known over the years, numerous individuals came in from the outside, some local, some from afar, to make varied contributions. The expression "visiting scholar" gradually came to refer to them all. Some detail will illustrate the caliber.

Probably the best-known visiting scholar at the college over many years was Professor John Emerton of St. John's College, Cambridge, England. Clare Birch (Amos) had originally encouraged her Cambridge lecturers to go to St. George's, and John later responded by making a visit. He then went annually over a long period, staying for a month, usually in July or August, and using the nearby École Biblique library. His published output over the years was more in scholarly journals than in books, and the École was ideal for his purposes. John was an Old Testament scholar who had lectured in Birmingham, Durham, and Oxford universities before becoming Regius Professor of Hebrew at Cambridge. A strong and traditional scholar of the Hebrew language, his lecture in St. George's courses was usually on the "Languages of Jesus." This became legendary and was an eye-opener for St. George's students. Always provoking lively discussion at the time, conversation arising out of it usually continued long after it was over. John's other famous lecture at the college was on Josephus, the first-century Jewish historian, which provided a good deal of useful background to biblical study. John became an honorary canon of St. George's Cathedral in 1984 and was highly respected by all who knew him. His wife, Norma, also a Cambridge academic (in science and religion), would often visit Jerusalem with him. Together, they were well-known members of the St. George's wider international family, supporting the annual British Friends' meeting in London every year as well as visiting Jerusalem.

Another noteworthy visiting scholar at St. George's during the 1980s and 1990s was Professor J. Robert Wright of the General Theological Seminary in New York City. General was a very well-known seminary of the Episcopal Church in the USA, and Wright was professor of ecclesiastical history. A colorful, dynamic, and highly-respected figure in the American church in those days, Wright would fly from New York to Jerusalem to lecture in St. George's courses. His areas of expertise were many. Primarily a patristics scholar, he had a special interest in the Eastern churches and in icons, particularly Russian. A participant in several American Episcopal-Oriental Orthodox dialogs, he was known internationally for his ecumenical work. Of course, his interests were deeply rooted in the history of his own church and he was the official historiographer of the Episcopal Church in the USA. J. Robert Wright, or "J. Bob," as he was affectionately known to his students, would mostly talk about the theology of icons to St. George's students, making the finer points of the classical debates over "image and prototype" and "worship and honor" come alive in the St. George's lecture room. Connections like this one gave St. George's College itself a status and a standard which enhanced the courses and left students feeling very well served indeed.

Better known in the UK was the Rev. Peter Walker. Peter trained for ordination at Wycliffe Hall, Oxford. He studied classics and early church history at Cambridge, England, and, after a curacy in Tonbridge, Kent, became a fellow of Tyndale Hall, Cambridge, an institution focused on academic biblical study. Peter visited Jerusalem during the 1980s and fell in love with the place. He was soon leading groups to the Holy Land, concentrating on the New Testament and early Christianity. He became one of the St. George's family and served the college in many ways, not the least through his various publications.

In later years Peter became professor of biblical studies at the Trinity School for Ministry near Philadelphia, Pennsylvania, in the United States. His books on the Holy Land include *In the Steps of Jesus: An Illustrated Guide to the Places of the Holy Land*.[8] The material in this book arose out of Peter's work with St. George's College, and in many ways typifies the

8. Walker, *In the Steps of Jesus*. See also Walker and Tomlin, *Walking*.

ethos and approach of the college's courses. His *In the Steps of Saint Paul: An Illustrated Guide to Paul's Journeys* is of a similar genre, and was used by St. George's in Turkey.[9] The books combine a love of the land with serious academic study.[10]

In addition to visiting scholars, the college always used the expertise of local academics in Jerusalem. Over the years, there was a wide variety of speakers from the local institutions in Jerusalem including the École Biblique, Tantur, Hebrew University, and Al Quds University, in addition to independent writers and speakers. Thus, a scholar would be invited into the college either to lecture on a biblical subject or, more often, to address some of the finer points of the Palestine-Israel conflict. Owing to the complex political and religious matrix in which the college found itself, it was always felt that course members should be educated, as far as possible during their short stay in Jerusalem, in what was going on in the area. After all, as well as biblical and historical themes, there were the local communities, Jewish, Christian, and Muslim, all around the college. Interpreting the Bible in the local context was part of the college's commitment from the beginning.

From the days of John Wilkinson onward it was one of the college's aims in every course to have at least one speaker from "each side" of the Palestine-Israel conflict. Wilkinson decided in 1969 that this would be the most appropriate way of addressing the local political situation. Never pretending that there were only two sides, of course, the challenge was always considerable. In practice, it often turned out that there would be two speakers in every course: an Israeli Jew and a Palestinian Muslim or Christian, representing only two of the many views on all sides. Course members were often disappointed that not "all views" had been represented in a course. In practice, there were various and often surprising political views from both Palestinians and Israelis.[11]

One significant character known at St. George's College from the early 1980s onward was Dola Ben-Yehuda Whittmann. She was one of the five children of Eliezer Ben-Yehuda, the famous "father of modern Hebrew." Eliezer Ben-Yehuda basically created modern Hebrew from a mixture of

9. Walker, *In the Steps of St. Paul.*

10. See also Walker, *Holy City*; *Jesus and the Holy City.*

11. Background reading for such a broad political area might be: Lewis, *Middle East* and *Multiple Identities*, as well as Amos, *Peace-ing.* A sizable literature has also developed on the Christians in the Holy Land. See Dalrymple, *From the Holy Mountain*; Aburish, *Forgotten Faithful: The Christians*; Ateek et al., *Forgotten Faithful: A Window*; Hummel et al., *Patterns*; O'Mahony et al., *Christian Heritage*; O'Mahony, *Palestinian Christians*; O'Mahony, *Christianity and Jerusalem.* See also Anglican Consultative Council, *Land of Promise.*

biblical Hebrew and transliterations from numerous other languages. He also made up quite a few words! The new Hebrew then became the language of the modern state of Israel. Eliezer's daughter Dola was one of the first native speakers of the new language. She died in 2004 at the age of 102. John Peterson recalls her visits to St. George's College to address groups on the Hebrew language and other matters of the Jewish faith.[12]

In later years, a frequent visitor to the college on the Israeli side was Yehezkel Landau, a graduate of Harvard Divinity School. Along with his wife, Dalia, Yehezkel founded "Open House," a house of encounter, hope, and reconciliation in the Tel Aviv area.[13] Yehezkel came into the college on many occasions to talk about the conflict, and the St. George's group would often go to "Open House" in Tel Aviv for a lecture and lunch. Another Israeli friend was Daniel Rossing, who at one stage worked in the Israeli Ministry of Religious Affairs in Jerusalem, dealing with visas. Later he was a freelance speaker with a great interest in Jewish-Christian dialog. He founded his own organization, the "Jerusalem Center for Jewish-Christian Relations" (JCJCR). Daniel would come to the college frequently to give his lecture on "the in-between"—the place of Jerusalem between heaven and earth, between past and present, and between East and West. As an American from a Lutheran background who had refound his Jewish faith, he always communicated well with the college's English-speaking groups and was much appreciated.

Other Israeli Jewish speakers included Ophir Yarden, director of education at the Interreligious Coordinating Council in Israel (ICCI), and a young man called Yakir Englander, who had grown up in one of the local ultra-Orthodox Jewish communities in Israel. In the first decade of the new millennium, Yakir was completing a PhD at Hebrew University in Jerusalem. He had passed through the trauma of leaving his home community in ultra-Orthodoxy, and was pursuing issues in the philosophy of gender and sexuality in Judaism. His involvement with St. George's College was not just in the lecture room. He was director of Kids4Peace in Israel and Palestine (see part 4), and in 2011 received an award from the Israel Council for Higher Education for his efforts.

A distinguished Israeli speaker at the college on one occasion was a man called Uri Avnery, a well-known and controversial peace activist who had become famous for crossing the lines in Beirut during the 1982 Lebanon War to visit the Palestinian leader Yasser Arafat. It was often said that Avnery was the first Israeli Arafat had met. Avnery had fought for the Irgun

12. In private conversation.

13. The story of "Open House" is told in Tolan, *Lemon Tree*.

in his early years and had later served twice in the Knesset. His crossing over to meet Arafat in Beirut was a tremendous risk and, of course, lost him the confidence of most of his countrymen: he was accused of treason. But following the war he edited a newspaper and continued to seek peace with the Palestinians through dialog and negotiation. He founded the peace movement Gush Shalom (Block of Peace), and was one of the first proponents of a two-state solution to the Israeli-Palestinian conflict. The Anglican bishop Riah Abu El-Assal managed to get Avnery to come to the college to speak one evening, and the lecture room was filled with anticipation and excitement as he shared his vision of peace in the Holy Land.[14]

On the Palestinian side, visiting speakers included Zoughbi Zoughbi from an organization called Wi'am; Mustafa Abu Shway from Al Quds University; Bernard Sabella, a well-known local academic and writer; and especially Naim Ateek, who spent many years living in one of the college apartments with his wife, Maha, and their family. Naim was a Palestinian Anglican priest who had been born in Beisan (Bet Shean) in Galilee and whose family had been expelled from their home by Israeli military in 1948 and moved to Nazareth. They had gone unwillingly, of course, losing their identity and livelihood in the process. Naim was ordained and worked in Haifa before becoming pastor to the Arabic congregation at St. George's Cathedral. Living in the college building he was usually available to speak on the Palestinian experience from a Christian perspective. His book *Justice and Only Justice: A Palestinian Theology of Liberation* tells his story and is a symbol of his rating as the "founding father of Palestinian Liberation Theology."[15] He founded the Palestinian Liberation Theology Center known as Sabeel at St. George's Cathedral in Jerusalem, and was always an engaging and enlightening speaker.[16]

Another Palestinian who became a great friend of St. George's was Ali Qleibo, a local Jerusalemite Muslim anthropologist, writer, and artist who was a frequent speaker at the college and guide out in the field. He was a lecturer at the Al Quds University in Jerusalem and a writer on local history and Palestinian rights.[17] He also contributed regularly to the popular Jerusalem weekly *This Week in Palestine*. His many paintings adorned the St. George's College building at different times. They reflect a soft and poetic Jerusalem, speaking through colorful images and evoking centuries of

14. His story is told in Avnery, *My Friend*.

15. Ateek, *Justice*. See also his *Palestinian Christian Cry* and *Palestinian Theology*.

16. Sabeel (Arabic for "the way" or "a fountain") eventually moved to its own building in Jerusalem. When Naim retired, he moved to the US to be with his family although he keeps close links with Sabeel.

17. E.g., Qleibo, *Jerusalem in the Heart*; *Before the Mountains*.

history. His canvases were for sale in the college over many years and quite a few of them were snapped up by course members.

Other "visiting speakers" might involve visits to places outside the college where groups were addressed by locals. One example is visits to nearby Palestinian refugee camps. In 1948, and again in 1967, many Palestinians lost their homes and ended up in different locations. Some returned later but didn't get their homes back. Many never returned at all and went to Jordan or farther afield. Many ended up in refugee camps in the West Bank in squalid and deprived conditions. Over seventy years later some of them and their families are still in camps that have developed some basic housing but without much decent infrastructure or clean water. Regular visits to the camps in the Bethlehem area (Aida, Dheisheh) to hear accounts of residents' lives were more than enlightening for St. George's course members and gave a sense of the Palestinian experience and the need for justice, well beyond what a lecture in Jerusalem could give.

On the Israeli Jewish side, courses would sometimes visit the Great Synagogue in West Jerusalem for either a Friday night or a Saturday Shabbat service, depending on the emphasis of the course. It was always a stimulating encounter with Judaism. Sometimes another synagogue might be found, such as the rather more liberal Orthodox one in Baka between Jerusalem and Bethlehem. Dr. Deborah Weissman was a member of that synagogue and would often come to the college to give a lecture or lead a seminar on Judaism or Israeli affairs. She would also arrange for groups to go to local Jewish houses for a Shabbat meal on Friday nights. Another thing was that groups might travel to West Jerusalem when speakers, for political or perceived safety reasons, would not go to East Jerusalem. Visits to the houses of local Israelis including settlers (for example in Gilo or Efrat) would give a sharp sense of right-wing Israeli views.

There were also visits to local Christian liturgies—a feature of most of the college's courses. Because of the location of the college, there were always opportunities, even if the course was not actually on liturgy or the Eastern Christians, to attend the Sunday services in local churches in Jerusalem. Course members were always encouraged to go on a Sunday morning at the crack of dawn to the Church of the Holy Sepulcher in the Old City for the numerous liturgies among the six denominations that use the church and which were just beginning. Another popular one was the Ethiopian service in the "round church" in West Jerusalem, very early on a Sunday morning. Courses would also frequently go to the Old City to attend vespers at St. James's Armenian Cathedral in the late afternoon, any day of the week. A staff member would often accompany such visits but sometimes they would simply be recommended. It might be that course members would attend such services even if they were not listed in the schedule. Encounters with local Christians always formed part of the backbone of St. George's courses, and such visits would be preceded or followed by a lecture or briefing on the community concerned.

These examples of visiting scholars, local speakers, and visits illustrate clearly the richness and variety of college life and learning over the decades since the renovation.

EDUCATION MATTERS

St. George's College is an educational institution offering a serious "educational experience" in the broadest sense of the expression. As we have seen from the days of John Wilkinson, there have always been multiple dimensions of learning in the courses. These have included academic study, fieldwork, travel, lived spirituality, and community bonding. The different subject areas have included the Bible, history, archeology, church history, liturgy, Eastern Christians, and other faiths. Pilgrimage—the sense of participating in a journey to holy places—is a significant dimension of the St. George's experience. The history of pilgrimage and pilgrimage literature have usually had a key place in courses. The educational genre of courses might be called "experiential" or "holistic." John Wilkinson, Gilbert Sinden, John Peterson, and their successors have all sustained the vital combination of academic and devotional elements. The St. George's experience isn't just a class or a course—it's an all-embracing journey, usually changing participants' attitudes and perspectives on a variety of fundamental matters.

Students and pilgrims at St. George's inevitably arrive at the college with their own agendas, expectations, and emphases. Some are "more academic," others "more religious," in their approach. The separation of academic study and personal spirituality has a long history in Europe and North America, and this can influence the overall experience of visitors to the Holy Land. The use of the title "study-pilgrimage" at St. George's is intended to capture something of a holistic approach, bringing the whole variety of elements together.[18] Enabling a smoothly-managed, multilayered, holistic, experiential learning process in a short period is the challenge St. George's staff faces in every course.

To make the learning process as smooth as possible, a number of educational features were put in place early on. Lectures in St. George's lecture room, out in the field at archeological sites or holy places, or on the bus

18. The college course director, Rodney Aist, has said in private conversation that the title "pilgrimage-course" might be better.

in short sound-bite portions remain a consistent feature. In the early days, educational aids were few; however, books are important in courses. The development of the college library helped enormously, especially after the renovation. Booklists and particular course books enhance the learning process. As described previously, in John Wilkinson's days his own books reflected the content of college courses. Usually, selected bibliographies are sent to students before they arrive at the college. Through the passage of time and the explosion of publishing, bibliographies have lengthened. Staff keep lists up-to-date with current biblical and theological scholarship.

One very important book from the early days and currently is Jerome Murphy-O'Connor's *The Holy Land: An Archaeological Guide*, which has gone through several editions during the last forty years.[19] Moreover, college staff have often recommended books that they have written themselves. Other books will be mentioned in other sections but some of the classics for use on St. George's courses have been: Kathleen Kenyon's *Archaeology in the Holy Land*; Herbert G. May's *Oxford Bible Atlas*; E. P. Sanders's *The Historical Figure of Jesus*; James A. Michener's *The Source*; Collins and Lapierre's *O Jerusalem*; and David Shipler's *Arab and Jew*.[20] A selection of the standard guidebooks is usually recommended. Devotional material is provided by the college when students arrive, but Archbishop George Appleton's *Jerusalem Prayers for the World Today* and John Peterson's *A Walk in Jerusalem: Stations of the Cross* have been used a lot.[21] The college chapel has the American and New Zealand prayer books, and mostly uses the American Episcopal hymn book *The Hymnal 1982*.

In addition, in the early days, the college developed a system of course handouts. Very early on there was no technology to produce such things. John Wilkinson made his own charts, maps, and models, and eventually created a slide archive. Along with Ted Todd and Clare Birch, John started producing handouts. Gilbert Sinden and John Peterson created more. By the early 1980s, there was a whole series of introductory handouts relating to each site visited and on arrival at the college, course participants were given a folder containing them. A system of numbers identified locations and subjects so that students could select the appropriate material for each day.

In the late 1990s, with the help of more sophisticated photocopying machines, the content of these handouts was incorporated into two

19. Murphy-O'Connor, *Holy Land*.

20. See Kenyon, *Archaeology*; May, *Bible Atlas*; Sanders, *Historical Figure*; Michener, *Source*; Collins and Lapierre, *O Jerusalem*; Shipler, *Arab and Jew*.

21. See Appleton, *Jerusalem Prayers*; Peterson, *Walk in Jerusalem*.

booklets, one for Jerusalem and one for Galilee. Later, books of material were also created for foreign courses. All these were quite detailed with historical, archeological, and biblical material succinctly laid out. They also included maps and timelines. At one stage, a very useful liturgy booklet was put together, containing words for services out in the field. There were also several small books of hymns for the same purpose.[22]

Another introductory booklet created to help course members was *The Cultural World of St. George's College Jerusalem*.[23] It contained very useful material on living in East Jerusalem, including general cultural practices and expectations, and some basic phrases in Arabic. The same was done for West Jerusalem in another chapter, with some basic Hebrew. Material on Arab and Jewish identity and history as well as some basics on Judaism and Islam was also included. There was also information on some of the many different Christian groups in Jerusalem and the Holy Land. Most course participants from the West would be unfamiliar with the Orthodox Churches such as Armenian, Syrian, Coptic, and Ethiopian. The booklet included simple introductions to these. There were also population statistics and other details. With this information, course participants would be gently eased into the new and sometimes confusing surroundings they suddenly found themselves in at St. George's.

An important educational dimension of courses at the college is the audiovisual. By the 1980s, there was a sizable slide archive in the college, and, with the turn of the new millennium, PowerPoint presentations appeared in college lectures. In the first decade of the new millennium, an entirely new audiovisual system with a large screen covering one wall of the lecture room was installed. Dramatic PowerPoint presentations were used to introduce sites and holy places. Music of many different styles and traditions was often used in lectures, and reflections, too, and this greatly enhanced people's experience. Recordings of some of the music of local Holy Land churches were popular, and sessions in the lecture room could come alive with both traditional and popular music. Gradually, Wi-Fi was used more and more, while staff and students brought their own laptop computers. The introduction of visual material as well as music could turn lectures and discussions into very stimulating and informative events. Today, if there is Wi-Fi on the bus, course members can access all manner of online information about sites while traveling. Since the turn of the millennium, the college has been capable of quite sophisticated, high-quality educational presentations.

22. All these can be found in the college archive.

23. In the college archive.

One identifying feature of St. George's courses from the beginning was the experience of being in a group. Learning was not individual but corporate. This was inevitable, of course, as the group traveled and worshiped together daily. The sense of "bonding" was strong, and fundamental to what the college was about. One aspect in evidence in the later stages of the college's life is the sense of "group activities" inside the college—and out in the field. As we shall see, the "Explorations in the Old City" exercise in The Palestine of Jesus course is an excellent example of this type of learning. Another significant group activity was the use of a Gospel "synopsis" for New Testament study. The synopsis is a large book with the Gospels laid out side by side in parallel columns. The course would divide into small groups and go into different parts of the college building and garden to look in detail at the relations between the different accounts of a Gospel event. They would study, for example, the "cleansing of the temple" or Jesus' "entry into Jerusalem," and by using the synopsis could see instantly the similarities and differences between the various Gospel accounts. The small groups would then report back to the large group. A morning doing this provided a creative experience of biblical study and helped bring some modern critical study of the Gospels into college courses.

In the years following the "Comes of Age" renovation, there were attempts to try to bring the college courses into line more formally with modern educational standards. One element in this alignment was the development of the course evaluation. All participants completed a form asking questions about their experience at the college and handed it in when they left. The style of the evaluation was typical of the genre and asked questions relating to accommodation, food, staffing, teaching, chaplaincy, and the general organization of the college and management of the course. All participants usually filled in a form, and staff made every attempt to improve things, taking into account the suggestions made. It was a useful way of taking a critical look at courses and keeping the experience as honed as possible.

Another educational concern over the years, with more or less continual discussion in the 1990s–2000s, has been whether the college's courses could be accredited in some way by an external institution. The overall genre of the courses has always been "holistic" and "experiential" which has mostly not been recognized by academic institutions, colleges, and universities in the main feeder countries. Also, the infrastructure in Jerusalem simply hasn't been strong enough to sustain such accreditation. Groups or individuals coming to the college could usually get institutions back home to give them credit, as happened when a group from King Alfred's College, Winchester, arrived to follow a Holy Land Studies module which I designed in the early years of the new millennium. This was a

Winchester module accredited by Winchester. But St. George's has never had an overarching institution to accredit its own courses. At one stage all the paperwork for accreditation by the University of Lampeter in Wales, UK, was prepared but at the last minute they withdrew. The formal relationship between St. George's College and Virginia Theological Seminary in the US has meant that students from that institution could receive credit but this did not extend to other students or courses at St. George's. The college still awaits the day when its courses might be accredited by an outside institution.

Another feature of the St. George's College educational strategy, present in all courses, has been the "group reflections." In many ways these symbolize the educational ethos of the college. Usually in the evening following dinner, or indeed at any convenient time of day and in any suitable location, a group gathers to share its experiences of that particular day. Held in the college chapel or lecture room when the course is in Jerusalem, or in a convenient room if elsewhere, the procedure is as follows: a member of staff, usually the chaplain, opens the session by making some comments about the day's experiences. The leader then invites people to share their experiences with the group. But participants are asked not to react to what anyone says, not to interrupt or contradict or say anything back to the speaker. Each group member is invited to speak if they wish or simply to listen. The session is not a seminar, discussion, or debate. There are other opportunities for that.

Participants' contributions to these reflections are offered to the group in a contemplative style, inviting everyone to share an insight or reflect on an experience before God in a prayerful space. The effect of this procedure is that each person is heard for what they have to say, without contradiction or challenge. What each person says is thereby valued and appreciated. Mostly, people share a religious insight from something during the day, a political shock, or an aesthetic appreciation. Group reflections following a visit to the desert or to Galilee, to the Church of the Holy Sepulcher or to Yad Vashem (the Holocaust memorial in West Jerusalem) can be profound and moving. The sessions are usually concluded by the leader drawing together things that have been said, and culminating in a short prayer or perhaps the office of compline. The St. George's reflections sessions are usually held several times during a course, with one toward the end to share all that has happened. The reflections contribute to the college's overall ethos of open-ended, mutually respectful teaching and learning.

In this chapter, we have seen something of the overall structure and educational strategy at the college and have met some of the many dynamic characters who have passed through its doors as visiting scholars. In later chapters, we shall find out more about courses. But first, we pick up the story of the college's deans and staff from the end of part 2.

6

Staff: Continuing Story

In this chapter, we return to the point in 1994 when John Peterson left St. George's College. Following a search for a new dean, the Rev. Dr. Frederick Schmidt from the US was appointed.[1] It was hoped that Fred would "shadow" John for six months in Jerusalem in order to provide some continuity. Fred originally hailed from the United Methodist tradition. He had been ordained into the Episcopal Church in the USA and had completed bachelor's and master's degrees in theology. Furthermore, he had completed an Oxford doctor of philosophy degree (DPhil) and written a good many articles and books. He was already a well-known academic and in later years published various books on ministry. Fred arrived in Jerusalem for a sixth-month immersion process, getting to know the college and traveling with the courses. But owing to personality clashes and differences in expectations and aspirations, things did not work out and he left Jerusalem well before the sixth months were completed, leaving the college without a dean once again.[2]

Following Fred Schmidt's early departure there was an interim period when the college was governed by a "management team." This consisted of the college staff, including Bishop John Bayton, who was chaplain at the time, and the dean of St. George's Cathedral, the Very Rev. John Tidy.[3] Dean Tidy held his cathedral role for four years (1993–1997) and was involved in the life of the diocese in several significant ways. Very familiar with the Holy Land, he supported the college during a difficult time and would do

1. *Bible Lands* 23:1 (Easter 1995) 25. Records Fred Schmidt's installation as a canon residentiary of St. George's Cathedral.

2. See the announcement in *Bible Lands* 23:2 (Winter 1995) 67.

3. It should be noted that there are usually two deans at St. George's: one at the cathedral and one at the college.

so again in the years to come. When he left the cathedral, he returned to England to be vicar of St. Mark's and St. Andrew's, Surbiton, near London. During the period of the management team at the college, a search was conducted for a new dean, but it would take a while for the right person to be found. The management team tried to steer an even pathway forward through a difficult period.

DEANS AND STAFF

In 1995 Henry Carse joined the staff of St. George's College as course director. Before the appointment he had been invited by John Peterson to teach some of the college classes since Henry was already living in Jerusalem. Henry played a considerable role in the college, contributing a great deal in different ways for a decade and a half. He became course director in 1995 and was involved with the college until 2010. An outline of Henry's background will illustrate why he was so well placed on the St. George's College staff and how he contributed so much. Originally from Vermont, US, Henry's journey to Jerusalem went back to the late 1960s when he traveled through some of the pilgrim sites in Europe, including Lourdes and Rome, and ended up in Jerusalem in 1970. He was nineteen years old and fell in love with the Holy Land, making it his home for over forty years. Henry married a young Israeli woman, had three children, and ran a farm in Galilee. He became an Israeli citizen and inevitably became embroiled in the local political scene. He left for a year to do a master's degree at the General Theological Seminary (GTS) in New York, and returned to Israel even more equipped to lead pilgrims through the land.

Henry was trained as a local guide in the course offered by the Israeli Ministry of Tourism, a qualification that enabled him and St. George's College to function smoothly in the land once he was course director. During that time, he completed a PhD in the field of applied theology as an external student at the University of Kent, Canterbury, UK. The thesis was entitled "Creative Ambiguities in the Pilgrimage Process."[4] A postmodernist theological study of contemporary personal pilgrim narratives, it involved interviewing some of the many course participants at St. George's on their experience of pilgrimage in the Holy Land.

Henry's background and experience qualified him as course director in a way that none before him had been qualified. Fluent in Hebrew and with some Arabic, he was an Israeli as well as an American, and had the much-coveted guide card which allowed him to move freely and with

4. A copy can be found in St. George's College library. Carse, "Creative Ambiguities."

respect among other guides out in the field. No previous member of St. George's College staff had been qualified as an Israeli guide, although some had thought of trying to do the course.[5] Furthermore, Henry had skills as a teacher and leader, especially in the desert, as well as in Jerusalem and Galilee. Equally fundamentally, he had a deep appreciation of the Israeli-Palestinian conflict which enabled him to steer pilgrim groups through the murky waters of local politics. On the ground, Henry's Hebrew and experience as a local could be very helpful, particularly in the periods of Palestinian uprising and increased Israeli security.

Henry's time at St. George's included some periods as "director of special programs" when someone else was course director. This role gave him chance to develop programs that were of particular interest to him. He was especially drawn to the desert and later wrote up his experiences in *Sinai: The Abundant Emptiness*.[6] With a deep and wide commitment to the spirituality and, above all, the experience of the desert, he helped many course members through an experience they would never forget. Henry's other publication reflecting his involvement with the people of the Holy Land was his 2010 *No-One Land: Israel/Palestine 2000–2002*.[7] As we shall see later, he also played a key role in the origins and development of Kids4Peace.

Another person who helped at the college during these years was the Rev. Bill Broughton from the US. He was American chaplain to Bishop Samir Kafity at St. George's Cathedral, and was very well known and respected in Jerusalem across many different communities. He had been a chaplain in Vietnam and was a keen archaeologist. He helped on many a college trip to the desert and was keen on theology and college life. Bill was a lively, enthusiastic, and eccentric character, who contributed a great deal to St. George's courses academically and pastorally over many years.[8]

In 1996, the right person was found for dean of the college: Bishop Bob Gordon Jones of Wyoming, US.[9] Bob brought a great deal of stability to the college. He had visited the Holy Land several times before becoming dean and had been on a ten-week course in the 1970s. He had been a missionary for sixteen years in Alaska, and bishop of Wyoming for twenty years. Bob

5. Expatriate course staff at the college have usually operated on the "spiritual leader card" (or "green card") issued for clergy and others by the Commission of Christian Pilgrimages, in Jerusalem.

6. Carse, *Sinai*.

7. Carse, *No One*.

8. He died in 2022 in San Diego, California, aged ninety-three. His ashes are buried in the grounds of St. George's Cathedral in Jerusalem. See his obituary in *Bible Lands* (Winter 2022) 20.

9. See the announcement in *Bible Lands* 23:4 (Winter 1996) 147–48.

had met the Rt. Rev. Samir Kafity at the Lambeth Conference in 1978, and knew the diocese of Jerusalem well. In fact, Bob had been involved with the "Comes of Age" project in the 1980s and had raised significant sums of money for the college. The "Judy Jones Worship Center," or chapel, on the second floor of the renovated building was dedicated to Bob's first wife. Bob married his second wife, Mary-Page, in 1993. When Bob attended the consecration service of Bishop Riah Abu El-Assal in 1996 in St. George's Cathedral, Bishop Samir Kafity asked Bob to be dean of the college. He and Mary-Page arrived in August 1996. Bob brought pastoral experience and episcopal weight to the role.

When Bob Jones arrived as dean, Ann Quirke, from Kilkenny City in Ireland, was registrar. She looked after the whole process of student applications and registrations, and a lot more besides. Ann was enthusiastically efficient and brought numerous management skills to the task, providing a bright and positive front-of-house experience for students. She had first arrived in Israel in the early 1970s with her husband who worked for the United Nations. Ann herself had worked at the British School of Archaeology in Jerusalem for a period and was looking for full-time employment. She came to know John Peterson through friends and did a few short stints of work at the college before being appointed full time as registrar in 1993. Ann brought stability to college management and sensitivity to the needs of all who passed through. During her time as registrar, she shared an office with Geraldine (Gerry) Kennon from All Saints' Church, Beverly Hills, California, who was warden.

When Ann Quirke left in 1996 to work at the Anglican Communion office in London, Ginny Ross from Virginia replaced her. Carolyn Tuttle from Colorado, a seminarian at VTS, arrived as course assistant. Later in the year, Todd Berkenfield took over as course assistant. It was a lively and creative team in an exciting and fast-moving community.

At this point, in 1996, I became senior lecturer at the college, my background being in academic theology. I had taught New Testament studies and Christian doctrine at Chichester Theological College and was senior lecturer in theology at La Sainte Union College in the University of Southampton, UK. Complementing this, I had broad experience in academic research and had completed a PhD in systematic theology at King's College, London. Back in 1981 I had attended a month-long St. George's College course entitled The Bible and Its Setting led by Gilbert Sinden, and had been a volunteer at St. George's Cathedral briefly before the course began. In the summer of 1987, I had taken part in a month-long archeological dig at the Old Testament site of Lachish, southwest of Jerusalem. I had also been a visiting scholar at Harvard Divinity School for a year (1993–1994), and felt well prepared to engage with American students. Most important of all, I had fallen in love with the Holy Land and the chance to join St. George's College staff was a dream come true. I took a year's leave from my Southampton job and headed to Jerusalem.

My first responsibility was to join the August 1996 class, a month-long course very similar to the one I had done in 1981, soaking up the sites, observing the teaching and learning, and taking notes! Entitled The Bible and the Holy Land, the course got me thoroughly immersed in the swing of college life and everything it did. Henry Carse was director of studies. The key difference for me on the teaching front was teaching out in the field and on the bus. My first presentation for St. George's was on the Jerusalem temple at the Second Temple model of Jerusalem, at that time in the grounds of the Holy Land Hotel in West Jerusalem. The session culminated in a discussion of E. P. Sanders's view of the "cleansing of the temple" narrative in the Gospels. It was an exciting and challenging context in which to be teaching.

The course was enriched by the then chaplain, the Rt. Rev. John Bayton. John was a great character with admirable wisdom and experience who, as already mentioned, was an icon specialist. He had one of the offices on the middle floor of the college in which he would see students, as well as work on writing icons. His enthusiasm knew no bounds and his combination of teaching and chaplaincy was invaluable. Icons were a regular feature of his lectures in the college lecture room as well as out in the field. His sense of humor and fun, linked with his serious theological interests and reflections, gave the courses a healthy flavor which was important to the college's ethos. People needed to enjoy themselves as well as learn something important. John helped bring that about.[10]

Through the 1990s the courses offered by St. George's evolved into different shapes and sizes. The ten-week course, previously mentioned, gradually disappeared. The market demand had changed. Instead, month-long, three-week, and two-week courses were offered. Ten days was the most popular. Courses were being adapted to the wider needs and requirements of potential participants. The Palestine of Jesus course still attracted the greatest number of participants, although there could be subtle changes under that title each time. In those days numerous ten-day courses ran in rapid succession: seven nights in Jerusalem and three in Galilee, focusing on the life, ministry, death, and resurrection of Jesus. In addition, new courses tried to consider some of the contemporary developments in biblical studies, for example, The Social Landscape of the Bible. This was a

10. Bishop John Bayton died in Australia in 2022.

three-week course whose lectures focused more on social issues during the biblical period.

In the mid-1990s, Bishop Ken Genge, from Canada, arrived to be chaplain. He was accompanied by his wife, Ruth, who became warden. Ken had recently retired as bishop of Edmonton in Canada, and recalls how their appointment came about. At the end of 1996, just before he retired, Ken dropped in on a meeting of Canadian bishops in Edmonton. In a recent autobiography (2019), he writes,

> Jim Cruickshank, then bishop of Cariboo, handed me a letter. It was from Bob Jones, then Dean of St. George's College, Jerusalem. Bob Jones was looking for a Canadian bishop to volunteer for a year as chaplain at St. George's College. Bob had asked Jim to be that chaplain—or to suggest a bishop. The College needed someone as quickly as possible. Jim had recommended me to (Bishop) Bob Jones. The job was mine if I wanted it . . . with no salary, airfare Tel Aviv/return, board and room and job expenses, and starting 1 February 1997.[11]

Ken and Ruth arrived and did a wonderful job in the now-established roles allotted to them. As chaplain, Ken led stations of the cross frequently, provided meditations in and out of the college building, and made himself available to course members for pastoral counseling. Ruth looked after course participants arriving and leaving and, in conjunction with the Palestinian staff, provided all their domestic needs while they were there. The Genges became part of the college family, sharing their experience and spirituality, and enriching the courses. They left early in 1998.

By the time I returned to teach theology in Southampton after a year's leave in Jerusalem (1997), I could see opportunities at the college which I would dearly love to seize. I had learned a great deal form Henry Carse, a wonderful teacher and storyteller. He managed the courses well and was excellent in the lecture room and out in the field. With my natural disposition to historical-critical biblical study, I wanted to contribute this to the courses at archeological sites and holy places. Even though I resumed teaching at Southampton, I wanted to return to Jerusalem as soon as possible. I met Henry for lunch one day in London at the new British Library at St. Pancras and we shared our visions for the future of the college. Henry felt that he had been course director for long enough and wanted to develop a layer of "special programs" beyond the basic Palestine of Jesus idea. He suggested I might return to Jerusalem and take up the course director's position, learning more of the administrative ropes while still doing some teaching. In

11. Genge, *How We Got*, 421.

England I had enjoyed teaching the New Testament, early Christianity, and Christian doctrine in a classroom, but to be able to teach out in the field had been magic! Lecturing on the parables of Jesus while traveling through the Jordan Valley on a bus, for example, or teaching about first-century synagogues in the archeological site at Capernaum, or about the meaning of the Caesarea Philippi text in Caesarea Philippi itself, surpassed all the teaching locations I had ever experienced. Excited by all this, I felt it would not be long before I was back in Jerusalem.

Following a difficult period in the college, Dean Bob Jones's task was to calm the waters and provide stability and confidence not only among the college staff but between the college and the wider Cathedral Close. In addition to management and pastoral responsibilities, Bob played a part in the courses. Developing an interest in the Crusader period in the Holy Land, he would sometimes do a presentation on the Crusades at Acre, if the course was there, or at the Horns of Hattin, the famous location in Galilee where Saladin defeated the Crusaders on July 4, 1187. Bob's other interest was in some little-known Canaanite altars underneath the Church of the Transfiguration on Mount Tabor which the course visited frequently. Bob and Mary Page provided the stability they promised and the college flourished under their leadership. Mary Page contributed more than a reasonable amount of the hospitality expected of a college dean's wife, playing her part in courses, keeping the group together, and helping the college fulfill its vocation as a place of fellowship and caring. Bob's nephew Michael Jones served as course assistant for a short period at one stage. After a successful few years, Bob and Mary Page left in 2000.

When I left the college in 1997, I was replaced as senior lecturer by the Rev. Dr. Calum Gilmour from New Zealand. Calum had been tutor and lecturer in Greek language and ancient history in the University of Auckland's Department of Classics and Ancient History. He was also a priest from the diocese of Auckland, and had played a significant part in clergy and lay training in New Zealand. He was accompanied by his wife, Raewyn, who had taught in a school in New Zealand. Calum put a good deal of effort into building up the academic side of college courses but sadly left within a year. He later produced a small book on pilgrimage sites in Turkey, published by his own independent publishing business in New Zealand and used on college courses.[12]

Around the same time there were other appointments to the college staff. Two Palestinian staff served as librarians at different times. First, Adel Moghrabi, a Roman Catholic, and, second, Simone Qumri, wife of Iyad

12. *A Pilgrim in Turkey* can be found in the St. George's College archive.

Qumri, a very well-known local guide who also served at the college as course director for a short time. Iyad is the brother of Rana Khoury who has worked in the college office for many years. They were both members of the St. George's Cathedral congregation. On the expatriate front, Shirley Hughes arrived from Australia as warden and executive secretary to Dean Bob Jones. Shirley had lived in several different countries and cultures. In the same period, Ginny Ross, the registrar, left and the position was filled for some years by a young Armenian lady from Ramallah, Katia Ohannessian. Polly Hodgins from the US became warden, and Rodger Featherston from Australia, accompanied by his wife, Finola, became chaplain for a period. There may have been a good deal of transience, but there were also dynamic and creative contributions all around.

Another person who should be mentioned here, though he has never officially been on St. George's staff, is a great friend of the college: Ibrahim (Abraham) Abu-Rakbeh. Known simply as "Abraham," he runs a small souvenir shop near St. George's School on Nablus Road. Abraham is a local Palestinian Christian whose shop contains all manner of olive wood religious items, icons, and other things of interest. The shop's location is such that course members returning to St. George's through the cathedral gate must pass it and mostly call in. Not only that, they are invited to sit down and drink Arabic coffee, making the whole experience memorable. So much has Abraham's small, enticing store been part of student life at the college that it often feels like the college shop! Indeed, Abraham has sometimes been invited into the college on the first evening of courses to meet participants.

THE NEW MILLENNIUM

In the summer of 1999, I returned to St. George's as course director and Henry Carse became director of special programs. This meant that he was able to spend more time on desert programs, for example, while I ran the regular courses. Bob Jones was still dean, John Bayton had left, and there were just two teaching staff: Henry and me. The course director is responsible for the management and running of all the regular courses and for making sure all arrangements are made and all teaching is covered. The course director is arguably the most important person in the course team and without that person the courses really cannot run. Indeed, the course director has always done about two-thirds of the course teaching, and sometimes all of it.

Bringing a good deal of teaching experience into the college from my past college and university teaching in England, and knowing St. George's quite well through having been there for a year already, I was able to rise to the occasion. I soon got to know the archeological sites and holy places better and developed a popular teaching style, especially out in the field. The joy of teaching in the Holy Land was immense and I set my sights on bringing biblical criticism and critical theology into the pilgrimage context of the courses, both in the lecture room and out in the field. The combination was enlightening and maturing as the foundational college ideology came into its own: bringing heart and head together in the context of a pilgrimage community of travel and worship.

A significant learning curve for me was on the administrative side. What I had not fully appreciated before was that the course director was responsible for making all accommodation bookings a year or so in advance for trips to Galilee and, when necessary, to Sinai and Jordan, and, indeed, anywhere else we went. This meant dealing constantly with tour operators, hotels, and buses. Every excursion had to be planned, arranged, and paid for. It was important to keep good relations with everyone involved, including bus drivers and guides. Friendship, humor, and trust helped everything run smoothly. We used a variety of businesses over the years, including Universal Travel on Salahedeen Street opposite the college, led by Naim Tarazi, and then Guiding Star, a local East Jerusalem tourism business founded and run by Gabriel and Delia Khano and their family.[13] They were a much-respected Palestinian business which served us extremely well, and were thought of as part of the St. George's College team.

In the early part of 2000, as I relaxed into the course director's job, Sally Johnson (later French) arrived at the college as course assistant. Sally was in the process for ordination in the Anglican Church of Canada and was looking for an internship until her ordination. St. George's College was recommended to her as a possible place to offer her services. She wrote to Dean Bob Jones, and was appointed. In the event, she arrived in Jerusalem soon after being made deacon and stayed just over a year. In the role of course assistant, Sally did the many practical things that needed doing in courses. But as a deacon she also brought pastoral and teaching interests and soon developed a wider role in the college. Henry Carse was away on sabbatical at this time writing his PhD thesis. In the same period Bob Jones left, and there was a transition to the next dean, Ross Jones (no relation). The chaplain, Rodger Featherston, also left about this time. It was during this period also that the second Palestinian intifada, or uprising, began (2000–2005) and affected course numbers and college morale. Very often

13. Their story is told in Khano, *Eastern Windows*.

course travel was restricted and itineraries had to be rewritten out in the field.

Sally's involvement with local courses, as well as foreign excursions such as Sinai and Turkey, exposed her to a good deal of the college's life, to its models of learning and teaching, and to the importance of pilgrimage and spirituality in the Christian life. When she left in 2001, she returned to VTS and was ordained priest and later married Clarke French. Sally also pursued a DMin (doctor of ministry) degree at VTS, and wrote a thesis entitled "Becoming Pilgrims: Experience, Identity and Virtue in the Context of a Holy Journey."[14] The thesis examined the place of virtue in the context of a spirituality of pilgrimage. It grew out of experience in the Holy Land with St. George's College and reflects much of the college's educational ideology and methodology.[15]

When Bob and Mary Page Jones left in 2000, I became acting dean. It was a busy time as I also continued as course director, doing a lot of teaching. Henry was away on sabbatical. As acting dean, I became much more involved in college management and finance, and started to appreciate the responsibilities of all the staff. During this time, Kathi McDonald from Albuquerque, New Mexico, took up the position of warden. In fact, she arrived in Jerusalem to be public relations secretary to Bishop Riah Abu El-Assal, but it happened that the college needed a new warden and it was agreed that this new arrival would step in. She was an official missioner of the Episcopal Church in the USA and was efficient and proactive in everything she did. Going about her duties with energy and commitment, she looked after course members day and night, and supported the Palestinian staff. This "hands on" warden continued until the end of 2002 when she returned to the US. I was recalled to my job in England in 2001 and, as it was a tenured position, I returned to Southampton.

However, when I returned to the college later as dean (2005), NARC held its annual meeting at the college, and Kathi McDonald was secretary. Once again, the college needed a warden and once again Kathi stepped in, returning to the job for a further three years. Always on top of the task in hand, this now experienced warden could always be relied upon to get things done, and it was a joy to work with her and to share in her lively enthusiasm for college life. In a fast-moving and transient situation, she kept a firm hand on all domestic matters. Unfortunately, she broke a hip during her time as warden and went through quite a challenging period getting better. Feeling thoroughly at home in the college, she recalled in later years

14. There is a copy in St. George's College library. French, "Becoming Pilgrims."

15. Sally was elected bishop of New Jersey, US, in 2023.

how she became real friends with some of the Palestinian staff and their families, and learned a great deal from them.[16]

From time immemorial, the chef in the college was a Palestinian called Omar Abdullah. He did a superb job over many years and everyone loved his cooking. He had a presence that made him one of the highly respected Palestinian elders of the college. However, Omar eventually died and a new chef was needed. In due course, Joseph Arbeed was appointed. Joseph was a local Palestinian Christian who was cooking full time at Hebrew University and came to the college part time. In due course he and his wife had a child and Joseph decided that he could no longer cover Hebrew University as well as St. George's. He chose to leave Hebrew University and come to us full time. His cooking was wonderful, and it was his expertise with food that made so many other things run smoothly as well. We soon learned that if the food was good, everything else was good too! In conjunction with Jill Need, Joseph produced a St. George's College recipe book. When the college kitchen moved to the cathedral guest house in later years, Joseph became cook for the whole close. Sadly, he left in 2019.

One day in 2000, the Rev. Don White, president of NARC, aware that the college was looking for a new dean, rang an acquaintance of his who was rector of Trinity Church, Tulsa, Oklahoma, and asked him if he were interested in applying for the job. He was the Rev. Ross Jones, who by that time had been at Trinity for eight years. Ross had been an undergraduate at Tulane, New Orleans, and had trained for the ministry at the Theological Seminary of the South West in Sewanee, Austin, Texas. He also later completed a DMin degree there. He had served in a parish in Louisiana and been chaplain at Florida State University. Ross was expecting to retire but was attracted to the idea of going to Jerusalem.

In due course, he was interviewed at St. Matthew's Church, Westminster, in London, and was appointed dean, arriving at the college in August 2000. His wife, Gwin, became "minister of hospitality," a title that reflected the college's ministry of care for all who passed through its doors. Unfortunately, Ross and Gwin had not long been in Jerusalem before the second intifada broke out, with devastating effects on the courses. Once again, St. George's was in the thick of political turmoil. Numbers fell immediately and the college was hit financially. A spate of suicide bombings in West Jerusalem made the Holy Land seem unsafe to potential pilgrims. Fortunately, no Palestinian staff were laid off but many courses were canceled and Ross's entire time at the college was devoted to trying to keep its doors open. American travel to the Middle East and to St. George's College was further

16. In private correspondence.

affected by the bombing of the World Trade Towers in New York City on September 11, 2001.

Fortunately, the situation gradually steadied and some courses did run, though with small numbers. Ross was keen that seminarians should do a course in Jerusalem and encouraged this with the seminary in Sewanee. On at least one occasion during his time, The North American Conference of Cathedral Deans and Spouses held its annual conference at the college. During his years as a student, Ross had entertained the idea of becoming a professor and had developed an interest in teaching. He contributed in courses in Jerusalem and in Turkey on philosophical and other subjects. He also oversaw several important projects in the college building during his time as dean. In addition, during this period, Ross and Gwin were involved in serving local Palestinian needs in the West Bank on behalf of the college and the diocese of Jerusalem.[17] During Ross's time, I returned to England, and Henry Carse returned to his role as course director.

Another course director in those years was Fr. Kamal Farah, a Palestinian priest who also brought a great deal of expertise and insight to college courses. Kamal was fluent in numerous languages including Hebrew, Arabic, French, and English. He also read the biblical languages and knew the geography of the Holy Land inside out. Kamal was an Israeli Palestinian, meaning that he was a Palestinian from inside Israel—an Israeli citizen with an Israeli passport. This meant that, like Henry, he could command a difficult or serious situation, in Hebrew, and could steer a college course through security and other challenges out in the field. Kamal was an excellent teacher and, because of his language skills, course members were amazed at his knowledge and capacity for explaining difficult concepts.

Fr. Kamal also had another, personal contribution to make. He had for many years been a Maronite priest. The Maronites trace their identity back to St. Maron, a desert figure who lived in the Syrian desert, probably in the fourth century. The Maronites live mostly in Syria and Lebanon and are an ancient church which has always been in communion with Rome. They are the only "Oriental" church which does not have an Orthodox parallel. Unlike, for example, the Syrian Catholics which have the Syrian Orthodox as their partner, the Maronites have had a Catholic strand all along. The result is a combination of Eastern and Western cultural and religious elements, which is unusual. Fr. Kamal's background as a Maronite priest meant that he had great experience of the Orthodox as well as the Catholic Churches. However, he converted to Anglicanism some years before arriving at St. George's and had become immersed in Anglican theology and spirituality.

17. Ross Jones died in the US in April 2023 and Gwin in January 2024.

He worked in the diocesan office and at one stage managed St. George's Cathedral Guest House. His presence on the college staff as course director and as priest and teacher proved fascinating for most Western Anglicans/Episcopalians when they arrived in Jerusalem.

LAY AND ORDAINED

Following Ross Jones's departure in 2004, there was a short interim period. By that time, I had been senior lecturer, course director, and acting dean, and had kept regular close contact with the college through visits and teaching in courses. There was something of a natural progression, therefore, when I was elected dean in 2004. In 2003 Jill Dampier and I married in California.[18] I had met Jill twice on college courses. She had been a park ranger for twenty-seven years and took early retirement to enable us to move to Jerusalem. However, she needed to give a year's notice before leaving, and so the Rev. John Tidy, still vicar of Surbiton, commuted from London to Jerusalem on an almost weekly basis, serving as an "acting dean" and keeping an eye on the college and its well-being. John Tidy continued in this role until Jill and I moved to Jerusalem in the summer of 2005. Unlike previous deans who were appointed for an initial three years, I was given a five-year contract because a change of bishop was on the horizon and it was the view of the college foundation that five years would provide more stability.

The job of dean at St. George's College is very varied, and different deans have brought different skills. John Wilkinson had been an academic and a teacher. John Peterson had been a teacher and had raised funds for a new floor. Others had focused on keeping the building in good shape. When I was appointed, it was specifically as a "teaching dean," with the expectation that I would spend more time than previous deans on teaching and being with courses. The idea fitted my background perfectly, and the foundation felt that following the completion of a good deal of practical work on the building during Ross Jones's time, there should now be further "academic strengthening." Of course, administrative and fundraising elements remained very much a part of the job, and travel to the countries that provided students remained central. I traveled frequently to the US, UK, twice to Australia, and once to New Zealand during my term in office.

One of the administrative responsibilities of the dean at that time was the task of securing work permits for Palestinian staff at the college: not

18. John Peterson officiated at the wedding ceremony at Faith Church, Cameron Park, in Northern California. Other clergy also took part, including Bishop Bob Jones, Kent McNair, my brother Philip Need, and David Lowman.

all have the same political ID. This could be a long and frustrating process—not the least for those for whom permits were needed. The procedure concerned West Bank staff who had to travel into Jerusalem for work. Those who lived in Israel or East Jerusalem, of course, had passports or identity cards. But West Bankers had to apply for permission from the Israeli government if they had daily work in Jerusalem. Some of our Palestinian college staff lived in Bethany and elsewhere in the West Bank, so permits were needed. The emergence of Israeli military checkpoints in and around the West Bank from the 1990s onward, and the building of the separation barrier in the 2000s, meant that West Bank college staff with permits were passing through military checkpoints twice a day on their way to and from work. Without permits they were denied entry and couldn't get to work. Even with permits, they were sometimes turned back. Applications for permits had to be made by the employer, meaning that the diocesan bishop and the dean were responsible for overseeing the process for college employees. The dean's role in getting the permits often involved numerous difficult telephone calls over several weeks as well as visits to the Ministry of Religious Affairs in West Jerusalem or some other location. Because there could be endless queueing and waiting, the process could be humiliating, even for the dean. Individual permits were only for a few months at a time and often took so long to get, that new applications had to be started almost immediately after permits had been granted. All this was necessary for the successful running of the college—without the daily domestic staff doing their jobs in the building, courses could not run smoothly. In due course, online permit applications eased the process somewhat. But for many years, this tortuous procedure was a feature of college life, reminding everyone of the extremely challenging local political scene.

One of the most significant events of my time as dean was my ordination at St. George's Cathedral in 2008. I had been appointed the first lay dean of the college, and a good deal of discussion had gone on in the foundation about this. It was decided that even though I was not ordained, I was familiar enough with the college and its ministry to be the most suitable person for the job at that time. However, my ordination took place at St. George's Cathedral in Jerusalem three years later. My journey toward ordination had been long, beginning in my teenage years. I had attended King's College, London (then a theological college), from 1976 to 1979 and had been recommended for ordination. Instead, I went into teaching and research. I had not been thinking of ordination during my years in Jerusalem although I did, of course, have a strong teaching, pastoral, and administrative role in the college as well as different roles in the cathedral. When I was senior lecturer and course director in the college, I played the organ in the cathedral for the Sunday 11:00 a.m. English Eucharist. During one particular year, I played weekly. By the time I was dean of the college, I was also a server in the cathedral and preached occasionally at Sunday services. Relations between the college and the cathedral had sometimes been strained in the past and my involvement in services certainly brought some improvements. My own journey in faith was also deepening.

During the few years that led up to my ordination, members of the cathedral congregation were beginning to ask why I was not ordained, recommending that I should be. In 2007 when Bishop Suheil Dawani came into office, he also asked me about being ordained and, as we began to work together, he encouraged me in that direction. It was a tremendously creative and dynamic period when I began again to consider what God wanted me to do. By way of responding positively to Bishop Suheil and to the local community, I offered myself for ordination with the full support of all those around me, including the Palestinian Anglican clergy of the diocese. I could not at that stage be sent to a theological college and was by then, in any case, a "mature candidate." In the Middle East and in the diocese of Jerusalem it is the bishop who decides whether someone is suitable for ordination. I had the full backing of Bishop Suheil and the diocese.

However, by way of a period of training, I fell under the mentorship of the Rev. Robert (Bob) Edmunds, Bishop Suheil's chaplain (2008–2011). Bob trained at Berkeley Divinity School at Yale, and had been Rector of St. Andrew's, Edgartown, on Martha's Vineyard, Massachusetts. During a sabbatical from his parish (2007), he had served as chaplain on a couple of college courses, with his wife, Deb, as course assistant. They were both great supporters of St. George's and had returned to assist Bishop Suheil. During the period leading up to my ordination, Bob and I had regular meetings focusing on ministry and liturgy. Then, following a retreat at the Benedictine monastery at Abu Ghosh near Jerusalem, I was made deacon by Bishop Suheil in St. George's Cathedral on Maundy Thursday, March 20, 2008, at the Chrism Mass with many of the Palestinian clergy of the diocese present. College staff, Muslim and Christian, came to celebrate with me. It was a very significant and moving moment. From that time, I served as a deacon at Eucharists in the cathedral and led evening prayer—all under the guidance of the Rev. Dr. Kamal Farah, the Rev. Zaki Nasser, and the Rev. Hosam Naoum. I shall always be grateful for their wisdom and support.

Six months later, after another retreat at Abu Ghosh, I was ordained priest by Bishop Suheil in St. George's Cathedral on September 28, the day before Michaelmas Day. My brother preached. Being ordained was a major change and the immediate effect was that I was serving as an assistant priest at St. George's Cathedral as well as continuing as dean of the college. My life had come full circle but more particularly, from the college's point of view, there was an inevitable unifying effect between college and cathedral. I was now on the staff of both, and, although this made life extremely busy, it was deeply fulfilling. I had served three years as a lay dean of the college. I continued to serve three as an ordained dean.

During my time as dean, the usual turnover of staff kept the college lively and stimulating. Course assistants, chaplains and wardens came and went. One chaplain during my early years was the Rev. Bruce D. Griffith from the US. Bruce had trained for ministry at Trinity College, Toronto, where he was later a fellow and tutor. He had also studied at the General Theological Seminary in New York. On arrival in Jerusalem, he had recently retired as rector of Christ Church, Oyster Bay, Long Island, New York, and was on NARC. He brought a great deal of experience to the chaplaincy role at St. George's. In the 1960s he had participated in Jerusalem archeological digs under the direction of Kathleen Kenyon at the British School of Archaeology and knew the Holy Land well. He had a lively interest in Christian theology and threw himself enthusiastically into teaching and pastoral care on college courses. Unfortunately, due to limitations of time, Bruce stayed only six months.[19]

In 2008 the Rev. Lois Symes arrived as chaplain. She knew St. George's from the past and had been in the St. Paul and the Early Church course in Turkey. Lois had been an archdeacon in New Zealand and had a great deal of experience of clergy and of church management. During the course in Turkey, the idea grew that she would make an excellent chaplain at the college. She did, and stayed two years, working with course members out in the field at sites, as well as in the college. She celebrated the Eucharist in college and out in the field, though not, of course, in St. George's Cathedral. The fact that women cannot be priests in the local Palestinian Anglican Church often gave rise to surprise, distress, and even anger in women visiting from the Anglican-Episcopal Church and other churches abroad. But Lois rose graciously to the challenges involved and became highly respected, not the least in her role as counselor and pastoral friend to students and staff alike.

By 2011 we again needed new staff. Kathi MacDonald had left, and Barbara Flannagan had been twice. Sharline Fulton had also done a stint. The college was again looking for a new warden and a new chaplain. We appointed the Rev. Heather May Mueller who was rector of St. John's Church, Maui, Hawaii, as warden, and the Rev. Rod Jepson from Melbourne, Australia, as chaplain. Rod had been the drummer in a rock band at one stage

19. He later published work on patristics and on the Oxford Movement. See Griffith, "Yearning"; Griffith with Radcliff, *Grace and Incarnation*.

and was used to life on the road! The Rev. David Tilley, who had been a student at Kelham and who had been on a college course, returned as course volunteer for six months. There was turnover also in other roles. Ben Drury, who was course volunteer for a year, had difficulty getting a visa to reenter Israel and found himself in exile for months. A young ordinand from the Church in Wales, David Rabjohns, came for three months. Our niece and nephew, Elise and Warren Booth, also came (separately) during this period as course assistants, providing much-appreciated support to courses and participants. My wife, Jill, was also frequently a course assistant. This rapid turnover of staff contributed to a strong feeling of transience as it always did. But the cultural richness and variety gave the college a global dimension rarely encountered in more stable situations.

In the last two years of my time as dean, we appointed the Rev. Dr. Andrew Mayes as course director (2009). Andrew came with his wife, Ann, and they lived in the course director's apartment in the college. Andrew had been in the ten-week course at St. George's in 1979 and had studied at the Armenian Seminary in Jerusalem in early 1980. He knew St. George's College and Jerusalem very well. He had studied theology at King's College, London, trained for ordination at St. Stephen's House, Oxford, and served in several parishes in London, Essex, Birmingham, and Sussex. At various times, Andrew had studied at Heythrop College in London, done a master's degree at the Nazarene Theological College in Manchester, completed a DMin at the University of Wales, Lampeter (published as *Spirituality in Ministerial Formation: The Dynamic of Prayer in Learning*), and had published several books on different aspects of spirituality.[20] Andrew's wide interests and experience, his knowledge of Jerusalem and the Holy Land, and his broad awareness of pastoral ministry made him ideal for the job at St. George's. When he was appointed, he was the bishop's officer for continuing ministerial education in the diocese of Chichester. He duly took up the reins of course director in Jerusalem and was enormously popular with the groups. He left in 2011 to become adviser for spirituality in the diocese of Chichester.[21] He returned to St. George's College as chaplain for a short period toward the end of 2023.

Three years after my ordination, and after six years as dean of the college and three as assistant priest at St. George's Cathedral, my wife, Jill, and I decided to leave Jerusalem. Our five-year contract had run out and we had stayed another year. I had been a "teaching dean," and following the

20. Mayes, *Spirituality*. See also his later books incorporating material used on St. George's College courses, e.g., *Holy Land?*

21. He subsequently moved to Limassol, Cyprus, before retiring in 2020.

2008–2009 recession, it was clear that the college would need to focus on fundraising and management in the immediate future. The Israelis were tightening up on visas and the time seemed right to let the college move forward under new leadership. We left in 2011.[22]

FURTHER PROGRESS

Following my departure, Bishop Suheil Dawani and the college foundation appointed the Rev. Dr. Graham Michael Smith as dean of the college. Bishop Suheil and Graham had been together in the DMin program at VTS in the US, and had kept in touch. Graham was Canadian, having been born in Winnipeg, Manitoba. He grew up in New York, and graduated from Fordham University in Russian and political philosophy. He had done a master's degree at the Episcopal Divinity School in Cambridge, Massachusetts, and had been ordained, serving in parishes in Ohio and Illinois for thirty-seven years. His DMin degree from VTS focused on servant leadership and the theology of the Trinity. During his time at St. George's, every room in the building was renovated, all receiving new bathrooms.

Before Graham arrived, Bishara Khoury joined the college staff as "logistics and liaisons officer." Bishara was a tremendous strength to the college, knowing the land and the people from the inside. Married to Rana, who became finance officer at the college after Albert Noursi, Bishara contributed an enormous amount to the college through planning and traveling with courses. Having a local Palestinian, who knew the land well and was thoroughly organized, helped the courses run very smoothly. However, Graham appointed the Rev. Dr. Kamal Farah to serve another period as course director, and after him the Rev. Dr. Rodney Aist, with the result that Bishara's position was lost. During Graham's time as dean, therefore, the support of some strong figures enabled him to focus on finance and management. He worked hard to venture into some teaching but his focus was on renovations. His wife Sherry's hospitality was crucial and she played an important role in welcoming course participants. Graham's love of classical music (he was a keen violinist) was also an important part of their joint hospitality. Graham served as dean until 2015.[23]

Rodney Aist was already known to the college when he arrived as course director in 2013. He had been a visiting scholar at the Albright

22. I became part-time priest in charge of Stock and of West Hanningfield, in the diocese of Chelmsford in Essex, England, and taught theology at the University of Notre Dame (USA) in England.

23. He died in the US in 2020.

Institute of Archaeological Research on Salahedeen Street, not far away. Staff from the college would often attend lectures and events at the Albright, and Albright staff and scholars came into St. George's. Rodney had studied in several institutions and had a master's degree from Duke University. His main research interest was seventh-century Jerusalem, and his PhD from the University of Wales, Lampeter, was published later as *The Christian Topography of Early Islamic Jerusalem: The Evidence of Willibald of Eichstätt (700–787 CE)*.[24] Rodney's external examiner for the thesis was John Wilkinson. Rodney was also a United Methodist pastor and had a great deal of experience working with pilgrim groups throughout Europe. He had worked in the Orkney Islands and in Milan, and had published popular books on pilgrimage. His combination of academic and pastoral experience placed him squarely in the St. George's tradition. And so he joined the college staff and held the position for a couple of years.

It was during this period that the Rev. Mike and Judy Billingsley arrived at the college from America. Mike was chaplain and Judy served as course assistant. Mike had trained at VTS and was serving in two parishes in Massachusetts when he visited Jerusalem during a sabbatical. He spoke with Dean Graham Smith who suggested that he take a position at the college. Judy was a registered nurse in the US, and found herself providing first aid care in courses. They stayed for two years, playing an important part in the college's life. Mike recalls leading stations of the cross for courses, providing meditations at sites, and helping with the liturgy in the college and the cathedral, as well as providing ongoing pastoral care for course participants.[25]

When Graham Smith left in 2015, there was a challenge once again to find the right person to be dean. This time, he came from Australia. The Rev. Dr. Greg Jenks was known to the college for some time past and had been in a course during John Peterson's time. Like myself, Greg had met his wife in a course at St. George's, and had returned several times as a visiting professor. Greg was an academic and an archeologist who had published several books and many articles.[26] He had been academic dean at St. Francis's Theological College in Brisbane and senior lecturer in the School of Theology at Charles Sturt University in New South Wales. He was a fellow of the radical "Jesus Seminar" in California, and a member of the consortium for the excavations at Bethsaida in Galilee. He had regularly taken students from Australia to participate in the digs at Bethsaida. An archeologist-priest

24. Aist, *Christian Topography*. See also Aist, *Topography to Text*.

25. In private conversation.

26. For example, *Once and Future Bible*.

seemed ideal, and Greg was appointed in November 2015. He also became a canon at St. George's Cathedral.

It was during Greg's time that a new development emerged. As we have seen, there had long been a course volunteer or course assistant on the college staff. This person would carry out a variety of jobs, usually with the group out in the field. Sometimes administrative jobs in the college were included, and occasionally the person might teach or lead worship. Often the course assistant would be a person in training for ordination or thinking of pursuing this. Usually course assistants stayed for a year, though sometimes less.

The idea came to Greg that this role might become more official. Linking up with a longtime friend of St. George's College, the Rev. Nicholas Porter, who had once been Bishop Samir Kafity's chaplain, Greg Jenks created the idea of a "Porter Scholar." The Porter Scholar would be financed by the Rev. Porter in conjunction with Berkeley Divinity School at Yale, and was set up for ten years. It would be available to a student from Berkeley, lay or ordained, who would spend a year at the college. The vision was that the "scholar" would have a tripartite role as follows. The primary responsibility would be to assist the work of the college, through helping with groups and with teaching, pastoral care, and liturgy. Second, they would help one day a week in St. George's Cathedral, under the dean. And, third, they would spend one day a week working with the Rev. Nicholas Porter's "Jerusalem Peace Builders" organization in Jerusalem. The arrangement was set up but did not come into play until after Greg left.

Greg's strengths were certainly academic, and he did the course director's job for a season as well as carrying the full responsibilities of dean. He transformed the college web page and oversaw the digitization of the college library catalog. Inviting the dean of VTS, the Rev. Dr. Ian Markham, to design a strategic plan for the college, Greg implemented it in 2016. One thing that happened during Greg's time was that the college dining room was closed and course dining moved to the cathedral guest house where it had been in the days of the original 1962 building. The idea was to bring the college and cathedral communities closer together. This change affected some of the dynamics of the courses, although generally it worked well. It was during Greg's time also that St. George's College was first given the title "The Anglican Center" in Jerusalem or the Holy Land in some of its literature. However, Greg's attempts to turn St. George's into more of an academic institution than had ever been imagined were unsuccessful, and, in view of several personality clashes, he left the college and returned to Australia in February 2017.[27]

While Graham Smith was still dean, Susan Lukens visited the college on interview for the job of warden. She was appointed and arrived at the end of 2014. Susan had been in Tanzania teaching and, as well as being warden, soon undertook other tasks for the college. Initially, she served for seven months, and then returned to the US where she joined the North American Committee (NAC) of the college. She also continued some teaching in Tanzania. As Graham Smith left and Greg Jenks arrived, Susan was offered another position at the college, that of associate dean, a new position created by Greg and designed to support his own work. Susan arrived in this capacity on January 1, 2016. She spent most of her time on administration but also contributed to courses. Susan was to remain in the college as associate dean for some time and became increasingly involved in marketing and fundraising in the US and the UK. During this period, she was ordained in Tanzania. Her efforts at the college were richly rewarded when an application to Trinity Wall Street for a grant was successful and the college received sixty-five thousand dollars, specifically earmarked to fund a new course entitled Building Dialogue Across Conflict. After Susan left Jerusalem, she was made associate dean emerita, continuing to act as faithful ambassador for the college in the US.

During this period, the chaplain at the college was the Rev. John Reese who came with his wife, Hazel, from England. John had trained for the priesthood at Cuddesdon Theological College, Oxford, and had spent many years in parish ministry in Herefordshire, England. He had also worked in Malaysia for three years and had wide and deep pastoral experience. After retirement, John and Hazel were seeking ways of offering their services to the wider church and heard of the job in Jerusalem. They had been to the Holy Land once and were attracted to the idea of returning. They did two weeks' training before arriving at the college as CMS mission associates in September 2016. John carried out the usual responsibilities of the chaplain and Hazel volunteered and "filled in" both at the college and at the cathedral. John has commented since that "serving as chaplain to St. George's College was a transforming experience. . . . To accompany the pilgrims and to help them reflect as they ponder Scripture, and often wipe tears from their eyes, is a humbling privilege."[28] After serving for nine months, John and Hazel returned to England at the end of May 2017.[29]

27. He became dean of Christchurch Cathedral, Grafton, until he retired in 2022.

28. In an email on August 14, 2020.

29. It was during this time also (2016–2018) that Pauline Collier, from All Saints'

Greg Jenks left in 2017, as did Rodney Aist. Before Greg left, the Rev. Dr. Hector Patmore was appointed director of studies. Hector was a Targums scholar (the Targums are Aramaic translations of Hebrew Bible texts), and he and his wife, Lydia, had been in Jerusalem previously at Hebrew University and at the Kenyon Institute (previously the BSAJ). Hector was keen to return and took the job at the college just before Greg left. Hector had been an ordinand in the Anglican Church in Wales and a student at Cuddesdon Theological College. At the time of his appointment, he had already been ordained deacon and was working part time as a lecturer at Cardiff University and part time in a nearby parish. In order to take the St. George's job, he was seconded for three years from Cardiff University with the arrangement that he would work on a research project during his time in Jerusalem. While in the job, Hector was ordained priest in St. George's Cathedral (2017) and served on the staff there.

Arriving as the dean left, however, meant that Hector ended up doing all the teaching as well as a good deal of administration and management of the college. The ensuing chaos left him with a tremendous amount of responsibility. He was new to the situation and was still getting to know the sites. It was a considerable pressure but he rose to the occasion with admirable application. It had been hoped that visiting lecturers would help at the college but, because of financial constraints, many of these were canceled. Hector remembers desert courses, ordinands' courses, and a trip to Jordan, in addition to some new courses such as one devoted completely to the parables of Jesus.[30] Hector and Lydia had taken one son, Bertie, to Jerusalem with them. While they were there a second son, Duffy, was born at St. Joseph's hospital and was baptized at St. George's Cathedral on the same occasion as Hector's ordination to the priesthood, bringing great joy to the family and community. Hector and his family left St. George's in 2018, and went for a year to the Ecumenical Institute for Theological Research at Tantur near Bethlehem. He was able to keep up some involvement with the college and cathedral from there. The family left Jerusalem in 2019.

After Greg Jenks left, the Rev. Richard LeSueur was appointed interim dean. It will be recalled that Richard had worked at the college with John Peterson in the early 1990s. He returned this time to help manage a complex and stressful staffing situation. Arriving in October 2017, he stayed for nearly a year. In the years since first being on the college staff, he had formed his own pilgrimage business in Canada, had been a leader of desert

---

Church, Stock, in Essex, England, served as Archbishop Suheil Dawani's personal assistant. She lived in the college building, in a very small apartment created out of a laundry area on the flat roof of the college.

30. In private conversation.

programs for St. George's College, and had retained his interest in the Middle East. Now, he took up the leadership, but as an interim. The search for a new dean began again. Unfortunately, when Richard left, another period of instability set in and it was decided that the Palestinian dean of the cathedral (and later archbishop), the Very Rev. Hosam Naoum, who lived in the college building, should become "director" of the college, with Bishop Suheil Dawani as official dean. The next dean, the Rev. Richard Sewell, was appointed in 2018.

In this part of the book so far, we have seen something of the basic structure and staffing of St. George's College, the foundation and the regional committees, some of the many visiting scholars, and some educational elements. We have also seen how various deans and other staff came and went and how the college refined its vision in the years following its "Coming of Age." It is certainly true that St. George's has always been a busy and fast-moving institution. It has witnessed a long and changing procession of leaders and visitors. It has survived some political and financial challenges. It has plunged the depths as well as soared the heights. But the quality of those who have passed through its doors, both staff and students, is testimony to the richness of the institution. Before continuing the story, however, we turn our minds in the next two chapters to the college courses as they are lived and experienced day-to-day.

7

Main Courses

The courses at St. George's are its raison d'être. The college exists to offer courses and the courses are mostly why people go to the college.[1] In the previous chapters we have seen the growth and development of the Anglican presence in the Holy Land and the emergence of the college with its two phases of building. We have followed the deans and some of the other staff through various stages of the college's life. We have looked at aspects of the college's educational structure. Now we turn specifically to what the college does: the courses themselves. In part 5 we shall see that these courses might be described as a process of "faith seeking understanding." But here, we follow the courses themselves "on the ground," seeing what the experience is, and what makes those who have been in them say they are "life-transforming."[2] In every course, the emphasis is on the Bible and the land; Judaism and Islam; the Eastern Christians; and on forming a worshiping community of faith while traveling the land. First, courses in Jerusalem.

IN JERUSALEM

It is often joked at St. George's that the Holy Land is the college campus! In a brochure from John Peterson's years, the following words appear: "All around St. George's College lies its larger campus, the Holy Land. Dean John Peterson calls it 'the laboratory in the land where God's divine drama

1. There are, of course, those who stay at the college on sabbatical or retreat but most are in courses.

2. For a firsthand personal account of participating in a St. George's course, see Everhart, *Chasing*.

unfolded.'"[3] In a way, this captures the heart of the matter, as the key elements in the courses are the land and its people. It was never the intention for course participants to travel to Jerusalem to sit in the college building, not even in the library, to study there and never go out. Obviously, the purpose was to experience the land in all its richness and beauty, and to encounter those people who call it home. Also, the college is an independent institution not attached to any university or academic body, so the syllabus and curriculum have always been open-ended. Coupled with this opportunity for exploration and adventure, this flexibility gives opportunity for tremendous creativity on the part of the teaching staff. Personal interests can be pursued, academic projects explored, and changes made from one course, even of the same title, to another. The weakness of such malleability is that course participants themselves can sometimes set the standard and tone.

Courses at the college have never been purely academic, and this has been one of the strengths of the unique St. George's opportunity. Introductions given by college staff at the beginning of courses usually emphasize the "holistic" nature of what is about to happen. At the very least, there are several different types of teaching and learning in a course: lectures and discussions in the lecture room, short presentations on the bus, and on-site briefings and explanations. Visits to archeological sites and holy places are themselves experiences leading to new understanding and awareness. Encounter with the land itself is something that cannot be done in a lecture room. To be in the desert, on the Sea of Galilee, standing in the streets of Jerusalem, Bethlehem, Nazareth, Capernaum or indeed anywhere in the land, is the unique dimension that takes participants beyond the classroom into the "living world" of the Bible and the people. There are always readings of the relevant biblical passages at sites and, on some courses, students themselves do short on-site presentations.

Opportunities for daily worship and prayer provide another layer. Every course includes an opening and a closing service of some sort, usually a Eucharist. The daily worship of the cathedral is open to course members when there is no clash with the course. The beginning of every journey is marked by prayer on the bus. There is always prayer at the holy places, and singing too. "Silent Night" or "O Come, All Ye Faithful" in the cave in the Church of the Nativity in Bethlehem, at any time of year, can be one of the most moving and memorable moments. Such visits, as we shall see later, bring intellect and heart together in significant and moving ways. Then there is the bonding with people from around the world. A single course

3. In a marketing brochure in the college archive.

can have at least half a dozen nationalities represented, and this variety alone is part of the global learning in the course, alongside reflections and discussions throughout, morning, noon, and night. Because of the combination of all these dimensions, the courses are "holistic" and formative in ways that leave classroom teaching and learning feeling shallow and bereft.

A college course brochure from 1976 (not long after John Wilkinson left the second time) makes the following comments about courses, drawing attention to the various layers which make them unique:

> In Jerusalem and the Holy Land there is something unique to be gained by a time of planned fieldwork, study, and reflection. All courses, whether a minimum two weeks or a maximum ten weeks, encounter the land from Dan to Beersheba.
>
> Sixty to seventy-five per cent of every course is spent in fieldwork. Each facet of the fieldwork is carefully prepared for by briefings and followed up by summaries and discussions. The structure of the fieldwork is based on systematic and thematic development so that members may experience each site or journey within its larger context.
>
> The amount of exploration which can be done depends on the time available, and no attempt is made to "see everything". Rather the College helps members become familiar with a selection of sites representative of various geographical, archeological, and devotional considerations.[4]

The multifaceted aspect of the courses at St. George's has always been the "spark" in the college's "Jerusalem experience." From all these layers, woven together through traveling the land and forming a community of faith, the unique experience is born.

It has always been the practice of the college to produce a brochure containing a calendar of courses for the year, including details of staffing and how to make bookings. The 1976 brochure shows that there was a range of courses including the following: a three-week course entitled The Bible and Its Setting (three times), a two-week course entitled The Palestine of Jesus (four times), and a ten-week course entitled The Bible and the Holy Land: Past and Present (once). The 1976 brochure records that in 1975 there were course participants from twelve different denominations and twelve different countries.[5] These calendars or schedules give good examples of what the college offered once John Wilkinson had established the

4. The 1976 calendar can be found in appendix E at the back of this book. The full brochure is in the St. George's College archive.

5. Again, see the 1976 brochure in the college archive where other brochures can also be found.

courses. It is worth emphasizing that the courses consisted of visiting the same sites although the focal themes might differ. Obviously, the ten-week course provided the greatest opportunity to encounter all the layers, and in many ways was the college's primary course. In terms of geographical scope and associated themes, the shorter courses were effectively portions of the ten-week course.

THE TEN-WEEK COURSE

For many years, the ten-week course was an important part of the college's offering.[6] It was established, consolidated, and developed by John Wilkinson. Entitled The Bible and the Holy Land: Past and Present, it usually took place between September and December. In later years it included foreign travel. The length gave this course the feel of a college semester or term, and its purpose was broad. For example, the aims of the ten-week course in September–December 1979 are laid out in the course schedule as follows: "1. To explore and respond to the Holy Land and her people today in order to deepen our understanding of the Bible and our faith; 2. To allow the Holy Spirit to renew us through prayer and worship in the Holy Land; and 3. To begin to appropriate and relate this experience to our lives and work at home." The details also outline three overlapping phases in the course: Orientation (including questions for course members about identity and context); Investigation (including the Bible, and Christian, Jewish, and Muslim perspectives in the Holy Land); and Interpretation (including sharing experiences in the group).

Even ten-week courses varied in content, but the 1979 course included the following places:

- Jerusalem and environs (old and new cities); Bethlehem (Church of the Nativity); the Herodion (one of Herod the Great's desert palaces); Hebron (home of the patriarchs); Mamre (Gen 18:1–15); Beer Sheba (the southern limit of the biblical land); and Ein Kerem (birthplace of John the Baptist).
- A whole week in the Sinai desert (including St. Catherine's Monastery and the Mountain of Moses).
- Back to Jerusalem. Samaria (capital of the Northern Kingdom in the Old Testament). Masada and Qumran.

6. In the early 1970s, a three-month course was offered, sometimes twice a year.

- About a week in Galilee, including Carmel (Elijah); Megiddo (place of the final battle and many other battles); Caesarea Maritima (Herod's port city); Hazor (one of the Old Testament cities); Dan (the northern border of the biblical land); the River Jordan (Jesus' baptism); Mount Tabor (transfiguration of Jesus); Nazareth (Jesus' hometown); Capernaum (scene of several incidents in the Gospels); Chorazin (another New Testament town); the Horns of Hattin (where the Crusader kingdom was destroyed by Saladin in 1187); and the Sea of Galilee (with boat ride).
- Back to Jerusalem through the Jordan Valley including Beit Alpha (with its Byzantine synagogue floor) and Beit Shean (Hellenistic/Roman city with theater); Jericho (where the walls came tumbling down in Josh 5–6).
- Finally, back in Jerusalem: the Mount of Olives and its churches; the Church of the Holy Sepulcher; stations of the cross along the Via Dolorosa; and Abu Ghosh, one of the four places commemorating Emmaus. The final day saw a visit to a religious kibbutz and the Diaspora Museum in Tel Aviv.

The course included visits to synagogues, churches, and mosques. There were several days off for refreshment and rest as well as a retreat. The idea was to cover the area from Dan to Beer Sheba, the symbolic extent of the land in Old Testament times.

It is also interesting to note the scope of the lectures in the 1979 course, which included the geography of the Holy Land; Judaism, including Jewish prayer; Islam; the local Christians; and the political scene. There were several lecturers including Gilbert Sinden, who was leading, and Ted Todd, the dean. Others were a well-known New Testament scholar from England, A. R. C. Leaney (visiting lecturer), Archdeacon Samir Kafity (later Anglican bishop), Canon Riah Abu El-Assal (Rector of Nazareth and later Anglican bishop), Naim Ateek, Daniel Rossing, Sister Lucy from the Ratisbonne Monastery in Jerusalem, and the Rev. Murray Rogers, a visiting Anglican priest immersed in Indian religions, who lectured on spirituality in Buddhism, Hinduism, and Islam.[7]

A report from the final reflections on the 1979 ten-week course shows that participants have experienced the following: their sense of the Bible changed; their understanding of geography and texts shifted in meaning and focus; the Old and New Testaments became more familiar; and biblical texts became more immediate and personal. The sense of Jesus and

7. The 1979 course schedule is in the college archive.

his mission also changed: imagining him in geographical, historical, and political context revealed something of his purpose and aims. In short, the Bible came alive. Being in Jerusalem affected awareness of Judaism and Islam, and introduced different types of Christians and their worship. Local Middle Eastern cultures are appreciated more than before.

The same report shows that the group was international and, though there were divisions, a new awareness of the need for sensitivity toward others emerged. The value of being together in a worshiping community was greatly appreciated. The variety of countries represented in the course itself brought new awareness. In general, elements of history and faith held together better than before, and there was a sense that once you've been to Jerusalem, you're never quite the same again. The report shows that the college's contribution was greatly appreciated and there was much to take home. Participants said they would be processing the Jerusalem experience for the rest of their lives!

During the 1980s, ten-week course itineraries expanded to include two visits to Galilee (one focusing on the Old Testament and one on the New) and up to ten days in Cyprus. The inclusion of Cyprus followed the emergence of Christianity out into the wider world with St. Paul. The ten-week course was comprehensive and all-embracing, providing a feeling of stability and purpose for the college and students which the rollover of short courses often lacks. The downside of the long course was that the group could become claustrophobic and intense. Enough recreation time and days off were needed to sustain a healthy mood!

Sadly, the ten-week course ceased to exist in the mid- to late 1990s for several reasons. The WCC provided many grants over the years for African and Indian students to go to the college but the grants dried up. Also, it became increasingly difficult for African students to get visas to enter Israel. In addition, ten weeks, even for a sabbatical, was thought increasingly by many Westerners to be expensive and too long a time to be away from home. But even though the ten-week course gradually faded away, the different portions of it survived and developed into other courses. As we shall see later in this chapter, the roots of the foreign courses can be found in the ten-week course trips to Sinai and Cyprus. We shall, therefore, effectively encounter the essence of the ten-week course by looking in detail at the various portions that made it up, survived, and developed as separate units.

The courses described in the following sections of this chapter and in the next chapter, gradually emerged as the staple diet of what the college continues to offer today. In some of what follows, I shall use a simple present tense with the hope of capturing something of the dynamic, moving, and multilayered experience still typical of college courses in general.

THE PALESTINE OF JESUS

From the beginning, and still today, the basic short course at St. George's College has been The Palestine of Jesus.[8] This course has varied in length from ten to sixteen days. In what follows I give a full two-week possible scenario for this course in order to convey the flavor of the experience. However, depending on the timings and circumstances, the pattern might be different each time. During the 1990s, The Palestine of Jesus course was only ten days long and some of the following places weren't featured. However, for a month-long course (The Bible and Its Setting) the following schedule would be expanded to include more places, more time at sites, and perhaps more time in the college. A month-long course would also include five days in the Sinai. But for the present purpose, I describe a typical fourteen-day Palestine of Jesus scenario.[9]

Courses usually begin the night before the first day, starting with evening prayer in St. George's Cathedral and a welcoming reception in the college, with introductions and the announcement of essential housekeeping matters. Usually, people have traveled a long way, so it's early to bed in preparation for a fresh beginning the following morning.

Day 1: The first day begins with an opening Eucharist in St. George's Cathedral, followed by breakfast, and then a group gathering in the college lecture room for introductions and orientation. Students introduce themselves and talk about why they have come to Jerusalem and what their expectations are. They are then introduced to the college building, its library and bookshop, and there are further announcements about domestic arrangements. After a break there is an introductory lecture and discussion about the history and geography of the Holy Land or about pilgrimage.[10]

This is followed by lunch, after which the group sets off by bus to spend the afternoon in and around Jerusalem. The journey on the bus begins with a short prayer, a standard college practice on all excursions in all courses. During the next couple of hours, the bus stops at various vantage points to illustrate the topography of the city and to see some of the main sites. The Mount of Olives and Mount Scopus give participants perfect views of the city and of the desert. The panoramic view of Jerusalem from the Mount

8. From time to time at the college there have been discussions about the contemporary political implications of this title. No contemporary nuance was ever intended. Both "Israel" and "Palestine" were known in antiquity.

9. Material used in this and other courses in Israel-Palestine is published in Need, *Following Jesus*. See also Need, *Gospels*.

10. Typical material might be: Armstrong, *History*; Montefiore, *Jerusalem*; Wilken, *Land Called Holy*; or Turner, *Image*.

of Olives is everyone's dream, and provides good opportunity to introduce visitors to the history of the city. A reading of Ps 122 starts to help students make connections between biblical texts and geographical locations: "I was glad when they said to me, 'Let us go to the house of the LORD!' Our feet are standing within your gates, O Jerusalem" (Ps 122:1–2). With brief outlines, introductions, and explanations, the aim is to catch something of the flavor of the city, its history, and contemporary life. Then it's back to the college for a break, evening prayer in the cathedral, and dinner. In the evening the group enjoys a "sound and light" show of Jerusalem and the Holy Land, with commentary by a staff member using the state-of-the-art audiovisual equipment in the lecture room.

Day 2: The daily pattern of meals in the dining room and worship in the cathedral provides the structure while the course is in Jerusalem. On the second day, course participants are sent out to explore the Old City in groups. This is an exciting way of introducing students to the walled city and its people, and a good way of triggering some real encounters. First, a morning lecture on the four quarters of the Old City: Jewish, Muslim, Christian, and Armenian. This introduces students to some of the history and dynamics of Jerusalem. Some geography and some of the traditions of the various peoples are included. Then, divided into four groups, participants are given a quarter to explore, and the following list of questions and activities to help them:[11]

> Your assignment is to explore one of the Quarters with the following questions and tasks in mind. Be ready to compile a report of your discoveries to present to the whole group.
>
> Bring with you: a map of the Old City.
>
> 1. Describe the boundaries of your Quarter. Are they clearly defined? Is there a contrast with neighboring Quarters?
> 2. Can you find a high place from which to observe your Quarter? If so, what are your observations from there?
> 3. What is the major religious shrine in your Quarter?
> 4. Can you find another religious shrine? Visit and note your impressions.
> 5. Are there any excavations under way or restored ancient buildings in your Quarter?
> 6. What is your impression of the people? Can you discern different ethnic or religious communities in your Quarter? Strike up a conversation

11. "Explorations in the Old City," from the St. George's College archive.

with a resident (not a tourist). Ask them what it is like to live in that Quarter.

7. Bring back a small item to symbolize your experience in your Quarter.

Students leave the college and make their way to the Old City where they remain until the middle of the afternoon. By about 4:00 p.m. they gather in the college lecture room for an hour's debriefing. There is always great excitement as they share their many experiences of the rich cultural mixtures of people, buildings, and food! In a few hours they have met some locals and learned much about life in Jerusalem. They have soaked up some of the complex religious and political layers and heard some real-life stories. Also, they have brought back symbols of their experience: a menorah, a Jerusalem olive wood cross, a piece of Armenian pizza, and a "Call to Prayer" alarm clock! After evening prayer, a free evening enables further conversation and sharing of insights and awakenings within the group.

Day 3: Today is Bethlehem, and an opportunity to consider the birth of Jesus. A lecture on the New Testament birth narratives of Matthew and Luke and the tradition of Jesus' birth in Bethlehem in later writings kicks up some serious conversations about the relation between history and faith. Groups are usually very mixed in background. Some might have done some Gospel criticism, while this approach could be very new to others. Most participants probably do not realize the differences between Matthew and Luke. Someone else might have done a PhD on the subject! Once we had a Harvard Divinity professor in the group alongside others who had never really reflected on faith very much until then. Diversity makes for lively discussion and some steep learning curves.

On the bus to Bethlehem, only five miles south of Jerusalem, a staff member or guide gives a commentary on the city of Jerusalem, walls, and gates, as we pass through the traffic. Traditions relating to Elijah come up as we pass the Greek Orthodox Monastery of Mar Elias. The Ecumenical Institute for Theological Research known as Tantur, near Bethlehem, gives an opportunity to talk about other aspects of local and international life. And then students are quite shocked as we pass into the West Bank through the Israeli checkpoint and separation wall, especially when Israeli soldiers (with guns) get onto the bus to check passports. New depths in the local conflict are revealed and much discussion ensues, then and later.[12] Once

12. As already noted, Israeli military checkpoints appeared in and around the West Bank in the 1990s, and the separation wall later, in the 2000s. All college courses in the Holy Land are affected by these, and itineraries must sometimes be changed when entrance to Palestinian areas is denied. Over the years, tensions have increased and course visits to the West Bank have been less frequent since the building of the wall.

inside Bethlehem, the visual change is stunning. We are now in a different geopolitical and socioeconomic landscape.

On the way into town, we focus our minds on Jesus, King David (also born in Bethlehem), and St. Jerome who lived in Bethlehem for thirty-eight years in the fourth century and who translated the Bible into Latin here—the Vulgate. He also started a monastery with two ladies: Paula and Eustochium. We make our way to Manger Square and the Church of the Nativity, the traditional birthplace of Jesus. Outside the church we read a section of Matthew or Luke's infancy narrative, and then hear a brief outline of the history of the church—built by Constantine, rebuilt by Justinian—followed by questions.

Inside the church, we view the Crusader mosaics and visit the Cave of the Nativity. Depending on the time of year and the political climate, there might be a two-hour queue or we might get in straight away. Finally, we kneel, pray, and sing, focusing on the fourteen-pointed star in the floor marking Jesus' birth (Matt 1:17), leaving people speechless. Lunch somewhere on Manger Square and time for some shopping and immersion in the local culture is followed by the return to the bus and the ride back through the military checkpoint up to Jerusalem. On the way, someone reads on the microphone T. S. Eliot's *The Journey of the Magi* in prayerful mood.[13] An evening reflection, sharing insights and impressions from the day, brings out questions of faith, history, politics, and personal belief. St. George's Bethlehem day always works its miracle of activating hearts and minds, though course members are often left with nagging questions.

Day 4: Following the birth of Jesus, it is now time to think about John the Baptist.[14] This day starts with a lecture on John and his world, the New Testament narratives about him, and the many traditions associated with him. Then, off on the bus to Ein Kerem, the beautiful village in West Jerusalem associated since the early Byzantine period with the birth of John and with the visitation of Mary to Elizabeth. Unlike Bethlehem, Ein Kerem fell inside Israel in 1948 and so has a totally different cultural and political feel. Today, it is an attractive artists' village with cafes, restaurants, and many tourists. In the summer it is glorious. The visit for the group is to the two beautiful churches: St. John the Baptist, marking his birth, and the Visitation, marking the famous meeting between Mary and Elizabeth. As usual, there is commentary on the bus, introductions to the churches, and

---

Bethlehem is usually but not always accessible.

13. See Eliot, *Complete*, 103–4.

14. Sometimes the itinerary tries to follow Gospel chronology but this is not always possible.

appropriate Bible readings and discussion. What can be known about John? What was his relation to Jesus and his message? Did John belong to the Essenes, associated with the community that lived at Qumran? Much to discuss over lunch in one of the local restaurants.

The afternoon changes gear quite dramatically, for near Ein Kerem is Yad Vashem,[15] the Holocaust memorial, commemorating the deaths of six million Jews in Hitler's gas chambers during the Second World War. Course members are visibly shocked. No guiding is allowed at Yad Vashem but the couple of hours spent walking slowly through the memorial trigger deep emotions in course members. There is loud silence on the bus going back to the college, but an evening reflection on the experiences of the day brings forth depths of emotion and awareness that people never imagined they could have. Processing this experience will take the rest of our lives.

Day 5: Today we return to the Old City, this time early to get into the queue for visiting the Haram esh-Sharif (Noble Sanctuary), or Temple Mount. By bus to the Dung Gate and then into the queue. A long wait, and then security checks lead us onto the huge platform which formed the base of Herod's temple and which today is the location of the Muslim Dome of the Rock. A guide and a staff member speak about the Jewish past, the Muslim present, and the complex political crisscrossing of layers of history. It is an excellent location, to say the least, for outlining some of the important elements of Judaism and Islam. A tour of the site provides endless stunning views of Jerusalem in all directions. If permitted, we enter the Dome of the Rock and the Al-Aqsa Mosque. The visits are stunning and provide a tangible sense of Muslim prayer and tradition. Then, out through another gate to visit the Western or Wailing Wall. Men and women are separated, which brings some surprise to our group. The men can get right under Wilson's Arch to see some of the Herodian foundations. History and religion are all around us!

Then, a walk through the winding alleyways of the Old City brings us to the Lutheran Hospice for lunch. Afterward, cake and coffee in the sitting room while someone plays the piano. Then, a lecture on the history of the Church of the Holy Sepulcher with one of the best views in Jerusalem of the actual building through the large window of the room we are using. The lecture provides a truly amazing introduction. The Gospel narratives, the tomb of Christ, Constantine and Helena, the various destructions and rebuilds of the church, the Crusades, and finally the six Christian denominations that

15. Hebrew for "a monument and a name," from Isa 56:5.

use the church today are all covered. The aim is to illustrate briefly how the church grew into its present form.[16]

On the way out of the Lutheran Hospice, time on the roof provides more excellent views. We then walk round the corner for an hour's visit to the church itself: in from the roof, down through the Ethiopian Chapel. Following several focal points, the climax is naturally Calvary and the tomb of Jesus. Individual prayers at the tomb, if we can get in, are moving beyond words. Then, out of the church through the main door. There's no way of introducing questions about the death and resurrection of Jesus quite like this way. Provoking different reactions and emotions, different views and experiences, and different understandings of faith, this visit, like others, brings heart and mind into focused concentration. Walking back to the college through the Old City, we stop at Zalatimo's sweet shop to view some remains of the Constantinian church. Along the way, course participants share thoughts and experiences. An evening reflection session brings out more.

Day 6: Today we travel to Galilee. A very early breakfast is followed by an early start from Jerusalem on one of the main highways, taking us a couple of hours to reach Caesarea Maritima, the port city built by Herod the Great. It was also home to Byzantine Christians including Origen and his library, and of course the Crusaders. On the bus we share more biblical geography with a lecture on the Philistines, and then the political landscape of the world of Jesus leading us nicely to our destination, which was also home to Pontius Pilate when he was not in Jerusalem. A couple of hours in Caesarea take us through the famous theater and amphitheater, as well as Herod's palace, and the Byzantine and Crusader remains. It is a thorough immersion in the world of Jesus, the early Christians, and later Christianity.

By lunchtime we're in Nazareth, and, following lunch, visit the main shrines. The huge Basilica of the Annunciation is the starting point. An introduction to Luke 1:26–38 outside, along with an explanation of the church and its predecessors, leads group members into an interesting discussion about modern Nazareth. After a visit of up to an hour we meet outside for glimpses of the street level at the time of Jesus. Then a walking tour through the streets of Nazareth takes us to the little Greek Orthodox Church of St. Gabriel with its icons and frescoes, and the famous spring water. Participants drink the water and pray. We sing in the church and discover its wonderful acoustics.

After St. Gabriel's, we make our way to our lodgings for the night. Over the years, these have often been at the Sisters of Nazareth across the

16. I published material on this church in Need, *Jerusalem: Church.*

road from the Basilica. Frequently they have been at St. Margaret's Hostel on the top of the hill, with its glorious views over Nazareth, and which belongs to the Anglican diocese.[17] Very often in recent years, the group has stayed an hour away from Nazareth at the German Benedictine Pilgerhaus at Tabgha on the Sea of Galilee, a state-of-the-art retreat house fitting our needs perfectly with its chapel and lakeside altar.

When staying at the Sisters of Nazareth, another treat is possible. Soon after their arrival on the site in the nineteenth century, the nuns started some repair work on their building and workmen dropped down to a lower level. Further excavations uncovered a superb rolling stone tomb in very good condition, dating from the period of the Second Temple, and probably the best in the Holy Land. There were also remains of other buildings from the Byzantine and Crusader periods. One interpretation of the excavations is that they reveal the first-century house of Joseph (across the road from the house of Mary at the Basilica), with a tomb over which later churches had been built. The sisters never did make very much of their discovery, although in recent years it has come into scholarly focus through the work of the archeologist Ken Dark who thinks that the site may well include the childhood home of Jesus.[18] Seeing these excavations provides an excellent learning curve for course participants as they connect this experience to their visit to the Church of the Holy Sepulcher in Jerusalem and its tomb of Christ. St. George's College has had a special relation with the sisters over many years, particularly with Sister Claude and Sister Stephania who would often give guided tours of the excavations. Following the visit, there is lively discussion on the circumstances and meaning of Jesus' childhood, death, burial, and resurrection.

Day 7: When staying at Pilgerhaus on the Sea of Galilee, we start the day with an early Eucharist on the lakefront, followed by breakfast. Then we're off around the lake to the various key locations. Mount Beatitudes with its focus on the Sermon on the Mount, its glorious gardens, and spectacular views, provides an opportunity to read part of the sermon from Matt 5 and hear a short reflection and discussion relating the message to the modern world. The contrast between this place and some of the experiences in Jerusalem (the separation wall and Yad Vashem) is tangible. The Church of the Beatitudes was designed by the famous Holy Land architect Antonio Barluzzi and offers a rich opportunity for peaceful prayer.[19] Then it's off

17. Depending on time and course focus it has sometimes been possible, when staying in Nazareth, to visit Mount Carmel (with its associations with the prophet Elijah), and even Haifa (to see the Bahá'í temple).

18. See Dark, *Archaeology*.

19. Barluzzi (1884–1960) was an Italian who designed several churches in the Holy

to Capernaum to visit the town of Jesus with its reconstructed synagogue, Peter's house, and the modern church. Once inside the site, a half-hour lecture on the history of the synagogue raises all sorts of interesting points about synagogues at the time of Jesus. A visit to the reconstructed white limestone synagogue, knowing that this was not the synagogue Jesus knew, sees us reading Mark 1:21–31. With all the challenging historical questions before us, the context is illuminating to say the least.

Stopping at the Benedictine church at Tabgha, we visit the mosaics, including the famous "loaves and fishes" mosaic in front of the high altar. A reading of the Gospel story of the feeding of the five thousand (John 6:1–15) marks the spot. Then we move on to the little Church of St. Peter's Primacy, with a good half hour for personal prayer and reflection. Looking out across the lake from there is an experience well beyond words. Reading John 21:15–24 with Jesus' question to Peter, "Do you love me?" raises questions of the meaning of the text and Peter's character and role. A passage from Egeria is also read. If there has been no Eucharist in the morning, there will be one at one of these sites around the lake. In any case, we sing and are truly uplifted. Other visits in the area are Bethsaida, home to some of the disciples, and Chorazin, both cursed by Jesus along with Capernaum (Luke 10:13–15).

At some point during this day, we board a boat for a ride on the Sea of Galilee, either from Tiberias or Kibbutz Ginnosar where we can also visit the first-century boat from the time of Jesus. The present-day tourist boat travels out for about twenty minutes toward the center of the lake. We then get the driver to switch off the engine. A member of staff introduces the silence which is truly stunning. A good ten minutes' quiet is followed by a reading of the stilling of the storm (Mark 4:35–41), and a staff member reflects on the weather pattern of the region, the symbolism of the story, and the Christology: Who is he? The boat ride takes participants into another realm of experience—the peace of Galilee and the message of Jesus and the kingdom of God. Evening reflections once again draw the group into shared insights.

Day 8: Today focuses on Sepphoris and Caesarea Philippi. From Nazareth, we stop first at Cana, the location of Jesus' "first miracle." Here we read the account of Jesus turning water into wine at a wedding (John 2:1–11), and visit the little Franciscan church as well as the Greek Orthodox Church. The pilgrim wine in Cana is cheap but not too cheerful. Most of the group try it and some even buy a bottle. We then drive on to Sepphoris, the

Land during the twentieth century.

"Ornament of all Galilee,"[20] only a couple of miles away. This major archeological site is a wonderful eye-opener into the world of Jesus. We learn that it was excavated by the University of South Florida under the leadership of the inimitable Jim Strange, who we might even see, on occasion, at the site. The visit is full of the world of Second Temple Judaism, of Jesus and his contemporaries, and of questions of religious practice and influence. Archeologists have reconstructed the streets and columns, and the mosaics are stunning. The Roman house, with its triclinium, or dining room, and its "Mona Lisa of the Galilee" mosaic, prompts vibrant discussion about the circumstances of the Last Supper. Sepphoris isn't mentioned in the Gospels, but Jesus grew up in nearby Nazareth, and so questions of whether he ever visited Sepphoris and what effect his visits might have had on him are rife. We discuss: How educated was Jesus? What languages did he speak? Did Joseph work in Sepphoris? The answers could make a big difference to our sense of Jesus' social background, but the visit helps build up a general sense of his historical and cultural setting, bringing out his humanity and home life.

We then head out toward Caesarea Philippi, always a special but challenging visit. Driving northeast into the Golan Heights gives course members yet another taste of the different flavors of geographical and political life in the Holy Land. En route we hear about the Druze people and their history. About an hour northeast of the Sea of Galilee we arrive at Caesarea Philippi, the famous location in the Gospels where Jesus asks his disciples the question, "Who do people say that I am?" (Mark 8:27–38). We hear that in antiquity there was a water shrine here to the Greek god Pan, god of fertility, nature, music, sex, and dance. Water poured out of a spring in a cave and pilgrims came from far and wide to worship. Over the years before Jesus, many gods were worshiped in Caesarea Philippi. Herod the Great built a temple to the emperor Augustus. There's still a great deal of water here today, and to stand near the water in the archeological site and read the Gospel accounts of Jesus' question is challenging for faith and for discipleship. The reading, followed by a reflection on Christology and discipleship, again prompts significant, lively debate and questioning of Jesus' own purpose and message as well as its meaning for Christians today. Wandering around the site enables the group to appreciate the modern excavations but also to enter the world of Jesus and the evangelists. As in all these places, text and location come together in creative tension. We then drive back to the Sea of Galilee and on to our accommodation.

20. Or "security of all Galilee"—Josephus's description of Sepphoris in *Antiquities*, 18.27. See Josephus *New Complete Works*, 588.

Day 9: The final day in Galilee and the journey back to Jerusalem. A very early breakfast is followed by departure to Mount Tabor, the mountain of the transfiguration of Jesus. On the journey, a briefing on the bus sets the scene, covering Mount Tabor in the Old Testament (Judg 4), the importance of the transfiguration in the New Testament (Mark 9:2–8), and its place in the Orthodox Churches in icons and other art. To ascend the mountain, we leave the bus and get into taxis for the hair-raising journey up. In the past, the assent could be really frightening as the edge of the road was open, leaving little room for taxis to pass. In recent years both the road and the taxis have been greatly improved.

Once on top we disembark the taxis and gather for further reflection on the location, and possibly a Eucharist. We then visit the church, another designed by Barluzzi and built in 1924. It is Roman Catholic, or Latin, dedicated to the transfiguration, and run by a community of Franciscans. Inside, we discover two levels with the high altar set down below the rest of the church. The mosaics and stained glass are mesmerizing. Also, we see two chapels at the back of the church dedicated one each to Moses and Elijah. Outside, the views across the Jezreel Valley are staggering. Back down by taxis, and, after drinking coffee, we pick up the bus. It has been another faith-shifting experience.

Next, we embark upon a two-hour drive south, usually down the Jordan Valley, heading toward Jerusalem. Sometimes we drive through the West Bank through ancient Samaria and modern Nablus. In Nablus we visit the famous Jacob's Well and consider John 4. There might even be a visit to the Samaritan community on Mount Gerizim. On the Jordan Valley route we visit the remains of the superb Byzantine synagogue mosaic at Beit Alpha, again filling out aspects of the world of Jesus and the early Christians. We then stop at the impressive archeological site at Bet Shean. On the bus, there are further opportunities for staff to offer geographical orientation, political commentary, and theological reflection.

After two hours or so driving, we reach Jericho, the oldest and lowest town on earth, and a desert oasis. Often closed by the Israelis for political reasons, the place can be deserted even when we get into town. In good times there might be a crowd taking camel rides and having lunch. We visit Old Testament Jericho. Reading Josh 5–6 and the fall of the walls, on top of the Tel, is always dramatic. The first use, to my knowledge, on a St. George's course, of a mobile phone to read a scriptural text from a digital Bible took place at Old Testament Jericho. We then hear the story of the excavations of the Tel by archeologists John Garstang and Kathleen Kenyon of the British School of Archaeology in Jerusalem. Discussion of the excavations and their controversial impact on biblical interpretation continues over lunch. Do the Bible and archeology hang together or not?

Sometimes a look at New Testament Jericho and the remains of Herod's palace is possible, and then we make our way back to Jerusalem, sometimes along the old Roman road that Jesus knew, stopping, if possible, to overlook the Byzantine Monastery of St. George Kozibah in the Wadi Qelt for a short period of desert silence and a meeting with some Bedouin. The days in Galilee necessitate rest when we finally get back to Jerusalem, and so there is free time for refreshment and downtime before dinner. After dinner, a lecture from a visiting Jewish, Christian, or Muslim speaker introduces us to an Israeli or Palestinian perspective on the political situation in the Holy Land. Heated discussion arises.

Day 10: In some courses there might be a day off following the Galilee trip. Depending on time, there is always at least an option for a trip to the Dead Sea, Masada, and Qumran, either with a staff member or booked separately by course members. There could easily be a lecture the night before, or at some point, introducing the Dead Sea Scrolls. For the visit, we start early, driving back toward Jericho and then south down the Rift Valley or Arava. On the way down from Jerusalem (2,500 feet above sea level) to the Dead Sea (1,200 feet below), the scenery is stunning. The immersion in the desert is overwhelming. Here now is a chance to introduce the story of Masada with all its levels of history and conflict. Eventually the great fortress comes into view in the distance, a sight unparalleled in the Holy Land. Next, Josephus and his *Jewish War*[21] come in, as well as the story of the modern excavations of Masada in the early 1960s under Yigael Yadin, the "father of Israeli archeology." Also helpful, a chance to introduce desert monasticism: Byzantine Christian monks lived on Masada in the sixth century.

On some courses we walk up the mountain on the "snake path," taking frequent rests as we go. In recent years the cable car has made the ascent easier. A guided tour of the top, especially in blistering heat in the summer months, is exhausting, but we see the entire place with its views of the surrounding terrain. The whole morning is an immersion, once again, in the worlds of Herod and Jesus, the early Christians—and contemporary politics: Masada still has its symbolism for modern Israel whose young people were for many years sworn into the army here. Returning from the top of Masada, there is an opportunity to float in the Dead Sea, followed by lunch.

We then take our bus back north to Qumran, the home of the Dead Sea Scrolls. On the way, we hear a half-hour lecture from a staff member covering the whole fascinating story of the discovery of the scrolls in 1947

21. On Masada, see Josephus, *New Complete Works*, 925–32.

and the continuing dramatic tale of their eventual gathering and translation. A modern short film on the way into the site, and a guided tour, expose the world of the Bible again, and of the Essenes, bringing the history of this amazing place to life. It is exciting to see the actual landscape and the caves where the manuscripts were discovered. Until the 1980s Qumran seemed to be in the middle of nowhere. Today, there are retail opportunities galore, as there are also at Masada. On another day we might visit the scrolls themselves at the Shrine of the Book in the Israel Museum in West Jerusalem. Back at the college we rest, pray, and eat.

Day 11: The morning of this day starts at the Mount of Olives, getting dropped off by the bus at the "panoramic view" of the Old City. It is time for further instruction about the history of Jerusalem, and then a walk down the mountain into the Kidron Valley. On the way down, we visit the key churches, with introductions, explanations, singing, and prayer. The first stopping point is the little Church of Dominus Flevit, or "the Lord wept," commemorating Jesus weeping over the city (Luke 19:18). Another stunning view from the grounds of this church provides the opportunity for more commentary, and then a reflection on Jesus entering Jerusalem on a donkey or on his weeping over the city. Then inside the little Barluzzi church, where the acoustics are excellent, group singing, perhaps of Taizé and other chants and hymns. A mood of devotion and pilgrimage is mingled with history, archeology, and local politics. Back on the main path down, a real, white donkey greets the group.

Farther down, we pause at the Russian Orthodox Church of St. Mary Magdalene with its glistening golden domes. A briefing on the history of the Russians in the city is followed by time for quiet prayer in the church or the beautiful garden. Then finally down to the Garden of Gethsemane with its striking Barluzzi Church of All Nations and its olive trees. Usually very busy with tourists and pilgrims, a gathering somewhere in a corner enables a reading of the Gethsemane account from one of the Gospels (e.g., Luke 22:39–46) and an outline of the history of the churches on this site. The theme is Jesus' agony and his final days. Inside, more quiet prayer in the purple haze of the stained glass. Sometimes a visit to the nearby Tomb of Mary is included, with a presentation and discussion about its significance. We then return to the college for lunch, rest, and study.

Day 12: Today we start early (5:30 a.m.), walking to the Old City for stations of the cross along the Via Dolorosa. This moving devotional witness is meditative and reflective, just as the city is beginning to wake up. Beginning at the Church of the Flagellation, we make our way, carrying a cross (about five feet high) which is passed from person to person between the fourteen stations. The chaplain leads the way as course members read and pray, using prayers created by Gilbert Sinden and published later by John Peterson.[22] The stations relate biblical and other themes to the modern world, drawing in contemporary political concerns such as the poor and suffering in the Holy Land and around the world. Always a deeply moving experience, this slow, prayerful walk brings everything together. Culminating at the tomb of Christ in the Church of the Holy Sepulcher, the stations are exhausting emotionally and intellectually. Breakfast in the Old City is followed by free time to explore.

After lunch in the Old City, we visit the excavations at the Davidson Center and archeological park just inside Dung Gate. Entrance is through a center providing a short introductory film and a display telling the story of the Jewish temples and the surrounding area. After time spent reading the display boards, we pass through to the archeological site. Every area inside needs explanation but it is a wonderful opportunity to imagine Jesus in context within the Judaism of his day. An overview of the Second Temple street level and the buildings and *mikva'ot* (immersion pools) in the area leads to a walk along the actual street near the temple remains on the western side. Excavations following 1967 revealed the street level from the time of Jesus, and the rocks that had fallen from the temple when it was destroyed by the Romans. Course participants see huge Herodian ashlars still lying where they fell in AD 70—one of the most amazing moments in Jerusalem's history.

We walk round to the southern end of the temple platform and hear more explanation of subsequent history. The group then mounts the temple steps which formed the main entrance into the temple at the time of Jesus. Some of the actual steps form the basis of the reconstruction. We see remains of Byzantine buildings in the area illustrating later history in the city. This visit is truly a climax to the day as participants reflect in group prayer and in silence on the significance of where they are standing. Overall, little effort is required to imagine Jesus in his world and to make the connections with Christian faith today.

Day 13: At least one day in the course is a Sunday and the group is encouraged to join in morning worship with the Palestinian Anglican congregation at St. George's Cathedral next door to the college. First, the group hears a briefing on the history of Anglicanism in the Holy Land stretching back to Michael Solomon Alexander. In Jerusalem, the Eucharist at St. George's is always an eye-opener for people who are there for the first time. Parts of the service are in English to enable the greater participation of visitors but some of it is in Arabic. The unusual Arabic-English mix is a

22. Peterson, *Walk in Jerusalem.*

learning curve for most, and the service is followed by a chance to encounter some of the local Palestinian Anglicans over coffee in the guest house garden. Sometimes, the Eucharist is packed with pilgrims from around the world. In Galilee, when staying in Nazareth on a Sunday, we attend morning worship at Christ Church, the local Anglican church.

Sunday afternoon in Jerusalem sees the group visiting the model of Second Temple Jerusalem, created by Michael Avi Yonah, and for many years located in the grounds of the Holy Land Hotel in West Jerusalem but now in the Israel Museum. It is a magnificent teaching aid and reveals much about the city that is difficult to see when you're in it. An hour at the model summarizes (or introduces, if it comes early in the course) the history of Jerusalem. The aerial view of the model means that the city can be seen at a glance, making it possible to connect places visited in the course and see how the various valleys and walls fit together over time in Jerusalem's history.

Another possible Sunday afternoon visit is to nearby Bethany (before the separation wall made the journey longer) and Bethphage. The two lovely churches by Antonio Barluzzi give the group opportunity to see mosaics and frescos, and to hear the relevant Gospel readings. In Bethany, we consider Lazarus, Martha, and Mary (John 11) and visit the pilgrim "Tomb of Lazarus." In Bethphage we ponder Jesus' entry into Jerusalem on Palm Sunday (Mark 11:1–11) and see the Crusader mounting stone. Enthusiastic singing in both places raises our spirits—individual and corporate.

Day 14: This day focuses on the resurrection of Jesus through a visit to Abu Ghosh, one of the four places in the Holy Land associated with Emmaus. Some courses might visit one of the other Emmaus sites, but Abu Ghosh is beautiful with its Crusader church and garden. The day begins with a lecture after breakfast introducing the complexities of the history of the Emmaus sites and the theology of Luke's account (Luke 24:1–32). A reading and exegesis of the text raises some interesting features such as the textual variant concerning the place and its distance from Jerusalem. The importance of the story for understanding the resurrection and the continuing Christian journey of discipleship is underlined. Later, we arrive at Abu Ghosh and the glorious Benedictine Monastery of the Resurrection with its Crusader frescoes (restored in the 1990s) and its amazing acoustics. The town is Old Testament Kiriath-jearim where the ark of the covenant rested for twenty years (1 Sam 7:1–2). The monks allow us to celebrate a Eucharist which is a wonderful climax to a two-week course in the Holy Land, bringing the group together and sending them on their way. Sometimes we also gather in the Church of Our Lady of the Ark of the Covenant on the hill in Abu Ghosh.

Back at the college, final reflections in the late afternoon draw out many layers of experience and insight. The course has opened the eyes of participants in numerous ways yet to be articulated as people prepare to return home. The wisdom of St. George's College founding fathers shines through as participants reflect on the structure and content of the course. The "Jerusalem experience" has worked its wonders once again. Text, land, people, worship, and reflection have seeped into participants' awareness and faith, coloring their lives and sense of God's ways with the world. On the final evening, dinner and celebrations include the giving of a certificate and the famous St. George's College tile. Goodbyes and departures follow.

OTHER COURSES

The Palestine of Jesus course has been the staple diet of St. George's College from the early days, and the ethos and content I have described sum up what a typical St. George's course is like. The basic immersion in the land, with biblical and theological input and reflection, along with encountering the people of the land and the three faiths, are all part of every course. This basic essence which gives St. George's its unique balance is constant. But the course emphases and focal themes can differ, as can the length of a course and the way in which certain segments are put together. So the original ten-week course contained virtually all of what St. George's did in the early years until foreign courses were developed. The basic focus on Jerusalem and Galilee was constant. If the course was slightly longer, there could be more time in Galilee. If it were a month, there could be an excursion to Sinai and even Jordan.[23] Sometimes an optional foreign excursion (such as Sinai) might be added on the end of a Palestine of Jesus course for those who wanted to stay on.

Looking back over the annual course calendars the college printed for prospective course members, it is interesting to see a variety of titles, knowing that the basic substance was always there.[24] In addition to The Palestine of Jesus, other courses have included: The Bible and Its Setting, The Bible and the Holy Land, The Bible and Worship, The Bible and the Holy Land Today, The Bible and the Land of Jesus, and The Bible and Flowers. During the 1990s and into the early 2000s there appeared titles that followed academic fashion a little: The Social Landscape of the Bible;

23. This became possible following the peace deal between Israel and Jordan in 1994.

24. Most course calendars can be found in the college archive. See a selection here in appendix E.

and Jesus, the Gospels, and the Land. Then there were Pilgrimage and Spirituality, and Abraham: Yesterday and Today, as well as titles covering Easter celebrations such as Holy Fire! and Risen with Christ, which sometimes had a subtitle such as Eastern and Western Easter.

As the number of students attending courses increased, there was also the fact that some wanted to return. In the context of the need for more variety, when I was course director (1999–2001), Henry Carse became director of special programs and developed courses such as Ways in the Wilderness, a desert course which was Henry's speciality. In addition, there were increasing numbers of ideas from staff and, indeed, from participants as to what good subjects and titles for future courses might be. One different, stimulating, and energetic idea which did take place was a five-day Hike the Holy Land course, a "boutique" walking pilgrimage, largely in Galilee.

Sometimes courses designed and even advertised on the annual brochure might not end up attracting enough support for them to run. If the college looked set to lose financially, staff had to make the difficult decision of whether to cancel or not. Some courses advertised but eventually canceled were: Christmas in Bethlehem; Icons in Cyprus; Motherhood and the Holy Land; and Praying with Music. The latter took a great deal of planning involving major institutions in Jerusalem across the denominations and faiths, but never attracted enough participants to run. In recent years a wide variety of courses with attractive titles has been offered with visiting specialists from different countries. Some have been held and others canceled. We shall consider some of them in a later chapter.

Another interesting offering on the courses front relates to the Lambeth Conference. This conference is a ten-yearly gathering of primates of the Anglican Communion in Canterbury, England. It is a high-profile gathering of bishops of the Anglican Communion taking years of planning. The idea of a "Pre-Lambeth" and "Post-Lambeth" gathering at St. George's College made good sense to John Peterson who launched it in 1988. It was thought that some of the Anglican bishops traveling from the East could stop off in Jerusalem on their way to England. And others might want to travel to Jerusalem beforehand and afterward for preparation and reflection in the Holy Land. Where better to spend time in prayer, reflection, and retreat with one's brother (and eventually sister) bishops than in the Holy City of Jerusalem? The Lambeth Conference was later held in 1998 and 2008, but the St. George's course didn't attract enough participants to run in 2008. In 2018 the conference was postponed because of disagreements in the Anglican Communion and was later delayed because of the coronavirus pandemic. It eventually took place during July–August 2022, but there was no St. George's course. The Pre- and Post-Lambeth retreats at St. George's, like all the other courses, included the usual combination of elements, though with fewer site visits.

Growing out of the basic ten-week course, all these courses provided the fundamental "Jerusalem experience," whether in larger or smaller portions.

RISEN WITH CHRIST

One of the courses that has flourished in the college over the years is Risen with Christ, sometimes known as Holy Fire! This course focuses on the services of Eastern Easter, and the traditions, theology, and liturgies of the Orthodox Churches of Jerusalem. The date of Easter in the Eastern Churches usually differs from that in the West, and there have always been differences in how the East and the West calculate it.[25] Suffice it to say that although the two Easters occasionally coincide, they can be a few weeks apart. This difference enables St. George's College to offer a course on Eastern Easter and still allow Westerners to attend, especially if they are clergy with churches to look after. The coincidence of the two Easters makes for a very rich course at St. George's but can exclude many clergy who might otherwise attend.

Risen with Christ consists of a combination of lectures in the college and visits to exotic Orthodox liturgies in churches in Jerusalem. The course is also extremely devotional, a real keeping of Holy Week in the college with suitable offices and prayer. The visiting lecturer for this course has often been the Rev. Dr. Hugh Wybrew whose *Risen with Christ: Eastertide in the Orthodox Church* has been the course book.[26] Hugh Wybrew was vicar of St. Mary Magdalen's Church, Oxford, and for many years taught courses on Orthodox liturgy at the University of Oxford. He lived and studied in Romania, Bulgaria, and the former Yugoslavia, and knows the Orthodox world very well. He was also dean of St. George's Cathedral in Jerusalem for several years in the 1980s and knows the local scene intimately. In view of all this he has been an extremely appropriate visiting lecturer for this course, which has mostly been ten days in length.

The course has usually started on "Lazarus Saturday," the day before Palm Sunday, with Orthodox liturgies in Bethany, the home of Lazarus. Then (when the Easters have coincided) the Western procession on Palm Sunday afternoon from Bethphage into the Old City (marking the beginning of Holy Week) attracts thousands of people. The first few days of Holy Week are quiet for the course, with prayers, lectures, and other orientations

25. The East uses the Julian calendar while the West uses the Gregorian.

26. Wybrew, *Risen*.

in the college. The busy climax of the week consists of the three great days of Maundy Thursday, Good Friday, and Holy Saturday. During these days the Orthodox liturgies come fully into their own. From the point of view of the course, this variety presents numerous options for visits. Usually, members of staff go with small groups from the course to different liturgies around the city. So, for example, it is possible for someone to "look in" at several foot washing ceremonies in the Old City on Maundy Thursday.

The key event on Maundy Thursday is the Greek Orthodox foot washing ceremony at the Church of the Holy Sepulcher in the Old City. This begins in the morning. Course members go early down to the parvis, or courtyard, of the church where hundreds of people gather to witness the ceremony, which lasts several hours. In order to understand the Orthodox Holy Week liturgies fully, one needs to appreciate them as performance. Liturgical drama is very much in evidence and an element of theater is certainly something participants see during the course. The experience is like being at the performance of a play as the Gospel narrative is read and the Greek patriarch of Jerusalem washes the feet of twelve men. Sometimes it is possible to get very close to the platform upon which the action takes place. In the heaving crowds, one can hear the account in Greek of Jesus washing his disciples' feet at the Last Supper, and watch this being reenacted liturgically. On other occasions it might be more difficult to see or hear. One year, the small St. George's College group gathered at the top of the nearby tower of the Lutheran Church of the Redeemer and got a bird's eye view of the proceedings.

Several hours at a Greek liturgy might be too much for some. But others can dash off to visit the Ethiopian foot washing at the Ethiopian monastery on the roof of the Church of the Holy Sepulcher. Then, on to one of the most dramatic ceremonies of Holy Week: the foot washing in the Armenian Cathedral of St. James not far from Jaffa Gate. The setting for this ceremony is visually much like a stage with the characteristic Armenian curtain where the Greeks would have an iconostasis. Another long service, this is reminiscent of a Puccini opera with glorious Armenian chant sung by the choir of the Armenian Seminary or boys' school opposite. One fascinating feature of this service for Anglicans is that the Anglican archbishop reads the Gospel—a tradition that goes back to the nineteenth century and the beginning of the Anglican presence in Jerusalem when the Armenians were especially welcoming to Anglicans.

Following this ceremony, it is possible to attend part of the Syrian Orthodox foot washing at the little Church of St. Mark, associated by the Syrians with the room of the Last Supper. Feet are washed and the Syrian archbishop is lifted high up on a seat in honor of the Last Supper. Then, one can go to the Coptic church at the Coptic patriarchate back on the roof of the Holy Sepulcher. Each ceremony has its own particular cultural look, its own liturgical language and vestments, and its own traditions and unique music. In years when the Easters coincide, the day might then finish with the Anglican Eucharist and foot washing at St. George's Cathedral in the evening, followed by a silent walk to the Garden of Gethsemane for a meditation led by the dean of the cathedral. And there are numerous Western liturgies to attend, making the course extremely rich in liturgical offering, and potentially somewhat overloaded. Choices must be made.

More services are available on Good Friday. Again, when the two Easters coincide, the day begins with stations of the cross on the Via Dolorosa. Hundreds of pilgrims from around the world participate. Led by the Anglicans and the Lutherans (marking their unique historical relationship), it is open to everyone. Another dramatic liturgy is the Orthodox burial service at the Church of the Holy Sepulcher in the early evening. A procession with an image of the body of Jesus and a shroud in which he would be wrapped forms the focus. The dead Jesus is symbolized by the figure and is taken into the tomb. This moving ceremony forms another experience in which course members are caught up and moved in faith as well as in learning.

The crème de la crème of Risen with Christ is the service of "Holy Fire" at the Church of the Holy Sepulcher on Holy Saturday. This is possibly the most significant service of the year in the Orthodox world, and certainly in Jerusalem. To be present at it is an experience never to be forgotten. The first challenge is to get tickets, and George Hintlian, in the Armenian Quarter of the Old City, is the man to be in touch with. George was secretary to the Armenian patriarch of Jerusalem for many years and is a well-known historian of the Armenian Church. He is friend to everyone in Jerusalem, and St. George's College has had good relations with him over a long period. He would often visit the college and give a lecture during the Risen with Christ course, focusing on the history and significance of "Holy Fire." Lectures would also be given by another Armenian specialist, Dr. Roberta Ervine, when she was living in Jerusalem. Once contacted, George Hintlian would usually secure the number of tickets needed. There are usually several thousand people attending this unique event, so even with tickets there is always a question about whether the group will get in. In recent years, because of the need for crowd control, the Israeli police have taken over handling the event. The annual service dates to at least the ninth century and, sadly, it has not always been peaceful. Sometimes the St. George's group gets into the ceremony and sometimes it doesn't, often getting turned away at the last minute.

"Holy Fire" focuses on the tomb of Christ, and is held largely in the rotunda, or circular area, around the tomb. Usually, the St. George's group leaves the college at about 6:00 a.m. to get into the Old City and start queueing. Each participant carries a small cluster of thirty-three candles bound together, and purchased beforehand. This is lit with the new fire when the moment eventually comes. The thirty-three candles symbolize the years of Christ's earthly life. There can be a few hours' wait before getting into the church, and then a few more hours before proceedings begin. The police set up barricades preventing many people getting near the church. Once through the barrier you at least stand a chance. Then, finally, you're in. The hours of waiting inside the church are filled with excitement. Thousands of people from Orthodox countries all over the world are there, including, of course, Greeks and Russians. For locals as well, this is a major event. During the waiting, people read, talk, watch other people, and see local Palestinian Orthodox Christians shouting and banging drums, and sitting on the shoulders of others. The event has more of the ethos of a music festival than a church service and can be quite frightening because there are no fire escapes and the church gets seriously overcrowded.

Eventually, the tomb is sealed with wax and there are processions around it. Then, after much excitement, the Greek and Armenian patriarchs appear and enter the tomb for the "miracle of Holy Fire." There is always much speculation about how the new fire is started, but the tradition is that God sends down the fire. After more waiting, and the seeming chaos around the tomb, the first spark of fire is seen coming out of one of the holes in the side of the tomb. This initial flame is taken by people with candles and soon the whole church is lit with the fire. A priest from the Armenian community, often the patriarch himself, appears on the Armenian balcony above the tomb holding a cluster of burning candles high in the air.

The new fire symbolizes the resurrection of Christ and carries with it all the powerful religious symbolism of light and fire. These days, many of the candles are soon extinguished by Israeli police with fire extinguishers. But not before Russian nuns and others "bathe" their faces in the fire, and not before it has been taken out by a member of the Greek community to be transported down to Tel Aviv and flown to the main cities of the Orthodox world. After the ceremony, many locals leave the church, taking the new fire back home with them in their own individual lanterns. In the evening of this day, St. George's students might attend the resurrection liturgy at the Ethiopian Orthodox monastery on the roof of the Church of the Holy Sepulchre. It is alive with brightly colored garments and drums. Umbrellas symbolize the Holy Spirit!

"Holy Fire" on Holy Saturday is, of course, the Easter Day service of the resurrection for the Orthodox, and so the Sunday is usually quiet in the college with services at St. George's Cathedral. On Monday the course ends with a visit to the liturgy at the little Romanian Orthodox Church in the area of Jerusalem called Mea Shearim, not far from the college in West Jerusalem. Risen with Christ ends as usual with reflections, dinner, and celebrations.

The "Holy Fire" ceremony is an experience that stays with participants forever. St. George's course members are always truly amazed if they have been at it. There is, of course, great disappointment and embarrassment for the college if the course can't get into the ceremony. For those who do attend, the event is a cultural, religious, social, and aesthetic experience of Orthodox worship of such proportions that it constitutes a major learning curve in their lives. Indeed, it is a glorious part of the course and a fitting climax, giving participants multilayered insights into so many aspects of Orthodox Christianity, as well as into Jerusalem and its local life. The international significance of the event also comes through. This course at St. George's College is always very special for all who attend.

THE YOUTH COURSE

For many years there was a Youth Course at St. George's College. When I first joined the staff in 1996, this was an annual event. The Youth Course was the college's outreach to young people. Aimed mostly at seventeen-to-twenty-one-year-olds, there was a good deal of flexibility about age. Usually there were about twenty American teenagers and half a dozen local Palestinian Anglican Christians from the diocese of Jerusalem. The Palestinians were from inside Israel, unless West Bankers could get visas. One of the main challenges was getting them all to bond. At the opening gathering of this lively ten-day course, the different cultural groups would be in fear and trepidation of their differences. By the end, they were all weeping in each other's arms, not wanting to leave!

Because it was a Youth Course it was much more physically active than other courses. There were many of the usual activities such as visits to archeological sites and holy places, but there was also much more hiking than in the other courses: up and down Masada, up and down Mount Tabor, and out in the desert. There was also swimming: not just floating in the Dead Sea but at places where participants could swim properly. There were presentations and Bible studies both in the college and out in the field. As well as quizzes on the bus and tests in the college, pizza and ice cream were plentiful. There was little sleep, and staff could be exhausted after only a couple of days. In the best Youth Courses, groups brought their own leader to establish and maintain discipline.

One year, with the encouragement of the Rev. Bill Broughton, we were able to arrange to take the Youth Course to the archeological dig at Ashkelon. Archeology is the national sport in Israel, and to some extent in the Palestinian territories too. Fr. Bill was well known in the college and had amazing contacts in the local communities, both Israeli and Palestinian. He was well connected in the academic and archeology worlds too. He had an infectious enthusiasm for archeology and the Bible and quite a bit of experience on digs. As a young man, Fr. Bill worked with George Ernest Wright, one of the great American archeologists. He also happened to be longtime friends with Professor Larry Stager of the University of Harvard. Stager was Dorot Professor of the Archeology of Israel, based at the Semitic Museum in Harvard, and was one of the "godfathers" of biblical archeology. During the 1990s and 2000s he was known especially for his work at Ashkelon, one of the five Philistine cities of the Bible.[27] Steger headed up the Leon Levy Expedition at Ashkelon, and the dig was celebrated worldwide.

With Fr. Bill's connections, we were able to take the Youth Course to Ashkelon for a day's visit, including digging. The staff at St. George's knew there would be some physical exercise involved, and we set off early from Jerusalem to get to Ashkelon in good time. On arrival, we were given a guided tour of the site (including the famous middle Bronze Age gate), as well as an explanation of the history of the dig and some of the procedures of archeology. We then separated into groups and went to different parts of the dig to embrace some hard labor for the morning. The heaving and sweating turned out to be a major workout! Not something we ever did with adults, the physical digging added an element of participation that increased learning and overall fun. By late afternoon we were back in Jerusalem with a vivid sense of what biblical archeology out in the field is all about—and a renewed appreciation of some aspects of the Bible itself.

Another thing that made the Youth Course fun was the guitar. A simple and somewhat battered instrument enhanced the worship, giving it a lively and contemporary feel. And there could be a lot of accompanied singing on the bus and out in the field, as well as in the evenings in the lecture room and in the chapel. In the 1990s and early 2000s Fuad Dagher (later ordained in the diocese of Jerusalem) would often join the course as chaplain. Fuad was an excellent guitarist and would frequently ad lib at unexpected moments. The music bound everyone together in spirit and

27. Ashdod, Ashkelon, Ekron, Gath, and Gaza.

in purpose. Over the years, the college purchased more than one guitar, though they were only occasionally used outside the Youth Course.

Usually, we tried to take the Youth Course to the desert for a special overnight experience camping out. Immersion in the desert was another of those physical adventures that changed everyone's understanding of the Bible as well as of faith. A short trip to the Negev, to one of the Israeli Bedouin tent experiences, provided untold excitement. We would drop down to the Dead Sea area in the late afternoon in time to arrive at the tent for an introduction to Bedouin life from one of the staff. Camel rides and an evening meal drew us further into desert life. Early the following morning, a walk out from the camp for sunrise and a Bible study provided another layer of learning impossible in a classroom. Like the Sinai excursion, this short desert experience was a portion of the Youth Course greatly appreciated by all who took part.

For quite a few years the Youth Course was an important part of the St. George's College commitment to young people. It was also a much-appreciated part of the life of the Palestinian Anglican diocese. An opportunity for education and reconciliation, participants' eyes were opened in unexpected ways, both about each other and about the Holy Land. Both Americans and Palestinians discovered some of their prejudices about others on this course, though these faded during the time together. Sadly, during the years of the first and second intifadas, the Youth Course fell on difficult times, largely because of events inside Israel as well as in the West Bank. Political tensions made American parents nervous about sending their children to the Middle East. Over the last couple of decades, this course has fallen away from the college program—a great loss to St. George's.

This chapter has described St. George's main courses held in Jerusalem including the ten-week course begun under John Wilkinson, the ever-popular Palestine of Jesus, Risen with Christ, and the Youth Course. With something of the unique essence of these courses in mind, we turn in the next chapter to developments in other countries.

8

Foreign Courses

As the college grew and expanded, so did its ideas about where to take its students. In this chapter we turn to courses held in countries other than the Holy Land: the foreign courses. Once the basic menu was established, there were inevitably dreams and aspirations about where else courses might go. As already mentioned, the ten-week course went to Sinai and to Cyprus. Sinai and Jordan were sometimes featured as segments of other courses. A course entitled Ways in the Wilderness was also basically Sinai and Jordan, and much of the content of this course is captured in what follows. At various stages other countries and cities came into view as possible destinations—namely, Turkey, Greece, and Rome. Gradually these all developed as attractive additions to the college's portfolio of programs: St. George's College abroad!

SINAI

For the Sinai, we leave St. George's at about 5:00 a.m. Making our way south from Jerusalem, we drop nearly four thousand feet through the Judaean desert into the Jordan Valley, continuing south at Jericho by the Dead Sea. Then a five-hour journey through the Negev desert to Eilat on the Red Sea, including a stop for breakfast, possibly in Arad, and a stop at Beer Sheva to visit the Tel and consider Abraham and Abimelech (Gen 21:25–34). A Tel is a multi-layered archeological mound, and the view from the visitors' platform at Tel Beer Sheva gives a panoramic impression of the area. This is an experience of major psychophysical significance—a desert view few can have imagined before arriving. Some Americans have been in a desert before but many have not, and the Negev is breathtaking.

After Beer Sheva, the drive farther south to the border is broken only by a toilet stop and a desert stop, to consider what we are doing and why. The concept of desert spirituality is already beginning to make some sense. The coach is loaded up not only with people's cases but also with sleeping bags for two overnights under the stars. For Sinai, the college has almost always worked with an Egyptian travel outfit called Abanoub Travel under the direction of Dr. Rabia and his team of Bedouin assistants who provide everything we need, including Jeeps for travel through the desert. Arriving at the Red Sea is always impressive. Its color is a striking blue but the name probably means "Reed Sea"—the Sea of Reeds. Are we somewhere near the port of Solomon (1 Kgs 9:26)?

Whatever else, this is a stunning trip visually. From Eilat, even on the bus, you can see four countries without moving your head: Israel where we are; Egypt ahead, where we're going; the Hashemite Kingdom of Jordan to the left; and then Saudi Arabia, the land of the Prophet Mohammed, farther south to the left. Crossing into Egypt was primitive until buildings were erected early in the new millennium. But, in any case, the task is to get everyone through the exit from Israel and entrance into Sinai at Taba. Then we drag anything up to forty sleeping bags across the border! No mean feat in the summer sun at the Red Sea!

On the other side, Dr. Rabia and his men await us with Jeeps. We pile in, probably eight to a Jeep with four or five Jeeps. Usually, three or four college staff are present, including Henry Carse and myself and sometimes the dean and his wife. This is St. George's College on the road, capturing everything we try to do—immerse people in the land of the Bible. The plan is to spend the first night in the desert, sleeping out under the stars, and Rabia knows the best places. We pull off the road into a cove and make camp. After some orientation, course participants find a spot to arrange their sleeping bags and enjoy some quiet time. Rabia's assistants prepare a delicious Bedouin meal on a portable gas stove. Before dinner, a presentation of a biblical text, perhaps a desert passage from the book of Exodus, helps orient us. Sometimes a visiting lecturer accompanies this course. On one occasion Joyce Huggett traveled with us and offered a great deal of desert wisdom.[1] In the 1980s, the Rev. Dr. Andrew Mackintosh of St. John's College, Cambridge, often traveled with the desert course, contributing much to the experience. Study is followed by evening prayer. After dinner, we gather around a camp fire to hear stories and reflections until dark, when people retire to sleep. The stars over the Sinai desert are incandescent,

1. Among her many books, see Huggett, *Formed*.

one of the most memorable visual experiences in the Holy Land. Space is three-dimensional. Sleep is deep.

Around 5:00 a.m. we are awoken by a shepherd leading his sheep and goats through the camp. The bells around their necks ring loudly and we wake, remembering we are in the Sinai desert. Morning prayer and an early breakfast and we're off for the rest of the journey by Jeep to St. Catherine's Monastery. It is the ultimate destination in the Sinai, and the excitement of ascending Jebel Mousa, the Mountain of Moses, during the night for sunrise keeps everyone focused. Amid all the anticipation and expectation, a stop for lunch and toilets (behind sand dunes) is followed by a look at some graffiti, probably done by fourth-century Nabataean Christian pilgrims. We also visit the stone tombs known as the Nawamis, which contain bones possibly dating from 4000 BC. The twin peaks of the Mountain of Moses and the Mountain of Aaron can be seen for miles around, and discussions of the Exodus narratives and traditions start in the Jeeps. We arrive at St. Catherine's in the late afternoon and book into the monks' own guest house at the foot of Jebel Mousa.

There have been several waves of renovation since, but in the 1990s St. Catherine's Monastery guest house is still primitive. Probably three in a room. Showers exist but often don't work. The heat is a blistering 40°+C in the summer. Before dinner, we gather for a presentation on a biblical text, probably the burning bush, for this is the place where, according to tradition, Moses turned aside and saw the bush burning (Exod 3:1–22). The place has been marked since the fourth century. The Monastery of the Transfiguration was built by the emperor Justinian in the sixth century and Christian pilgrimage to this place has flourished ever since. After a delicious meal, a briefing about camels for ascending the mountain is followed by early sleep. At 1:30 a.m. we rise to ascend the mountain in time for sunrise between 5:00 a.m. and 6:00 a.m. Most people come unless they are physically unfit.

Leaving the guest house on foot at 2:00 a.m., course members make their way to the base of the mountain. There are two options for ascent: walking up or riding a camel. A flashlight is required either way. It is pitch black. Walkers leave immediately, following the winding path up the mountain. It takes at least a couple of hours and possibly more on foot. Camel riders wait in the camel park to be allotted a camel and camel driver. The ascent is a rare experience, again under the Sinai stars, with plenty of time for meditation and wondrous amazement at creation.

Toward the top of the mountain is an area known as Elijah's Plateau, associated with the prophet Elijah's visit to Mount Sinai (or Horeb, its other name). The "still small voice" or "voice of sheer silence" (1 Kgs 19:8–13) he experienced here is tangible. We gather at the plateau to celebrate a Eucharist just as the sun comes up. Seeing the host at the Eucharist elevated at the very moment the sun appears over a mountain cliff is an experience none of us will forget. The full and proper connection of the Eucharist with creation can finally be made both in minds and in hearts. After the service, for those who wish, we eat the packed breakfasts we hauled up the mountain trail with us. The other option is to climb farther to the very top of Mount Sinai for a reading (sometimes in Hebrew) of the Ten Commandments.

Following the mountain peak and breakfast, everyone walks back down. There are 3,750 steps down on another side of the mountain, and then a winding path back to the monastery. Getting back down can take a couple of hours and course members take it slowly, either alone or in small groups aided and assisted by the course assistant and other staff. We all meet at about 8:00 a.m. at the monastery Church of the Transfiguration for a guided tour by one of the monks. The monastery is, of course, Greek Orthodox, and after time in the desert, the color of the church is blinding, as the famous sixth-century mosaic of the transfiguration in the apse of the church shines out with stunning brilliance. We then see the small Chapel of the Burning Bush at the back of the high altar. On the way out we see the hundreds of skulls of previous monks of the monastery, and sometimes we can arrange a visit to the monastery library where the well-known Fr. Justin talks to us about the manuscripts held there. It was at St. Catherine's, of course, that the famous Codex Sinaiticus was discovered by Constantin Tischendorf in the nineteenth century.

After packing up possessions and preparing the Jeeps, we're off again for another night out under the stars. Rabia leads us to a different cove for an experience similar to before. This time there's a chance for everyone to share their experiences of the monastery and mountain, for other biblical presentations and studies, and for sharing impressions of the meaning of it all for life and for faith. The many traditions of the desert fathers, including John Climacus of Sinai (ca. 570–649) and others, come to life through the whole experience. There is now a real appreciation among participants of the physical mountain and its spiritual significance.

After dinner and another night sleeping out, we're off early the next morning to Nuweiba on the Red Sea, to a hotel for the final night. This gives course members a chance to freshen up and sleep well and, of course, swim in the Red Sea before heading back to Jerusalem. An early desert Eucharist on the beach the following morning with a short, reflective homily sends us back to the border for passport checks and dragging sleeping bags back into Israel. Somewhere just before that we stop for a final desert reflection, usually on creation and transfiguration. The seemingly endless drive back to Jerusalem follows, but we're home by midafternoon. The next day is certainly a day of rest!

JORDAN

On other occasions, the Sinai part of a course might be followed by several days in Jordan. If so, we board a boat in Nuweiba in southeastern Sinai, and cross the Red Sea to Aqaba in southern Jordan. Sometimes we stop at Wadi Rum, well known for its most famous visitor, Lawrence of Arabia. His role, and that of the British, in the area during the First World War inevitably come up in discussion.

We then make our way to the "rose red city" of Petra. It was John William Burgon who wrote those words, capturing something of Petra's charm and exotic lure as well as its ancient pedigree: "Match me such marvel save in Eastern clime, a rose-red city half as old as time."[2] Petra was inhabited from prehistoric times, and layer upon layer of history await us. The visit provides another rich learning experience. Petra is special! A visit to this place can be a turning point in life. There is nowhere on earth quite like it. For St. George's College, it's another glorious learning curve, involving another opportunity for widening and deepening our understanding of the ancient world and of contemporary faith. After checking in to a hotel near the entrance to this vast archeological site with all its treasures and color and its overriding mystique, we gather on the first evening for a briefing. St. George's is excellent at preparing people for site visits, and one of the staff gives a concise history of Petra in preparation for the following day.

Petra is the city of the Nabataeans whose empire arose in the sands of Edom (the red sands of the region) in the second century BC and lasted until the second century AD. The Nabataeans were an Arab people who spoke Nabataean Arabic. They were a desert people who knew their need of water and, indeed, their name probably means "drilling for water." They gradually came to control the region and the trade routes of southern Jordan and Saudi Arabia. They traded in spices and controlled the spice routes, dealing in frankincense and myrrh. Were the magi of St. Matthew's Gospel (and known to us from Christmas cribs as the "three kings") Nabataeans? Certainly, Herod the Great's mother Cypros was Nabataean, and the Nabataean king Aretas IV had a daughter whom Herod Antipas divorced for Herodias leading to John the Baptist's objection and subsequent beheading (Mark 6:14–29). Petra was destroyed by an earthquake in AD 393.

2. Burgon's poem "Petra" was written in 1845.

Then there is the modern story of the "rediscovery" of Petra by the archeologist and traveler John Burckhardt in 1812. Shared with our group the night before a full day's exploration of the site, the historical account gives rise to rich discussion and wide orientation in preparation for the following day's visit. Indeed, course participants are aware that they are entering another level of the biblical world and story. Night prayer closes the meeting, and we retire early in order to rise early.

Following breakfast, the day in Petra begins just as soon as the site opens. A local trained guide accompanies us throughout and provides historical and archeological background and detail. First, the long walk through the Siq, or alleyway, which is the entrance into the site, stopping along the way to look at the stunning color of the rock formations and remains of buildings. All are amazed at what they see. Some take a horse and cart, famous in the Petra Siq, all the way down to the so-called Treasury, the most famous of the many buildings. The group is already wilting in the heat, so "drink water!" is the order of the day to prevent dehydration.

The Treasury flickers into view in the sunlight as it appears. We pause to appreciate its majesty and to take photographs. Moving on into the main part of the site, we then see the remains of more buildings, caves, rock formations, and even a Byzantine church. The vivid stripes of color are imprinted on hearts and souls, and, indeed, minds, as our guide informs us about life in the ancient Nabataean capital. We learn of the ancient goddess of Petra, Dushara, and the practice of sacrifice. Picking up the theme later, a St. George's staff member leads half an hour's reflection on sacrifice and its place in Christian theology. Lunch at the site is followed by a long hike up to the monastery, another "must see" in Petra, so named because Byzantine monks lived there. The long walk back to the hotel takes us into the late afternoon. An evening reflection in the hotel on the group's experiences closes the day. Course participants have become aware, in a new way, of biblical geography, historical events, and people, as well as some perennial theological themes.

The following day sees another early start as we leave Petra, making our way north toward Amman. Within a few hours we arrive in the small town of Madaba for a rather different encounter. Like Petra, Madaba goes back to biblical times, and was controlled by the Nabataeans until it was taken by the Romans. It was the seat of a bishop in the early Christian period but was destroyed by an earthquake in the eighth century. In the nineteenth century (1884), while the site for a new church was being prepared, a Byzantine mosaic map was discovered in the floor and was restored.

Most visitors to Jerusalem, especially students, hear about the famous Madaba Map in Jordan. It's the oldest mosaic map in the world and the earliest map showing Jerusalem and the Holy Land in the sixth century. Unusually, it is oriented east-west and shows the main streets of Jerusalem and the churches built in the city before about AD 570. It is a fascinating introduction to the geography of the Holy Land. Those who hear of the map and see reproductions soon want to see the real thing. St. George's College courses passing through the area always stop to look. The map lies on the floor of the little Greek Orthodox Church of St. George, and a good introduction and explanation triggers lively discussion of the extent and characteristics of the Holy Land and Jerusalem in the sixth century. Originally consisting of some two million tesserae, the map is unique and provides a perfect educational visual aid.

Depending on the time available in Jordan, two other visits are possible. First, Jerash, one of the most famous of the archeological sites in the northern part of the country. It is a spectacular example of a Roman provincial town and its colonnaded streets and town center are world famous. Even a short visit gives the flavor of the place, and the imagination springs to work on what it might have been like in the first and second centuries. One important element is that Jerash is one of the ten cities known to us from the Gospels as the Decapolis. This location gives an opportunity for a good deal of teaching on the background to the New Testament, as well as on geographical places mentioned in the Gospels and associated with Jesus. In fact, Jerash has been thought by some to be New Testament Gerasa of the Gerasene demonic story (Mark 5:1–20). The complexity of matching the text with a location is itself a learning curve here, as there are other competitors for the actual place, and textual variants too! As always for St. George's students, being in the location makes all the difference.

The other location usually taken in before heading home is Mount Nebo. This mountain top, with its staggering views in every direction, is the traditional location of Moses looking into the promised land before handing over to Joshua, and then dying (Deut 34:1–12). It isn't difficult to see this location as the supreme vantage point for looking into the land. Linking up with the previous days in Sinai and the study of Moses at the mountain there, we focus next on the Old Testament texts relating to the entry of the Israelites into the land (Josh 1–5). A dramatic reading of the death of Moses on the site is memorable. Today there are remains of a Byzantine church with some notable mosaics, which we see. All of this takes us through various levels of learning, with geographical and biblical orientation. If there is time, we also visit Machaerus, the remains of the Herodian desert palace where, according to Josephus, John the Baptist was beheaded. The place provides yet another opportunity to read a New Testament text in historical context.

It takes time passing over the Allenby Bridge. We then make our way back into the West Bank and up to Jerusalem. Heat and exhaustion overwhelm the group. The modern political landscape continues to be as much of a learning curve as the ancient biblical one. But we make it safely, and by mid- to late afternoon we are back in Jerusalem at the college reflecting on the experiences of the past week and looking forward to a day off! Course participants will never forget Sinai and Jordan.

TURKEY

Before I left Jerusalem in 1997, after being senior lecturer for a year, Bob Jones, Henry Carse, and I had several conversations about the possibility of developing the college's courses outside the Holy Land. There was some concern about this expansion as the college's purpose was to provide courses in the Holy Land. But there seemed to be opportunity and need. Indeed, the "Holy Land" could be understood with some justification to include countries such as Turkey and Greece, as well as Egypt, Jordan, and Israel-Palestine. They are all "lands of the Bible" and might easily fall into the college's portfolio of courses. In any case, a foreign course could begin and end in Jerusalem and still take place mostly in the new country. Turkey was uppermost in our minds as a possible new destination. The idea of a "Footsteps of St. Paul" course looked attractive and possible.

Following my return to England, Bob and Henry went to Turkey, met with possible guides, and designed an attractive course. The first time it was offered, it was hugely successful. When I got back to Jerusalem as course director in 1999, I was very keen to take on the Turkey course as I had spent years teaching St. Paul and the councils of the early church, which all took place in locations now in modern Turkey. The potential seemed infinite, and the course soon became a regular feature of the college's offerings. When I became involved, I was able to transfer all my Southampton University lectures into the St. George's College bus and out into the field in Turkey. The combination of learning experiences proved spectacular and the course soared in popularity.

The first few times it was offered, the Turkey course was called St. Paul in Turkey. Beginning in Jerusalem, the group flew to Antalya from Tel Aviv and back again at the end. Starting in Jerusalem, we would head to Caesarea Maritima, with a focus on Paul leaving for Rome in Acts 27–28. In Turkey we would begin on the southern tip at Antalya and work our way up the western part of the country to Istanbul. However, we soon developed this course into St. Paul and the Early Church, to include both Paul and the seven ecumenical councils. For political and safety reasons during the early 2000s, we finally decided it was better to do the whole course in Turkey. Course participants were not signing up for Jerusalem because of political difficulties, and it seemed sensible to offer the Turkey course completely in Turkey. Also, the itinerary grew to take in much more of the new landscape. The "Turkey course," as it came to be known, has now been offered many times and is worth describing in detail.[3]

The new-style St. Paul and the Early Church course begins in Ankara, capital of Turkey, on the night before the first full day. Course participants come from the usual English-speaking countries. As with other courses, we aim to blend academic biblical study with theology, spirituality, and travel. We always have a few staff with us, including the main teacher, a chaplain, and a course volunteer, in addition to a Turkish guide, required by law. In almost every case our guide has been Mehmet Tanriverdi from Kuşadasi.

Day 1: The first morning kicks off with an introductory lecture in the hotel, focusing on St. Paul and his world. We then board the bus and, in true St. George's style, start the journey with prayer and making sure everyone is there. The morning includes a visit to the Ankara archeological museum and an overview of the city, providing background to the country through which St. Paul spent so much time traveling. If there is time, we might also visit the Atatürk mausoleum. One of the main features of this course is that I do quite a lot of teaching on the microphone on the bus, introducing the early Christian period. As we travel through Cappadocia, where we spend a night, I cover some background material, the Council of Nicaea in 325, and the three Cappadocian Fathers: Basil of Caesarea, Gregory of Nazianzus, and Gregory of Nyssa. Key lectures and reflections throughout the course are in hotels and archeological sites, and bring together the two strands of the course: St. Paul and the Early Church.

Day 2: The following morning, in a lecture in the hotel, I cover the basic theology of the Cappadocian fathers and read some of the poetry of Gregory of Nyssa. As we visit the amazing "fairy chimneys" of the region and the famous underground cities later in the day, we hear about and discuss the various phases of persecution of early Christians. Our guide, Mehmet, covers the history of Anatolia and modern Turkish culture and politics. Course members respond with excitement and immerse themselves in the unique environment. The group begins to bond well.

Day 3: As we travel south, we pass through Konya, or ancient Iconium. The most important thing to see there today is the tomb of Rumi, the

3. Among several books recommended for this course, the main ones have usually been Need, *Truly Divine* and *Paul Today*, as well as Murphy-O'Connor, *Paul: His Story*.

thirteenth-century Persian Sufi mystic. It is a "must see," but some course members wonder what the connection with Paul and the early church might be. After a presentation on Rumi and the reading of some of his poems outside the tomb, it becomes clear that the mystical element ties in with some of the strands in Gregory of Nyssa's poems: the mystery of God and the limitations of human language. It also raises some parallel questions about St. Paul's theology. Konya is an interesting city with a market and mosques. At some point in the course, Mehmet arranges for the group to spend an evening attending a session with the Turkish dancing dervishes, started by Rumi. This experience brings awareness and discussion of the theme of dance in theology and faith, and connects Muslim and Christian understandings of God.

Day 4: A single night in Konya and we leave, heading south and noting that as Paul went to Iconium (Konya) on his first missionary journey in Acts (14:1–7), he traveled north from Perge. We now travel in the opposite direction, south to Perge. Ancient Iconium has not been excavated but the place reconnects us with Paul, and starts us off tracing his journeys in Acts and comparing Luke's Paul with the picture of Paul in his own letters—more material for discussion and reflection. Arriving in Antalya, we visit the archeological site of Perge and tour the ruins under Mehmet's guidance. He shows us as much as possible in the time available, including the enormous ancient gateway to the city and the bathhouse. In the shade after the visit, I give a short talk on some aspect of Paul's theology or social world, often "St. Paul and Slavery." Lecturing in an archeological site known to Paul in Acts is an immense privilege, and we sift through biblical and theological issues culminating in lively debate.

Days 5–6: The same pattern prevails as we travel up to Yalvaç, or St. Paul's Pisidian Antioch, and then at Hierapolis and Laodicea, the latter immersing us in the first of the few cities of the book of Revelation that we will see on this course. These huge and impressive archeological sites occupy quite a bit of time. There might be a Eucharist at one of them. Historical and biblical details including more councils are covered at the sites and on the bus.

Days 7–9: The first part of the course culminates in our arrival in Ephesus, the jewel in the crown of ancient Asia Minor, and the metropolis. Three days in Kuşadasi enable us to visit Selçuk and the remains of the Byzantine Basilica of St. John containing, according to tradition, his tomb. A short lecture on the "Word made flesh" in that place is one of the most moving moments in the course. A full day's visit to the archeological site in Ephesus, including the little-known remains of the "council church" around the back of the tourist trail, fills out the background to a good deal of history already shared. On the bus we have had lectures on the Council of Constantinople. Now we are brought up to date by Ephesus, significant not only for Paul but for the series of early church councils too. This visit is important because Ephesus, so central in early Christianity, is also another of the seven churches of the book of Revelation. A day off in Kuşadasi enables people to rest and recover. But we are not leaving yet. A day trip to the island of Patmos is scheduled, with a focus on St. John the Divine and the book of Revelation.

Day 10: A very early start by boat from Kuşadasi leads us into a four-hour journey on the sea out to the Greek island of Patmos. There's just enough time to read the book of Revelation on the way! In reality we read sections and have a Eucharist on board. It is another unique and memorable experience, bringing all the seven churches to mind, too. When we arrive (now in Greece), we gather with a Greek guide for a visit to the cave where St. John is said to have had his vision and to have written the book of Revelation. We also gather for an introductory presentation on Revelation and its world of apocalyptic images. We then visit the Monastery of St. John with its stunning frescoes, icons, and manuscripts. A short visit, and then after lunch a brief wander around town, and we're back on the boat for the four-hour return journey. But the travel each way is soothing and meditative, giving time for individual reflection and social interaction. It's also a boating experience calling to mind Paul's own travel by sea. Overall, so many things come together in a very rich experience indeed.

Day 11: Leaving Kuşadasi the next morning, we make our way north to Bergama (ancient Pergamon). On the way, we pass through Izmir (ancient Smyrna). Both places are among the seven churches of the book of Revelation. In Izmir, we recall the second-century martyr Polycarp, and, if there's time, stop and visit one of the local churches and the archeological site. A dramatic reading of the account of Polycarp's death brings his story and significance to life. Then, on to Bergama, one of the great cities of antiquity and famous for its parchment. We visit the main archeological site and then the Asclepium, one of the centers of healing dedicated to the god Asclepius—much here to help us think about faith and healing. On one occasion a dog and a praying mantis attend our Eucharist, as well as the group! Then a look at the Red Hall, once a temple of Serapis, before retiring to a lovely roadside hotel for the night. It is here that our group activity, developing slowly throughout the trip, comes to a head: the "Creedal Project." This enables participants to think through the whole process of writing a creed. The group has been divided into smaller groups which are given clauses of the famous Nicene Creed to rephrase in modern language. At Pergamon the chaplain collects all the phrases together and reads out the new "group creed." The project is a revealing process, and another way into understanding the early church—and into doing some modern theology as well.

Days 12–13: After a lengthy coach journey, including more lectures, we arrive in Bursa where we eat the famous Iskander kebab and visit the Green Mosque. Shopping and exploring the town lead onto finding our hotel, once used by Atatürk. Some go out for a Turkish bath. The next day, we leave for Iznik, or ancient Nicaea. This lovely town sits on the edge of Lake Nicaea which is visually stunning. As with the Gospels and the Holy Land, and St. Paul in Ephesus, so in Nicaea, the famous council of 325 comes to life. Readings from Eusebius of Caesarea on Constantine and the council enable a vivid imagining of the event. We reflect upon its significance then and now. Visiting the lakeside, we see the alleged remains of Constantine's summer palace and debate additional aspects of the fourth-century council, including the Nicene Creed. Then off to the later church in town, which may have been the site of the Second Council of Nicaea in 787, the icons council. We also see some of the local Iznik pottery. On the bus leaving the area, a lecture on icons and their significance for faith focuses on the long-term significance of the Second Nicene council.

The next leg of the journey sees a boat trip across the Sea of Marmara into Istanbul, or ancient Constantinople. The time in this amazing city brings together everything we have done, especially at Hagia Sophia, the jewel in the crown of the whole course. Arrival in the city is breathtaking, and we take another boat trip, this time down the Bosphorus, to get orientation. "Sailing to Byzantium," indeed.[4] This is a superb way of viewing the city for the first time, and is another experience so memorable as to stay with course participants for the rest of their lives. The buildings up and down the Bosphorus, the bridges across the river, and the views of Hagia Sophia and the Blue Mosque all create a glittering experience and a fitting climax to the journey so far.

Day 14: The morning of the final day begins with a visit to the Chora Museum on the outskirts of the city. This thirteenth-century building was originally, like Hagia Sophia, a church, which was later turned into a mosque, and then a museum. It has recently become a mosque again (2020). One of the most amazing collections of frescoes and mosaics anywhere in Turkey, Mehmet gives us a thorough tour. We then spend time picking out more Gospel scenes and fourth-century fathers of the church from the mosaics and frescoes. Visually, this is one of the best experiences of the trip.

4. A poem that was often mentioned en route. See W. B. Yeats, "Sailing to Byzantium," in Larkin, *Twentieth Century*, 82.

The final visits are the Blue Mosque and Hagia Sophia. The Blue Mosque, with its towering arches and blue tiles, provides an unparalleled experience (for most of our group) of Islam and Muslim culture. Built in the seventeenth century, it stands as an icon of the Muslim faith and impresses itself upon us both in size and beauty. Then, across the road after a group photo, Hagia Sophia, or Holy Wisdom, the final visit of the trip (and, like Chora, turned back into a mosque in 2020). The overwhelming impact of this building, and its significance for Christians, form a perfect climax to our journey. After a historical outline, standing outside, the tour continues inside where we see rich and colorful mosaics culminating in the one above the exit: Constantine presenting the city of Constantinople to the *theotokos*, or Mary the mother of God, and Justinian presenting her with the church of Hagia Sophia.

But it is, of course, the significance of the place for the Christian understanding of Jesus—the Wisdom of God—which is key. At this stage all the strands of the St. Paul and the Early Church course come together: the biblical concept of God's wisdom; the theology of Paul; the theology of the councils; the book of Revelation; the development of the cult of Mary; and Christology, with all its fine tuning. All of these are now symbolized in one of the greatest buildings in the world. The story it tells includes the story of Byzantium, of Islam, of modern Turkey under Atatürk, and since. The visit to Hagia Sophia symbolizes everything St. George's College wanted to do in Turkey, and is a wholly appropriate place to finish.

On the final night of the course, there are lively discussions and presentations, including a college certificate, a tile, and a course photograph. The excitement concludes with a celebratory dinner, followed by goodbyes and farewells. Participants usually leave either during the night or the following morning—or stay in Istanbul for more exploration and adventure.

During the years I was dean of St. George's College, we did the Turkey course many times, sometimes twice a year. Occasionally, we tweaked it and did something different. On one occasion we started in Adana, visiting Tarsus for St. Paul, and Antioch for the councils and Paul. When we did that, the course lasted three weeks, a bit too much in a minibus with a small group! On another occasion we took in the Dardanelles and Gallipoli in northwestern Turkey, recalling the First World War and the many losses of human life there. The visit was especially moving for our Australian participants. On a couple of occasions, we met with the Greek ecumenical patriarch Bartholomew at St. George's Orthodox patriarchate in Istanbul.

It is not difficult to see in this account that what St. George's College does in Turkey is what it also does in the Holy Land: enable a holistic learning experience, combining the study of the Bible and Christian history with an understanding of the development of Christian belief in Jesus and its significance for today—all wrapped up in a first-class journey by land and by sea.

GREECE

As the idea of "St. George's College abroad" developed, and with the success of the Turkey course, we started to think of more places we could visit. One element in this consideration was the concept of "second tier" courses—that is, courses that students who had already been to the Holy Land could come back in. Turkey was successful, but we needed even more new programs and opportunities that would draw participants into returning and deepening their study-pilgrimage experience.

Two obvious possibilities were Greece and Rome, two locations that had significant importance in terms of biblical texts and Christian history. Indeed, participants in the Turkey course had often raised the question of the possibility of adding Greece onto the Turkey course. This would enable a more complete experience of Paul's world, and those coming from Australia and New Zealand, and even the US, might prefer to take in the two countries in one visit. The problem with combining them was that we would need at least three weeks to do justice to the scope of the material. Also, it might be difficult to dovetail the whole course together smoothly. For example, arranging a single guide to be with us for the whole time across the two countries, although not impossible, might not be straightforward.

In any event, we never attempted Turkey and Greece together in one course. Instead, we decided to try out a separate course entitled St. Paul in Greece, and, although this only happened a couple of times, and never really took off as much as the Turkey course did, it was still a roaring success for all who joined. The idea was to do what we were so used to doing in the Holy Land and in Turkey: bring together a study of biblical texts with an experience of the land; get familiar with the terrain through which St. Paul traveled and the context in which some of his letters were written; appreciate the country and its place in Christian history; and encounter the contemporary people of the land, Christians and others. So in every place in St. Paul in Greece, we considered and discussed Paul's visit to that location, the historical background, and the appropriate letters. As in other places we had a local guide with whom we worked to bring about a wholesome diet of culture, history, philosophy, and theology. Lectures in hotel rooms and on the bus, along with Bible studies, reflections, and prayers, all made it another special St. George's College experience.

For St. Paul in Greece, we begin in Thessaloniki, an appropriate place to fly into. Meeting course members on the first evening, we begin the study of Paul, focusing on his earliest letter, the first one to the Thessalonians. Most course members have not done the Turkey course, so basic introductions to the course and to St. Paul are made early on. There is no single, major archeological site at Thessaloniki, but it forms a convenient base from which to go forward to Philippi and Neapolis.

Philippi was originally known as Krenides, meaning "the springs," because there is much water in the area. On arrival, we head straight for the archeological site for a thorough tour and explanation. It is truly impressive, and we can only scratch the surface in a couple of hours. In Paul's day this was an important political and commercial center. Most of what can be seen at Philippi today comes from a time later than Paul, but the setting provides an enormous amount for the imagination to work with. In the Byzantine era, the city grew considerably and became a place of pilgrimage because of Paul. Its history, like many of the places we visit, begins several centuries BC, in this case in the sixth century. It was named after Philip II of Macedon, and then became a Roman colony.

As usual for a St. George's group, the field trip is an exciting, multilayered experience. Philippi is peppered with ruins of interesting buildings, including a theater, library, baths, fountains, colonnaded streets, temples to various gods and goddesses, and several churches, some substantial. Indeed, in the early Christian period, Philippi was the seat of a bishop. One interesting feature of this city is that the ancient Via Egnatia ran through it. This major road ran from this area west to the coast, and then on to Rome, turning into the Via Appia. Later it also ran east from here to Constantinople. Along with the site itself, the history gives a geographical orientation and a context for a study of Paul and his world, as well as of the later period. Acts 16 is one of the relevant texts. Paul was here probably on all three missionary journeys, but in this text it's the second. He comes to Philippi following his vision of a man from Macedonia, and founds the first church on European soil. Philippi was a vast multicultural, international city and it is not difficult to imagine Paul's purpose in visiting the place.

This is a good location to consider the two main sources for Paul: Acts and his own letters, in this case Philippians, with its famous "Hymn to Christ" (Phil 2:6–11). The study provides an amazing trigger for discussion of Paul's theology and his understanding of Christ and of God. Often the group includes clergy and teachers who have much to bring to the discussion. Following Phil 2, our attention turns back to Acts 16 and the story of Lydia from Thyatira, the worker in purple dye, who was baptized by Paul, as well as the conversion of the Philippian jailer, and Paul and Silas's own spell in jail. There is another opportunity for group learning too: a visit to a particular spot associated with Lydia. Nearby, there is a modern church commemorating the baptism of Lydia. The tradition that it was in this region that she was baptized goes back to Byzantine times. So, gathering around a body of water in glorious countryside, we read Acts 16 and launch a group discussion on the text as well as the meaning of our own baptisms. The discussion concludes with some communal singing and prayer inside the church.

From Philippi we travel to nearby ancient Neapolis (modern Kavalla), simply to note the place where Paul arrived on European soil. After leaving Troas he set sail and landed at Neapolis on his second missionary journey (Acts 16:11). It is implied that he visited again on his third journey, leaving there by boat (Acts 20:6). Although there is little of direct archeological value for our course, it is a refreshing spot with a modern church, and gives rise to good discussion about the relation between Paul's letters and the accounts of his movements in Acts.

The next leg of our journey takes us south, ultimately to Corinth and Athens. But on the way we come to the famous Meteora monasteries in central Greece, standing as they do on the plain of Thessaly and comprising a major UNESCO World Heritage site. Their relevance to a St. George's course is not only because their historical and geological interest is considerable, but also because of their significance in the history of Christian monasticism. The Meteora are huge natural pillars formed by vertical fault lines in the rock. They have been weathered for thousands of years, and from the ninth century attracted Christian ascetics who would ascend and live on the top. From the ninth through to the fourteenth century, a series of monasteries was built on these vertical rock formations, and in their heyday in the fourteenth century there were twenty-four. The parallels with the rise of monastic life in the deserts of Egypt and Judaea in the fourth century are striking. Today, the Meteora monasteries (only six surviving with a little over fifty monks and nuns) are second only to the monasteries on Mount Athos in their historical, artistic, and religious significance.

The main purpose of our visit to Meteora is to encounter something of the life of the monasteries through visiting some of the chapels. We begin, as usual on these courses, with an evening introduction and a lecture on the Orthodox Church or spirituality, including icons. This prepares us for the next day's ascent (by pathways up the rock formations, laid in the 1920s), to enter some of the monasteries and view the rich and vivid series of frescoes and icons. An awareness of Orthodox theology and spirituality gradually dawns upon participants as we have explained to us and pick out for ourselves some of the Christian theological themes of the artwork, including the lives of disciples and saints. We only have time to visit about three monasteries before setting off again on our journey. But this stop is a major part of the course, opening doors of perception for us that will surely remain open for some time to come.

The journey continues by bus, first to Delphi where an entire day is needed to visit the archeological site, including the various temples and, of course, the famous tholos in the Shrine of Athene, and the theater. This visit takes us off Paul's trail a bit, but deepens our appreciation of the Hellenistic dimension of Paul's thinking. The shrine of the Delphic Oracle, Pythia, initiates discussion about the gods of Greece and the business of foretelling. The beautiful shrine on the slopes of Mount Parnassus is followed by a trip to the Delphi Museum to see the famous statue of the *Charioteer* among many other artifacts. The entire visit enables another level of learning with appropriate briefings, lectures, discussions, and reflections.

Travel is always an important part of the St. George's concept of learning. Travel by sea as well as by land adds to the experience. Getting out onto the sea gives a sense of one of Paul's methods of traveling. Following Delphi, there is a ferry ride across from the mainland of Greece to the Peloponnese and to Mycenae, the famous home of Agamemnon and background to Homer and the *Iliad*. It is one of the largest archeological sites in the world and, like Delphi, immerses participants in some of the history and culture of Greece. The visit to Agamemnon's palace and tomb is one of the most visually striking anywhere. Another day is taken in this area to allow time for scenic Nafplio, and for some free time, and possibly an excursion to Epidaurus with its stunning theater. Then on to Corinth.

Once in Corinth we're back in thoroughly Pauline territory preparing for another major archeological encounter. Staying in a nearby hotel the night before the visit, we gather for an introduction. The following day is spent exploring the site itself. With the introduction and two important letters from Paul to the Corinthians, we are well equipped for what we find. Corinth is an impressive site. A day visit doesn't really do it justice, but, in any case, not all our participants are budding archeologists! There can be too much detail! So a general picture is adequate, with the experience of being in the place enough for some. As we walk through the site, text and location come together once again.

As I have indicated before, the places relating to Paul do for Paul what places in the Holy Land do for Jesus. The right balance and getting a good, clear picture of the situation means that people get a three-dimensional picture of the dynamic apostle to the gentiles. Somehow, Corinth is one of the best places because most church people feel more familiar with First Corinthians than with any of his other letters. The significance of Corinth lies in its location on the isthmus, connecting the mainland of Greece with the Peloponnese. The best way of appreciating this crucial, strategic position of Corinth is to climb to the top of the Acro-Corinthos, the mountain which overlooks the ancient city. Some participants take on this challenge! At the summit, the remains of the Temple of Aphrodite tell the story of the promiscuity and immorality addressed by Paul in 1 Corinthians (5:1–2). At the very top, we can see clearly each way, east and west across the isthmus, and appreciate the significance of this place as a crossroads of culture and commerce, both by land and by sea.

Below the mountain, there is also much to see. The history of the place is split. In 146 BC, Corinth fell in a war with Sparta. After a hundred years it was reestablished in 46 BC by Julius Caesar. Archeological remains from various periods include a theater, market, temples, fountains, baths, altars, statues, pillars, basilicas, houses, shops, and other unidentified buildings. A walk through the streets of ancient Corinth gives Paul and his letters a context which can't be imagined until we get there. Suddenly, there he is, in his world, and many aspects of his life and letters come alive. Suddenly, at moments in the archeological site, emphasizing the crossroads and the cultural, multiethnic, transient communities of Paul's day, the issues and problems of his community and his own responses emerge in multicolor.

A pause in the site for half an hour, in the shade if it is hot, enables a twenty-minute presentation on any aspect of Paul's Corinthian correspondence that a staff member might choose: splits in the community, worship, marriage and divorce, immorality, speaking in tongues, Paul's own authority, Paul and women, the cross and resurrection, or any other current aspect of Pauline studies. The combination of archeological site, reading of text, and the lectures and discussions enable an unparalleled appreciation of Paul and his theology. Talk about bringing the Bible to life! Evening reflections on the day's experience then bring out many of the things people have seen, thought, and experienced. Participants share the impact of the visit on understanding and belief. Usually, radical changes have occurred in people's perceptions of Paul—and of their own faith.

The next morning, we're off over the Corinthian Canal—itself a teaching aid with all its history and significance—to Athens for another encounter with history, archeology, and philosophy. The change from the rural mood of the Corinth area is striking as we enter the bustling, polluted capital. But here is another major stop on the Pauline trail, another opportunity to appreciate his world and his thought. The focus, of course, is the Acropolis with its various buildings and remains. We head for the Parthenon. A good guide covers the history, including something of the Greek philosophical tradition stemming from Plato, Aristotle, and others.

A reflection from a staff member (if possible, on the site) brings text into context. This time, Acts 17 and Paul's address to an "unknown god" on the Areopagus hill is central. The theological dimensions of the passage can be taken up in discussion either on the site or later in an evening reflection. Some free time enables participants to visit other antiquities or go shopping. One crucial recommendation, if not actually part of the course, is a visit to the Byzantine and Christian Museum in Athens. It holds some twenty-five thousand artifacts from the Byzantine period and beyond, including icons, frescoes, mosaics, manuscripts, and many other exciting and illuminating items. Many choose this option over retail therapy!

A final Eucharist and a meal in a restaurant in the city bring the course to a close. As with the other courses, the combination of travel, inspirational locations, and important biblical texts has worked its way into people's awareness. A thoroughly holistic learning experience comes to a close with a new appreciation of St. Paul and his world, as well as of Christian faith and its many different dimensions. St. Paul in Greece is an eye-opening experience and a stomping success.

ROME

Quite often at St. George's College there was conversation and discussion about a possible course in Rome. It seemed an obvious choice as a new location, given that city's significance in the New Testament and in Christian history. In many ways Rome parallels Jerusalem, and we often thought that a course in the "Eternal City" would attract interest and complete our portfolio. Over several years the dream gradually became clearer, and we started to discuss when we could do it and what should be included. One of the Palestinian Anglican clergy in the diocese of Jerusalem, the Rev. Nael Abu Rahmoun, had studied in Rome and spoke fluent Italian, so we liaised with him. Italy was more expensive than we realized but gradually a course came together focusing on early Christianity in Rome and, of course, on Paul's Epistle to the Romans. There were numerous possibilities for a course title, but we settled on The Church and Rome. The course ran in 2010, lasted about ten days, and included Assisi. It attracted about a dozen people.

There is much to do in Rome and, again, choices must be made. Each day begins with morning prayer in the hotel meeting room, followed by an introductory Bible study, lecture, or discussion. The theme is Paul's Epistle to the Romans, or the importance of Rome in the Acts of the Apostles and in early Christianity—a good, solid start to the day. Focusing on some of the early Roman fathers of the church helps fill out the picture. The idea, as usual, is to cover as much as we can from the framework of our overriding theme. After breakfast, we're off out into the city on foot or by bus.

Visits over the following days include obvious places like St. Peter's with the excavations, or *scavi*, underneath, showing us the traditional tomb of Peter. Then the other three of the four main churches: St. Paul Outside the Walls, containing the traditional tomb of Paul; St. John Lateran, the Cathedral Church of Rome; and St. Mary Major, with its reliquary containing wood from the crib of Jesus, and its Chapel of St. Jerome.[5] With hundreds of churches, we are selective, but the fascinating San Clementi with its Temple of Mithras underneath is included, as well as a few others en route as we walk the streets. The classic St. George's combination of learning styles and emphases comes into play.

We also spend time in the Vatican Museum and at a papal audience. The Wednesday afternoon general audience with the pope is well known and we get tickets and attend, seeing Benedict XVI in the "popemobile." This is an opportunity to think about the papacy and its significance, as well as Benedict's theology and its emphases. On one evening, we take a short walk to the Waldensian church, a group originally founded in the twelfth century and with numerous traditions in a variety of places. It is one of the most significant non-Roman churches in Rome. The visit to their center and a presentation from one of their leaders sparks off heated discussions. We also visit the Anglican Centre for a guided tour and an introduction to its work.

Assisi is nearby, and a couple of nights are arranged there. The focus changes to St. Francis and St. Clare, and the many rich traditions of this unique destination. With only one day for actual visits the time is limited, but we manage to see most of the important churches and shrines, led by a local guide. The Basilica of St. Francis with its stunning Giotto frescoes and the tomb of Francis leaves lasting impressions, as does the Basilica of St. Clare and her tomb. Visiting the crucifix that spoke to St. Francis is very special. And the Portiuncula,[6] where the Franciscans first met, is fascinating. Indeed, the whole story of Francis and Clare and their engagement with creation and with the poor is spiritually moving and uplifting. Even in a single day their dynamic spirits are felt among us and prayer somehow seems more alive. New senses of faith, understanding, and spirituality emerge and we make the most of our short visit, culminating in numerous discussions on the bus back to Rome.

5. Jerome died in Bethlehem in AD 420 but tradition has it that his remains were later taken to this church.

6. Meaning the "little portion" of land.

The final day in Rome is free. Course participants explore further and prepare to depart. A concluding seminar and Eucharist, along with certificates and college tiles, bring the course to a close. Reflections, as usual, bring out important experiences and insights. Rome has worked its magic, and this has been a stimulating immersion in Christian history, texts, and theology. Modern Rome has also been encountered, and questions of Catholicism and ecumenism have been discussed. Sadly, the college is out of pocket following this course, and it is not repeated. But, in any case, it has been a glorious educational success for all who took part.

The "foreign courses" at St. George's, including Sinai, Jordan, Turkey, Greece, and Rome, have played a key role in the college's history and offerings over many years. They do more than simply "bring the Bible to life." They bring the whole of Christian history to life and enable serious theological reflection on faith in numerous important, colorful, and exciting locations. This combination of courses in the Holy Land and courses abroad gives St. George's College a truly international feel.

In part 3 we have considered some of the many dimensions of college life at St. George's including basic framework and staffing, educational matters, and the rich contributions of a variety of individuals. Two chapters have outlined college courses both in the Holy Land itself and in the wider region, capturing something of the essence and dynamism of St. George's out in the field. We turn now in part 4 to consider some further elements of the college's broadening vision: reconciliation, celebration, and an interfaith element.

PART 4

Reconciling and Rekindling

9

Kids4Peace and an Unusual Conference

Two other important developments at St. George's College have been Kids4Peace (K4P), a project which spread through the diocese of Jerusalem and the college to become an international movement, and Rekindling the Spirit, an event held in 2009 in North Carolina. The first was a project for reconciliation between the peoples of the Holy Land. The second was a college reunion.

As the name suggests, K4P is a course for kids. But it has been more than a course and has stretched well beyond St. George's College. Indeed, over several years it developed numerous important and powerful tentacles outward into the lives of adults and communities both in the Holy Land and farther afield. The roots of the concept lay in the summer youth camps of the diocese of Jerusalem. Canon Suheil Dawani, Arabic pastor at St. George's Cathedral (1997–2004) and later Anglican archbishop, worked with the idea in its early stages. Then Henry Carse became interested, and got St. George's College thoroughly involved.

Basically, the idea of K4P was for a peace camp that brought young Palestinians (Muslims and Christians) together with Israeli Jews. There were strong feelings of despair and hopelessness as continuing violence erupted on the streets of Jerusalem and the West Bank during the second intifada. The hope that Israelis and Palestinians might come together for peaceful dialog still seemed a long way off. When I became course director at the college in 1999, Henry Carse became director of special programs, a new position, as we have seen, which concentrated on a second tier of courses. Henry's speciality was the desert but he also spearheaded a new wave of interest in reconciliation across the faith communities in the Holy Land through K4P.

Henry arranged a series of meetings, events, and activities in the college. Parents and children were interviewed and individuals were selected from the different communities to take part in a St. George's-based encounter across the divides. The Jerusalem events introduced families to the idea of operating across divisions and imagining a different way forward in the conflict. K4P became immensely popular and grew beyond all expectation. Before long the idea of launching a K4P summer camp outside the Holy Land was born, following the example of other such movements (one being Seeds for Peace, another peacemaking movement that often visited the college to speak about its work and which later joined with K4P). The idea of taking young people outside the conflict zone for a neutral encounter was popular and was thought to be the best way forward for K4P. Soon the leaders had decided on a summer camp in the US.

The expansion of K4P in this way spread across the next few years, and St. George's was always involved at an official level: the college dean was ex officio on the governing board. Bishara Khoury was involved in running the camps in Jerusalem and abroad for a period. The first camp took place in 2002 at Camp Allen near Houston, Texas. Twelve youth, four each from the Jewish, Christian, and Muslim communities in the Holy Land, flew out and shared a two-week camp experience, which included all the activities of a classic American summer camp as well as cultural and religious encounter and dialog. By the end of the camp, potentially lifelong friendships were established and serious differences overcome. It was a stunning and emotional change in the lives of participants. Those who had been unable to imagine that an enemy could be a friend, that the conflict they had grown up with could dissolve in another situation, or that they could embrace aliens and "terrorists" as friends and family, now saw the world in a new way.

Pilgrims on St. George's College courses soon encountered K4P and became enthusiastic in the desire to make a difference to the Middle East conflict. They would return to their respective countries with great determination to make a difference. K4P was a way of doing this and of contributing to global peace. Laity, clergy, and bishops in the US soon became active, and, in later years, with the momentum established and a good deal of financial support, other camps were held in Atlanta, Vermont, and Boston, and later in Canada and France. An enduring problem, however, was knowing how to sustain friendships made in another country once the participants were back in their conflict zone. This was the most challenging element, and inevitably many, though not all, participants lost touch because of the conflicted situations they went back to in Israel and Palestine.

Reunion meetings were held at St. George's College but the need was greater than the capacity to deal with it.

In the years following the first decade of K4P, the growth was more in North America than in the Middle East and the program turned more toward domestic conflict resolution in the US. As far as St. George's College is concerned, K4P was the first full-scale development in relation to the local conflict in Israel-Palestine. And it involved local non-Christians in a way that none of the courses ever has. Sadly, after Henry Carse's departure, the college ceased to have any connection with the movement.[1] The last K4P event involving St. George's was in 2010.

The second part of this chapter concerns the college's 2009 reunion event, Rekindling the Spirit. During the closing years of the first decade of the new millennium, there were excited and exciting conversations among St. George's College staff about the possibility of organizing a reunion of some sort for alumni. With so much support in the English-speaking world, the college was well placed to provide an event or occasion at which participants could get together for a few days to touch base and share experiences and memories. The sense of an international family has always been strong at the college with so many people having shared a formative experience of the Holy Land through St. George's. Staff realized that the college and course participants would benefit from an event that would rekindle the experience and celebrate the unique opportunity the college offers. The unexpected global recession of 2008–2009 triggered an awareness of the need for marketing and fundraising to encourage support for the college. Also, if anyone felt unsure about traveling to the Holy Land because of concerns about safety, St. George's College could go to them!

And so the idea of a reunion was born. But where would it be? To have it at the college itself would present a challenge because it was hoped to attract more people than St. George's could accommodate. Inevitably, because of the strong support from the United States and issues of travel, it was decided to try to find an appropriate venue in that country. Jill Need, along with Rana Khoury and Genia Stephan, took the lead in searching the internet for appropriate venues and contacting them. After looking at several possibilities, including Estes Park north of Denver, Colorado (home to the famous Cheley Summer Camps), it was decided that the Episcopal Church Conference Center at Kanuga, North Carolina, would be the most suitable location for the event. Its leader, Stan Hubbard, was already known to the college.

1. Henry retired to Vermont in 2008 but was involved with K4P until 2010. He still leads pilgrimages in the Holy Land with Fr. Kamal Farah.

Kanuga is well known in the US, and has a stunning setting of fourteen hundred acres in the Blue Ridge Mountains near Hendersonville, North Carolina. It includes a thirty-acre lake, twenty miles of hiking trails, and staggering views. Open for individuals and groups, camps, and retreats, it offers organized conferences and events for large numbers, church groups, or individuals. With accommodation for four hundred forty guests, its beautiful rural setting looked perfect for what St. George's was considering. The Chapel of the Transfiguration would be the location of services and there were plenty of large and small venues for lectures and discussions. The date was set for February 19–22, 2009. The event would be called "Rekindling the Spirit," and would be a reunion and celebration.

When the time came, and following much preparation, several college staff, Palestinian and expatriate, flew out of Tel Aviv to the US for the event. The reunion attracted nearly a hundred participants including ex-deans and course directors. The American, British, and Australia/New Zealand Regional Committees were represented as follows: Bishop Allen Bartlett (NARC), Bishop Robin Smith (BRC), Bishop Keith Slater (ANZRC), and Bishop James Tengatenga of Malawi (ACC representative). The reunion was Thursday evening to Sunday morning, and so provided two full days of talks, discussions, and worship, as well as the major opportunity of meeting up with people at receptions and meals.

The flavor of Rekindling the Spirit can be seen from the lecture titles and speakers at the event. Having left the college in 2008, Henry Carse attended and gave the opening lecture on a subject related to his PhD: "The Ethical Edge of Pilgrimage." Henry also spoke on his favorite subject: the desert. Gregory Khalil, a Palestinian originally from San Diego, California, but then working for the Palestinians in Ramallah spoke on the Israeli-Palestinian conflict. The Rev. Canon John Peterson spoke on St. George's College in the context of the Anglican Communion, and led the stations of the cross through the Kanuga site. I did a PowerPoint presentation on the history and development of the college buildings using numerous old black and white photographs from the days of John Wilkinson.

Other sessions included two on journaling led by Daphne Grimes, a great friend of St. George's who had attended numerous courses and was an active ambassador for the college. Daphne founded and headed up a retreat house called the St. Thomas the Apostle Center, near Yellowstone Park in Cody, Wyoming. Journaling was always encouraged at the college and played a key part in courses. Daphne's experience and insights were much appreciated.[2] Another session was led by Dr. Mitzi Gardiner. Mitzi

2. She wrote up many of her experiences at St. George's College in Grimes, *Journeys*.

had been a course assistant at the college and had completed a PhD at the School of Oriental and African Studies in London (SOAS). Her subject was the Israeli separation barrier. Mitzi had lectured on this at the college on more than one occasion. Her other presentation at the reunion was on the political symbolism of the olive tree.

I led two sessions: "Images of Faith" was an illustrated journey through the holy places of the Holy Land considering how images of places such as Jerusalem, Bethlehem, and Nazareth change when pilgrims see actual locations. The second session was based on the college's St. Paul and the Early Church course in Turkey which had recently celebrated its tenth anniversary. The college's Palestinian staff led an open discussion on life at the college. And the St. George's College Executive Committee led a session called "St. George's College: The Best Kept Secret." It was often claimed that there were millions of people who had never even heard of St. George's College. The reunion was interested in how to reach them in the future.

The element that held the reunion together was, of course, the worship. The college's connection with the SSJE brothers has already been noted, and they very kindly offered to take care of the worship at the Kanuga conference. Brothers James Koester and Jonathan Maury had been to the college several times and knew its courses and ethos extremely well. They handled the management and leadership of the services, producing an admirable worship booklet containing prayers and all the music—except that played by the Bent Grass bluegrass band which provided musical entertainment one evening.

Rekindling the Spirit turned out to be a joyous occasion marking another line in the sand in the history of St. George's College. Many people met again after years of not seeing each other. There were numerous chances for the college to share news and hopes for the future. Stories were told and memories shared. Worship provided an opportunity to be thankful to God for all that St. George's had achieved over the years until that moment. Of course, there were some who were not able to attend, but the event had the effect of binding together many who treasured the college, its work, and ministry. Everyone left refreshed and reinvigorated. The spirit of the college had been rekindled, and the staff were ready for another chapter. Participants were given a special Rekindling the Spirit tile made by Stefan Karakashian.

K4P and the reunion at Kanuga demonstrated the college's commitment to reaching out beyond its usual boundaries. The next chapter explores further developments on its horizons.

10

Changing Perspectives

AFTER NEARLY TWO DECADES into the new millennium, another new dean was appointed at St. George's College. The Rev. Richard Sewell and his wife, JulieAnn, arrived in October 2018 from the diocese of Southwark, England. Richard knew the Holy Land a little already from living as a volunteer at the Scottish Hospice in Tiberias during the 1980s. He had worked for the Anglican mission agency USPG as a mission educator with additional responsibilities for USPG's relationship with the churches in Pakistan and Bangladesh. He studied theology at the University of Birmingham, England, and trained for the priesthood at the South East Institute of Theological Education (SEITE), now the St. Augustine's School of Theology. Richard had set up and run an interfaith project in London, and had been rector of the team ministry in Barnes, South London. He had been on a St. George's course already and knew the college. He was an ideal candidate for the multifaceted role of dean.

His wide experience meant that Richard had multicultural and interfaith awareness which stood him in good stead for what would face him in Jerusalem. Expecting correctly that the local Palestinian-Israeli conflict would play centrally into the dynamic at St. George's College, he soon found that expatriate cultural clashes were also part of daily life there. Over the years St. George's has become very Americanized, with predominantly American participants in courses. But the varied overall cultural landscape of staff and students, involving Americans, British, Australians, and New Zealanders, as well as local Palestinians, is a significant part of the dynamic of the college and mostly needs to be navigated with care and caution by those in charge. Introducing course members to the internal cultures at the college as well as to the surrounding cultures and conflict is always a challenge.

Richard inherited a variety of things from his predecessor, Greg Jenks. As we have seen, the idea of the Porter Scholar was set up in Greg's time. It only came into practice when Richard Sewell arrived. The idea was to have a framework in which the hitherto "course assistant" role might become more established and developed. Since the Porter Scholar role began, there have been several occupants starting with Della Wager Wells and Stephanie Burette. Each of these was already ordained deacon before arriving at the college and so was able to carry out liturgical duties as well as practical and administrative ones. The Porter Scholar idea has proved constructive and supportive in all sorts of ways.

Other things that Richard Sewell inherited from Greg Jenks included the idea of having a series of visiting lecturers to take care of courses. This went beyond the practice launched by John Wilkinson and John Peterson of having resident academics to contribute to courses. Greg's idea was to have a visiting lecturer more or less doing the job of course director on selected courses. Also, the idea of new courses with dynamic and attractive titles came up again during this period. Some of these courses have run once or twice, while others have never run. The ones that have survived will be considered later in this chapter. During Richard's time in office, also, the link with VTS has continued, and they have often taken the first course slot in January each year. The British Regional Committee has also increased the flow of British students in recent years, not the least in an important course for seminarians. During Richard Sewell's time there has also been practical work on the building, such as the renewal of the air conditioning and heating. In general, the college continues to function smoothly and efficiently with a strong feeling of cohesion between the college, the cathedral, the diocese of Jerusalem, and the Anglican Communion.

In 2018, the Rev. Canon Dr. Mary June Nestler from the United States was appointed as "Course Director and Lecturer in Contextual Biblical Studies." She was on staff when Richard Sewell arrived. Mary June was no stranger to St. George's College. Her involvement with courses goes back at least to the mid-1980s when she was frequently a visiting lecturer. Her qualifications for the position were exemplary, for she had not only been involved in the higher echelons of the Episcopal Church in the USA, but had also been thoroughly involved in clergy training there, as well as with archeology in Israel.

Mary June's academic background meant that she brought high standards with her to the college when she arrived. She has qualifications from: the University of California, Los Angeles; St. Mary's Seminary and University Ecumenical Institute, Baltimore; the General Theological Seminary in New York; and the Curtis Institute of Music in Philadelphia. In matters archeological, she has taken part in many digs and been a consulting archeologist and area supervisor for the Mount Carmel Project, as well as area supervisor at Sepphoris and at Capernaum. Mary June is no armchair archeologist!

On the clergy training front, she was ordained to the priesthood in 1979 and served in several parishes. She was a member of the faculty at Claremont School of Theology and the dean and president in the 1980s and 1990s. She was canon for ministry formation and then canon to the ordinary of the Episcopal Diocese of Utah in the US, and had been deputy to the General Convention in the dioceses of Utah and Los Angeles. In 1993, she was a member of the archbishop of Canterbury's Anglican/Oriental Orthodox International Dialog. It is clear from Mary June's experience that she was in a prime position to step into the St. George's course director role in 2018. Her contributions to the college courses since have been immeasurable and appreciated enormously by course participants. In the summer of 2022 Mary June retired from the position and was replaced by Rodney Aist who, after writing some lively and interesting books on pilgrimage and teaching at Drew University, returned to St. George's for a second period.[1]

It is worth reiterating here that the development of new courses and the running of existing courses have been affected many times during the college's history by the volatile dynamics of the political surroundings. Local conflicts have usually led to participants canceling and waiting for things to calm down. Cancelations in response to the long-running Israeli-Palestinian conflict, including frequent outbreaks of violence, events in Gaza, suicide bombings in West Jerusalem, and other incidents, have often had severely detrimental effects on college finances. As we have seen, this broad context gradually led to the growth of foreign courses at the college; if students would not travel to Jerusalem, they might travel with the college in Turkey or elsewhere.

But, fortunately, there were the prosperous years as well. What if course numbers were booming and the college couldn't accommodate everyone? It was during these times that staff members started to think of another level of courses that might be operating away from the college simultaneously with a Palestine of Jesus course. There might, for example, be a Ways in the Wilderness course traveling in the desert while a Palestine of Jesus course was in the college in Jerusalem. Also, on occasion it has been possible to run a second-tier course in Jerusalem staying in a local hotel, while a basic course was running in the college itself. Much depended on staffing but simultaneous courses have been quite successful in several

1. See Aist, *Jerusalem Bound*; *Pilgrim Spirituality*.

periods of the college's history. Indeed, this idea was the basis of Henry Carse's "Special Programs" concept which was so successful. The fact that students frequently wish to return to the college for new experiences has, of course, played an important part in this.

During 2017–2018 creative ideas were rife and the need for visiting lecturers helped give birth to some new proposals for courses. One of the main ones introduced was The Holy Land and the Arts, a course focusing on aspects of the Holy Land in art. Subjects included Jerusalem, Abraham, Jesus, and Muhammad, and themes from their lives. Examples from mosaics, icons, frescoes, olive wood, stained glass windows, and other media have been used. This course stretches across the three faiths, Judaism, Christianity, and Islam, and has been very popular. Dr. Barbara Drake Boehm, senior curator at the Cloisters section of the Metropolitan Museum of Art in New York, has been the leader.

Another popular course has been Women of the Bible. From the time of the rise of modern feminism in biblical studies and theology there has been scholarly concentration on the women of the Bible. Focusing on major themes and major women from the Old and New Testaments, this course visits the same places as other courses but focuses on the appropriate biblical and other narratives. Another course that has grown out of the wider interests developed around the time of the millennium is the St. George's Walking the Jesus Trail. The college did a five-day Hike the Holy Land course in the first decade of the new millennium, and this proved very successful. Both courses are ways of encountering the land by foot. Following the Galilean ministry of Jesus, the walking course takes in about eight to nine miles a day, finishing in Jerusalem, and focusing on Jesus' final days.

Throughout the years, St. George's has always offered the opportunity for a parish, college, or institution to bring its own course, closed to anyone else. Indeed, this has happened frequently. For example, over many years, the Canadian Jesuit priest J. P. Horrigan brought his own parish group from the Church of Our Lady of Lourdes, Toronto. The chaplain of St. John's College, Oxford, the Rev. Liz Carmichael, also brought a group to St. George's, as did the well-known metropolitan Kallistos Ware from the Eastern Orthodox Church. On one occasion the college organized a course with the Council for World Mission. These courses could be the basic Palestine of Jesus or have a specially-designed focus. A different type of course was Building Dialogue and Community Across Conflict. Enabled by a grant from Trinity Church, Wall Street, this course included eight representatives from four different institutions: Msalato Theological Seminary in Tanzania, Virginia Theological Seminary in the US, Cuttington University in Liberia, and St. George's College, Jerusalem. Each group came bringing its own regional conflict, sharing experiences, and trying to move forward through encounter and discussion. The course focused on dialog and peacemaking, with the aim of training leaders for the future. In all these courses, basic trips out to key places were related to important texts and ideas, using St. George's unique location.

Perhaps the most successful of the more recent courses at St. George's, however, is the very popular Sharing Perspectives. This Christian-Muslim-Jewish encounter program seeks to develop the college's offerings in an interfaith direction. But before looking specifically at Sharing Perspectives, it is worth saying something about the history of interfaith courses at St. George's.

Originally, of course, with its Anglican Christian foundation, the college courses were populated solely by Christians. It is important to bear in mind here the history of the Anglican diocese covered in part 1 of this book. Bishop Alexander's aim had been to convert local Jews to Christianity. Later bishops had converted Orthodox Christians and others to Anglicanism. But participants in college courses had always been Christian. College courses began as mostly Anglican, and then opened out ecumenically, seeking encounters with people from other Christian denominations. We have noted the wide breadth of countries and denominations eventually represented on college courses. But interfaith was another matter. There were, of course, Muslim as well as Christian Palestinians on the college staff. The possibility of locals attending courses was always there, and the Youth Course had local Palestinian Christians. Occasionally, local Israeli Jews would inquire about coming in courses, but never appeared. Overall, interfaith course participants took a very long time getting to the college.[2]

However, the desire to have a course that would be open to Jews, Christians, and Muslims is longstanding in the college, and has often been discussed and debated by staff. The difference between local Jews and Muslims and, for example, American or British Jews and Muslims, was always part of the discussion. Western liberal Jews and Muslims might be more likely to attend than locals in the Holy Land, given the political situation. One development in this direction was the introduction of a course focusing on Abraham which ran in the 1990s and into the new millennium. It had titles such as Children of Abraham and Abraham: Yesterday and Today.

Abraham was a good focus for a course hoping to attract an interfaith group. In 2002 Bruce Feiler published his popular book *Abraham: A*

2. The St. George's College "Comes of Age" brochure lists several different religious traditions represented on college courses, including Jewish. These were probably few, and from the US.

Journey to the Heart of Three Faiths.[3] This soon became a course book for the St. George's Abraham course. As the "father of all nations," and important in the literature and theology of the three faiths, Abraham was a friend to everyone. The Abraham course was immediately successful. It visited places important to the three faiths (for example, Hebron, Jerusalem, and Bethlehem). It had Jewish and Muslim visiting lecturers who led participants through important parts of the holy books of the three faiths. It also visited communities of the three faiths in homes or places of worship in the Jerusalem area.

The Abraham course was undoubtedly excellent at unleashing diverse opinions and provoking heated discussions. There would be study of the Genesis narrative, especially of the meaning of the *Aqedah*, the so-called sacrifice of Isaac, in Gen 22. There would be an unraveling of the place of Abraham in St. Paul's theology in Romans and Galatians, and of Abraham's place in the Qur'an. There would be discussions of interfaith issues, broadening horizons for all taking part. However, this course never had any Jewish or Muslim participants other than visiting lecturers, and this was felt to be a real weakness. Such participatory breadth was only to come later, in the second decade of the twenty-first century, when a new course entitled Sharing Perspectives was born. In many ways this was a natural development of the Abraham course.

Sharing Perspectives was spearheaded by the Rt. Rev. Dr. Richard Cheetham, bishop of Kingston in the diocese of Southwark in London, England, from 2002 to 2022. Bishop Richard studied in Cambridge, England, and completed a PhD at King's College, London, on religious belief in contemporary Britain. He had been a teacher at Eton and had interests in education and learning across boundaries. He was involved in Christian-Muslim dialog in the UK and was already cochair of the Christian-Muslim Forum in England, which had been set up following the sad events of 9/11. He had been on several pilgrimages to the Holy Land and had taken part in more than one St. George's course.

In 2011, Bishop Richard became chair of the British Regional Committee of St. George's College and saw an opportunity to make additional contributions to interfaith education. His main hope was to help provide a positive framework for bringing Christians and Muslims together not only in dialog but in a shared space in which they could begin to grow into each other's experience. He brought these interests to the BRC and spoke to Dean Graham Smith at St. George's about the possibility of a shared Christian-Muslim course. Graham was immediately interested and supportive,

3. Feiler, *Abraham*.

as were Bishop Suheil Dawani and the college staff. Bishop Richard got together with Graham Smith and the course director at the time, Rodney Aist, and started to design a course. The college's friend Dr. Mustafa Abu Shway, of Al Quds University in Jerusalem, was also involved from the planning stages and throughout.

The first of these courses was entitled Sharing Perspectives: Muslims and Christians in the Holy Land. It ran from March 21 to 27, 2014. Extremely successful, it was nevertheless limited in resources, and in the time available from the participants' side—it ran for only a week. The participants were a group of Christians and Muslims, all of whom had already had some involvement and experience with interfaith dialog in England. A great deal of preparatory work had to be done in London before the course got off the ground. Bishop Richard's personal assistant in Southwark, Margaret Humphries, managed the travel and visa arrangements for all participants and, because of security in Israel, the process was not straightforward. Grants from the BRC and from several Muslim charities in England helped make the course possible.

On arrival at St. George's College, the mixed Muslim and Christian local Palestinian staff offered hospitality, which turned out to be a key part of the course. Meeting local Christians and Muslims was important and enabled the process of sharing to broaden and deepen. Visitors to the Holy Land are often struck that local Palestinian Christians and Muslims generally get on very well, bound together as they are by their common ethnic identity. It is not always so in other places. In the course, there were lectures on Jerusalem and the local political scene, and orientation around the city including the Muslim and Christian quarters of the Old City. They visited the Haram esh-Sharif and attended Muslim prayers at the Al-Aqsa Mosque, prayed at the Church of the Holy Sepulcher and along the Via Dolorosa, and also visited the Mount of Olives and a local mosque at Ras El-Amoud. In the wider area they visited the tombs of the patriarchs in Hebron, including nearby Mamre, focusing on Abraham and Gen 18. The group also went to Bethlehem and the Church of the Nativity, as well as to Galilee, visiting the Sea of Galilee and Nazareth. They discussed Jesus and Muhammad, the love of God and of neighbor, and the ascension of Jesus (present in both the New Testament and in the Qur'an) in Christianity and in Islam.

One of the most moving elements in this course was sharing worship across the two faiths. Christians attending Muslim worship observed objectively and with respect. Muslims attending a Eucharist did the same. The group also heard the views of young Christians and Muslims at St. George's School and in private homes. One of the most enlightening moments was a conversation between two young Palestinian women—one Christian and one Muslim—discussing their backgrounds and their perceptions of faith and life growing up in their two respective faith traditions in the Holy Land. There was also, of course, the feature which so often helps make St. George's courses so special: the bonding of participants through conversation at meals and on the bus, in the lecture room and out at sites, and in the common room and wherever and whenever they were together. In the light of traveling around the land and the holy places, participants were able to "share perspectives" as they lived together in the college. This course was not just a trip or even a pilgrimage but a real personal interfaith encounter at several important levels.

The course ran three times under Bishop Richard and started to grow in scope. It was soon hoped that if this could be done with Muslim and Christian participants, it might well be possible to include Jews. Even though there had been significant input from Rabbi David Rosen on one of the courses, attracting a Jewish contingent who would go to Jerusalem on a trip organized by Christians was never going to be easy. In fact, the Rev. Dr. Karen Hamilton from Canada, with a good deal of Jewish-Christian-Muslim interfaith experience, became involved and helped the course attract Jews as well as Muslims and Christians, bringing the original vision and hope into a three-way interfaith reality.

Bishop Richard Cheetham wanted Sharing Perspectives to get into the DNA of St. George's College, and after the first three courses this happened. The bishop's hope of generating "well-equipped, interfaith practitioners"[4] has now been achieved. Participants return to the UK having undergone a real change of outlook. The quality in terms of education and experience has been unparalleled—an illuminating shift in perception and perspective for all involved. Overall, this course has been hugely successful and has remained in the college's program despite being demanding and challenging to plan, arrange, and carry out. For the participants, it has broadened and deepened their understanding and appreciation of people of other faiths as well as enhancing their continuing work back home.

In 2020, the staff of St. George's College, under the able leadership of Dean Richard Sewell, decided to hold centenary celebrations for the college, recalling Bishop Rennie MacInnes's educational vision following the First World War. It will be remembered that MacInnes made several appointments of scholarly canons at St. George's Cathedral with a view to consolidating the idea of a "Collegiate Church." Now, a century later, much had happened that needed celebrating. On the weekend of January 24–26, 2020, therefore, previous staff (including deans, course directors, and chaplains)

4. In private conversation.

and course members gathered in the college with cathedral staff, friends, and locals to mark the occasion and to give thanks. Following evening prayer in the cathedral, a welcoming reception was held in the college and an opening dinner in the cathedral guest house refectory. There were some present who had known the college for forty years.

The following day, participants went on a field trip to Mount Zion to see the excavations around the Essene Gate, led by two archeologists from the German Protestant Institute of Archaeology in Jerusalem, as well as visiting the Church of the Holy Sepulcher to see the famous *Domine Ivimus* graffito in the depths of the Armenian section of the church. The visit typified St. George's College excursions out into the field. After lunch there were two short lectures in the college lecture room. First, as a previous dean, I spoke on "The Many Faces of St. George's College." Second, as course director at the time, the Rev. Dr. Mary June Nestler spoke on "Pilgrims on St. George's Way." Both lectures drew attention to the life-transforming effects of St. George's courses on participants.

Later, evening prayer in the cathedral was followed by a celebratory banquet in the MacInnes Hall. During the meal there were speeches from the dean and from the chairs of the various regional committees. In addition, messages were read out from the archbishop of Canterbury (patron of the college), the Rev. Canon Dr. John Peterson (previous dean), and from VTS, with whom the college continues a close relationship. The climax of the celebrations came on the Sunday with a Eucharist in St. George's Cathedral celebrated by Archbishop Suheil Dawani, accompanied by several bishops. The sermon was preached by the Rt. Rev. and Rt. Hon. Sarah Mullally DBE, bishop of London. Participants in the college centenary celebrations were joined in the cathedral by a range of independent pilgrim groups, and the cathedral was packed. Afterward, photographs were taken for the record. A centenary college tile was given to all who took part.

Sadly, following the 2020 celebrations, the coronavirus pandemic struck, and the college had to close its doors. They remained closed for two years as international travel ground to a halt and a totally new and unanticipated worldwide crisis unfolded. The whole of Jerusalem and the Holy Land was, of course, in the same situation as pilgrims and tourists disappeared from the landscape. Fortunately, no jobs were lost at the college and care for the staff was maintained.

But Dean Richard Sewell refocused the college's sights and, along with Mary June Nestler, developed online material for college supporters worldwide. A particularly successful Lent course in 2021 attracted large numbers online, and Sewell's book of Lenten meditations, *River Through the Desert:*

A Lenten Journey in the Holy Land, followed.[5] During this period also, a past course member left St. George's College a sizable financial legacy, providing a much-needed element of stability, something the college had always lacked. After a very difficult period and the two-year closure, the college opened its doors again during the early months of 2022. The Rev. Andy MacBeth from the US became chaplain and his wife, Sybil MacBeth, was appointed minister of hospitality. Other chaplains during this time included the Rev. Joe Rivers, the Rev. William Allberry, and the Rev. Ken Dimmock.

A new and exciting development in this period was the idea of a "Writer in Residence" at the college. The well-known Welsh writer and broadcaster Rhidian Brook was appointed, and he and his wife, Nicola, moved into the tower apartment in the Cathedral Close for a year. In the same period, through work with the regional committees, Richard Sewell sharpened the ministerial training side of the college's courses, introducing the notion of ministerial formation through pilgrimage. This meant that a larger percentage of the college's courses would focus on ministerial training.

But despite reopening and turning a new corner, by the end of 2022 the college was still affected by the coronavirus pandemic, and by the middle of 2023 new waves of political violence in the area took their toll. In October 2023 the Israel-Gaza war broke out, throwing the whole region into political chaos. Numbers of course participants at the college fell; some courses were completely canceled. Palestinian staff had difficulty getting through checkpoints to work. By the end of that month the college had closed its doors completely and its future was thrown into kaleidoscopic uncertainty. Toward the end of 2024, no courses are running at the college. However, through all the challenges, staff have continued to provide online resources for the international St. George's family. At the same time, Richard Sewell has launched "Let light shine out of darkness: The Campaign for St. George's College," aimed at raising $1.195 million to help the college through many financial challenges and into the future.

For well over half a century now, in a specially designed building, and often against considerable political and financial odds, St. George's College has provided a breadth of courses and a flexibility of curriculum that have attracted a wide variety of participants from around the world. The scope for holistic learning continues to develop today, enabling the enriching and enhancing experiences that form the college's fundamental character and identity as it reaches out across new horizons.

5. Sewell, *River Through the Desert*.

11

Epilogue

St. George's College, Jerusalem, is a truly unique, life-transforming institution of the Anglican Communion. Having evolved within the Anglican diocese of Jerusalem, it functions as an ecumenical and interfaith hub for the global church and beyond. It is a center of learning, ministry, and reconciliation in which faith can be informed, grow, and come to maturity. The location, of course, has always been favorable for it sits in the heart of Jerusalem, the mother city of all Christians. Its purpose has always been focused on the land that surrounds it, on the Bible, and on the local people. The pull of Jerusalem on pilgrims has always been magnetic and St. George's College has played a key role in enabling many Christians to experience one of the most fascinating destinations on earth.

This book has traced the origins and development of St. George's College over the inside of two centuries, from the first political and missionary interests of the British in the Middle East, through the many twists and turns of their presence in the region, to the establishment of an Anglican diocese based in Jerusalem. The book has followed the engaging story of the first Anglican bishops with their interest in converting local Jews and Christians. It has shown the turning points along the way as Christ Church gave birth to St. George's, and as ministry and mission enthused the various players in the drama to expand the possibilities of pilgrimage to the Holy Land.

Education was always high on the agenda, and the concept of a Collegiate Church and the dream of an Anglican college were always present in the minds and hearts of the early bishops. As the college came to birth, courses were run for local ordinands and foreigners with some leading academics playing a part. As the political sands shifted and the challenges of the surrounding context bore in, the British became more established in the area, not the least through the Mandate government in Palestine in the first half of the twentieth century.

Eventually, under the leadership of Archbishop Campbell MacInnes and the Rev. John Wilkinson, a building was erected in Jerusalem and the college was established. Arriving at St. George's, students followed in the footsteps of archeologists and pilgrims across the centuries. Wilkinson also created the St. George's courses and refined them, leaving a legacy that still plays an important part in the college's life today. As the idea and the reality grew and courses filled up, it was realized that the building needed extending and renovating. The diocese continued to develop, too, as it expanded and became part of a province. John Peterson led the "Comes of Age" project at the college in the 1980s, raising sufficient funds to add a third floor and renovate the existing two. The building was reopened in 1990.

Courses were refined, developed, and eventually expanded into "foreign" trips through Sinai, Jordan, Turkey, Greece, and Rome. The college's mission stretched outward through Kids4Peace and interfaith courses. There has been much cause for celebration, and still the college's potential knows no bounds. Today, St. George's is a flourishing ecumenical, interfaith institution, still riding the many political storms of the region—most recently the Covid pandemic and the Gaza war. However, through all this, the college has continued its work and remains a treasure to all who know and use it.

Within two centuries, St. George's College, Jerusalem, was born, grew, and developed into what it is today. Its location, purpose, and ministry remain a powerful part of the journey of faith for all who attend its "study-pilgrimages." Long may it transform the lives of all who pass through its doors!

PART 5

Faith and Understanding

12

A Pilgrim Theology?

As we have now seen in some detail, St. George's College, Jerusalem, offers a series of courses or "study-pilgrimages" throughout the year, enabling participants to encounter the Holy Land and its people, read the Bible in new ways, and reflect on their own and others' faith. The courses bring heart and head together in a holistic process which group members say is "life-transforming." From the early days of the college there has been a serious interest in combining learning with prayer and devotion. There have always been both academic and devotional elements in courses, and participants study and pray together throughout. From the beginning, the style of teaching and learning at St. George's has been multilayered, with various activities both inside the college and out in the field. So the following elements have always played an important part: lectures and reflections in the college lecture room, briefings out at sites, short presentations on the bus as courses travel around, visits to specific places of archeological, historical, and religious interest, and prayer and worship in holy places. And although participants might sometimes be called students, it would be fair to say that most would recognize themselves, to some degree at least, as "pilgrims."

But how might this broad educational process be imagined theologically? What understanding of pilgrimage might be appropriate for instructors and participants as a framework for the college's teaching and learning? Interestingly, there has never been an official, written St. George's College educational policy. Certainly, people like John Wilkinson knew clearly what they were doing. Deans and course directors have had a breadth of experience as teachers and leaders, and have articulated clearly how they have seen their task. There have, of course, been different emphases over the years, sometimes more on academic learning, sometimes more on pilgrimage and devotion. But statements of purpose and course outlines make it clear that the various elements mentioned above have always been there. The word "experiential" has often been used to capture the breadth and depth of the whole operation. For all those who take part, the courses are truly uplifting and refreshing, deepening understanding, and affirming faith.

Even so, there can be major surprises, challenges, and disappointments in the Holy Land. Visits to holy places can fracture images treasured since childhood. Expectations and hopes can be dashed as contemporary reality sets in. Through this very process, however, new levels of understanding emerge, deeper senses of the reality of God begin to dawn, and faith starts to feel rather different. Although a "theology of St. George's College courses" might begin in a variety of different places, this experience of disorientation and reorientation provides a particularly rich opportunity for reflection on what the college is doing in its programs. In this final chapter, I suggest that St. George's College courses might be understood in terms of St. Anselm's notion of "faith seeking understanding"—a multilayered "conversation" in which new perceptions and new insights are born. Further details of this idea are spelled out using concepts from the classical theology of icons.[1]

PILGRIMS' PROGRESS

We have already seen in chapter 1 that St. George's College course participants might be thought of as standing in the long line of pilgrims across centuries who have made their way to Jerusalem and the Holy Land. In recent years, the distinction between "pilgrims" and "visitors" or "tourists" has often been discussed at the college, prompting reflection on what individuals and groups think they are doing when they travel to the Holy Land. Are they on a religious journey or on a holiday? Are they travelers and tourists seeking knowledge and information, or pilgrims on a spiritual quest? The writer Cynthia Ozick has commented, "A visitor passes through a place; the place passes through the pilgrim."[2] This distinction has often enabled participants in St. George's courses to think more deeply about their intentions, hopes, and expectations.

A tag like Ozick's, of course, begs definitions and there have been many different understandings of pilgrimage. Is a pilgrim simply someone on a journey to a holy place? Or should they have an articulate sense of what being a pilgrim is? Isn't the spiritual journey more important than

1. This is not an official statement by or for the college, but a personal reflection on how its ministry might be imagined theologically. This chapter is based on Need, "Jerusalem Pilgrims."

2. Quoted in Prior, "Pilgrimage to the Holy Land," 169.

the physical? Should there be physical and spiritual hardships as there were on pilgrimages over many centuries? The comfort of modern travel would certainly disqualify many twenty-first-century journeys to holy places if this were the case. Then there are questions about when a pilgrimage begins or ends, what pilgrims take with them, and what they leave behind, as well as what they encounter as they travel. Further questions are about personal agendas and group expectations. Clearly, there are different kinds of pilgrims. And other than those on the journey itself, who is to say which definition is best?

My sense is that, whatever answers we give to these important questions, the breadth and depth of the St. George's College "study-pilgrimage" qualify participants as "pilgrims." Leaving behind familiar comfort zones, they are on a physical and a spiritual journey. There is prayer and worship at holy places, study of Scripture, and engagement with the land. There is ecumenical and interfaith encounter with locals and others in the course. There is discussion, debate, and reflection on matters historical, archeological, and theological. And hopefully, through the wide variety of experiences, pilgrims grow into new levels of awareness of God. The courses at St. George's are "experiential" and "holistic" in the sense of "not narrowly academic" but incorporating many different levels and styles of learning. This sumptuous feast makes "pilgrims" out of most of those who take part in the college's courses.[3]

FRACTURED IMAGES

So what do pilgrims on a St. George's College "study-pilgrimage" really experience? We have seen much of the answer to this question in previous chapters. There are many exciting and uplifting elements. Pilgrims are able to get a three-dimensional sense of biblical stories and texts. They can get an immediate sense of the relation between places in the Bible, and soon start to benefit from a sense of the geography of the Holy Land. They can quickly and easily "imagine" the Gospel stories. There is a powerful sense of spirituality in the land as pilgrims are immersed in the physical places known to them from Scripture. Being in the places that Jesus and the disciples knew triggers an unparalleled physical and spiritual journey. Pilgrims come to a greater sense of the significance of Jesus' birth in Bethlehem, a greater understanding of his message of the kingdom of God in Galilee, and a more profound awareness of the meaning of his death and resurrection

3. For further discussion of the nature of pilgrims and pilgrimages, see Aist, *Jerusalem Bound*; *Pilgrim Spirituality*.

in Jerusalem. Following the stations of the cross along the Via Dolorosa reignites faith in a unique way. Being a pilgrim in the Holy Land not only brings the Bible to life, it transforms and renews the spiritual life at deeper and deeper levels the longer one stays.

Upon arrival, however, pilgrims are usually also hit by some major surprises. The country is new and unfamiliar. The contemporary landscape is not the biblical one. The modern state of Israel and the West Bank look very different from how the area might have appeared in the first century. Course participants often comment that things seem smaller than they imagined, and that places are closer together. In addition, different cultures interact and conflict in an incomprehensible political maze. Pilgrims are often shocked and dismayed. Presuppositions are upset, and faith and understanding are disturbed. Images are fractured or broken. "This is not what we imagined," they proclaim. But even as this happens, the process of shifting images and changing perceptions brings about new possibilities of appreciation and insight. New thresholds emerge as pilgrims cross into a "liminal" zone.[4]

Most pilgrims arriving at St. George's College for the first time do so with clear images of places in the Holy Land and events in the Bible. Often subconscious, such images can be extremely powerful. In fact, most of them are images of biblical places picked up in childhood, at Sunday school, through singing hymns in church, and through hearing Bible stories read in various contexts. Particular hymns have usually been influential in this process. "There is a green hill far away, without a city wall," written by Mrs. Alexander in the nineteenth century in Ireland as she looked out of her window onto her own local "green hill," has influenced generations of people in English-speaking countries. "O little town of Bethlehem, how still we see thee lie," written in the same period by Bishop Phillips Brooks of Massachusetts, has done a similar job for the birthplace of Jesus.[5] Many such images are reinforced by popular films about Jesus such as *Jesus of Nazareth* and *The Passion of the Christ*.[6]

The visual imagery of film and art mingles with biblical texts, permeating faith and understanding. When course participants arrive in the Holy Land, they usually have long since "imagined" the major biblical places. But these images of Jesus' birth town and crucifixion location are nineteenth-century creations, stemming from a particular ethos of spirituality and

4. The concept of "liminality" has been used by anthropologists and scholars of religion to refer to crossing a threshold (Latin: *līmen*) into a new, ambiguous spiritual experience. See Turner and Turner, *Image*.

5. These hymns can be found easily in most modern hymn books.

6. Both widely available on DVD.

religious belief. They were written on the other side of the world from the places they mention, with the purpose of encouraging faith and inspiring worship. There is no "green hill" or "little town" in the Holy Land as imagined in the hymns, and when pilgrims arrive for the first time they can be surprised and even shocked by what they find.

Visits to the Church of the Nativity in Bethlehem and the Church of the Holy Sepulcher in Jerusalem can be a steep learning curve for many. In Bethlehem, course participants realize that the "little town" image they brought with them is no longer historically credible for them. At the college, they study the birth narratives in the Gospels of St. Matthew and St. Luke, as well as some early traditions about Jesus' birth. They realize that accounts vary and traditions change. But a visit to an ordinary cave in the Bethlehem region starts to help reimagine Jesus' birth, showing how he was more likely born in a cave than an inn. Similarly, in Jerusalem, a visit to the Church of the Holy Sepulcher, linked with a study of archeology and relevant texts, shows that the original place of Jesus' crucifixion was a quarry outside the city, and that centuries of development and building have changed the appearance of the site. No green hill—but a wider and deeper awareness of the crucifixion and burial of Jesus. In Bethlehem and Jerusalem, traditional images crumble in the light of new awareness.

BIBLE AND ARCHEOLOGY

Another level at which pilgrim images move on a St. George's course is in the relationship between biblical texts and stones at archeological sites and holy places—as well as between different biblical texts. One of the most well-known moments in Holy Land archeology arose from the excavations by Kathleen Kenyon at Jericho in the 1950s. Famously, this legendary archeologist concluded that stones at the lowest and oldest town on earth, thought to be those that fell in the time of Joshua (Josh 6), in fact dated from several hundred years before his time: middle Bronze Age (ca. 2100–1550 BC), rather than late Bronze Age (ca. 1550–1200 BC). Her conclusions triggered a conflict between the Bible and stones that has never settled down in archeological circles.

A similar problem arises with the so-called Solomonic Gates at Megiddo, Hazor, and Gezer (1 Kgs 9:15). Are they really from the reign of King Solomon, as has been claimed? Archeological evidence suggests a later date, and the Old Testament texts concerning them turn out to come from a much later period. Questions inevitably arise over the relation between the texts and the stones. This uncomfortable disparity suggests that the Bible isn't quite what it seems. So, is archeology trying to "prove the Bible" or simply discover what is really there underground? Issues of interpretation are all-important: stones mean different things to different people. St. George's College mostly visits Jericho on its courses and sometimes Megiddo and Hazor (less often these days). But disagreements between texts and stones raise difficult questions about the historical reliability of the Bible—and might even provoke a change in a pilgrim's image of the Bible itself. Is it history or literature, and what is the story of its own evolution?[7]

More serious still are the questions that arise in relation to close study of New Testament texts and locations. Jesus' birth in Bethlehem comes to mind once again. The appearance of the place can bring challenges, but what about the associated texts? The birth in Bethlehem might seem undisputed for most Christians until the details in the Gospels are examined closely. The story of Jesus' birth appears only in the Gospels of Matthew and Luke. No other writer in the New Testament seems to know anything about it. And because Bethlehem is also King David's birthplace, some scholars have argued that Matthew, especially, wanted to connect Jesus to David by having him born in Bethlehem. In other words, Bethlehem is a literary and theological symbol, not the real historical birthplace of Jesus. He is more likely to have been born in Galilee, probably in Nazareth, where he seems to come from in Mark, the earliest of the Gospels. This question, prompting much discussion for many in the St. George's College groups, creates discomfort. Faith and understanding start to shift significantly if it appears that Jesus might not actually have been born in Bethlehem.

In Jerusalem, a similar discussion arises at the Church of the Holy Sepulcher and the Garden Tomb. The church is the traditional location of the death, burial, and resurrection of Jesus. Since the nineteenth century, however, the Garden Tomb, popularized by General Gordon, has also been part of the discussion. Which is the real historical location of these events? Either, but not both—and maybe neither. The Church of the Holy Sepulcher has everything on its side as the likely place. But the case is not water tight. Again, discussion can create anxiety for some course members who come expecting to see "the exact spot." Similar anxiety can occur in Nazareth where course participants are shown two locations for the annunciation: the Roman Catholic Basilica of the Annunciation and the Greek Orthodox Church of St. Gabriel. Also, there are four locations in the Holy Land for the account of the resurrection appearance of Jesus at Emmaus.

Along with the challenging appearances of biblical places, therefore, questions of the authenticity of sites and of the way biblical texts should be

7. For a comprehensive account, see Barton, *History*.

read also affect inherited images, triggering lively but sometimes uncomfortable changes of perception. The long-expected image, the long-sought-after picture, treasured since childhood, collapses. Certainly, a stronger sense of the Bible as literature starts to dawn, along with a realization of the complex relation between history and story. But the building blocks of faith move, and although for some specific places and texts don't matter too much,[8] for others the experience is quite unsettling.

FAITH SEEKING UNDERSTANDING

Though uncomfortable and challenging, such moving images and shifts in perception can, however, open new levels of awareness which affect faith and understanding in a positive way. I suggest that the pilgrim journey on a St. George's course might be seen as a process rooted in a growing awareness of God but open to uncertainties in matters of historical knowledge, texts, stones, sites, and holy places—a maturing faith, carrying the possibility of different and moving layers of understanding and meaning.

Thus, using a phrase developed from some words of St. Anselm (ca. 1033–1109), abbot of the Benedictine monastery at Bec in France and later archbishop of Canterbury, we might say that pilgrims at St. George's College are on a journey of "faith seeking understanding." This basic concept has roots in the theology of St. Augustine (354–430) but appears in Anselm's *Proslogion* where he says he first inhabits faith and then looks for understanding, rather than trying to understand everything first and then believe. For Anselm, faith is prior to understanding and enables it. He writes, "I do not seek to understand so that I may believe, but I believe so that I may understand; and what is more, I believe that unless I do believe I shall not understand."[9]

In the modern Western world, people often imagine the opposite to be true: that faith should be based on understanding, that the human intellect must first understand everything before faith is possible. Anselm's position enables us to see that faith is a perspective which can carry growth in understanding. Questions, doubts, uncertainties, revisions of knowledge, and new discoveries are all held in the process of faith, which itself grows in relation to understanding. There is more of a sense here of a "conversation," perhaps, than if the process worked the other way around. Following Anselm's view, all aspects of learning are seen to be engaged in a constant

8. See Macaulay, *Towers*, 195, where Laurie seems not to mind in Bethlehem or in Jerusalem "whether the shrines are rightly identified or not."

9. Ward, *Prayers and Meditations*, 244.

process of revision, and faith is expanded in the light of changing knowledge and deepening insight. Each aspect influences and nurtures the other and, even though there may be a great deal of uncertainty in knowledge, faith and understanding both grow significantly and together in this process.

I suggest, therefore, that on St. George's College courses, pilgrims be thought of as entering an ongoing "conversation."[10] They embark upon a journey of exploration, adventure, and growth in which traveling is more important than arriving. The multilayered experience includes conversations between history and texts, people and places, intellect and emotion, head and heart, and ultimately between the human and the divine. The experience spreads out in numerous directions, opening new levels of perception. Just as in general life, conversation enables relationships to develop, leading to growth in knowledge and awareness, so in the pilgrimage experience, a living, moving conversation characterizes the overall process of "faith seeking understanding."

THEOLOGY OF ICONS

How then might this "conversational faith seeking understanding" be explained in more detail? In trying to articulate the inner dynamic of this process for St. George's College course members, the classical theology of icons provides a most useful tool. Pilgrims in the Holy Land encounter icons in churches everywhere, especially churches in the Eastern traditions. The holy places in Bethlehem, Jerusalem, and Nazareth are alive with the color of icons, and icons form a vivid part of the spirituality of many of the local churches. In the Orthodox traditions, icons are "doors of perception" or "windows into eternity." They are colorful artistic representations of religious themes including the Trinity, Jesus, Mary, and the saints. Popular events depicted from the life of Christ are the nativity, baptism, transfiguration, crucifixion, and resurrection. Icons are essentially something to "look through" rather than "look at." Icon means "image" in Greek, and the image bears the presence of the one imaged. When praying with an icon, head and heart are brought together in a conversation between the human and the divine.

It was St. John of Damascus (ca. 675–ca. 749) in the eighth century, writing from Mar Saba monastery near Bethlehem, who first officially

10. Conversation plays an important part in Hans-Georg Gadamer's notion of knowledge and understanding. See Gadamer, *Truth and Method*, 325–41. I follow his basic ideas here.

defended the making of icons in Christianity.[11] During a wave of iconoclasm (the breaking of icons) in the Byzantine empire, he formed a theology of images that has prevailed until today. Some people felt that making and using icons was idolatrous. Since human beings are created in God's image (Gen 1:26) and Jesus Christ is the image of God (Col 1:15), they said, no more images were necessary or needed. But John argued that the incarnation indicates that God has been enfleshed in the material world and that God himself, therefore, is an image-maker. John stresses the importance of God in creation and in Jesus, and emphasizes that his presence in icons is in continuity with his other actions in the world. For John, the icon is a location of incarnation, drawing the human and the divine together. To deny the legitimacy of icons, he maintains, is to deny the incarnation itself. John's theology was to influence the decisions of the Second Council of Nicaea in 787, a council that affirmed the use of icons in Christian worship.

John's basic insight was reinforced by another Greek writer, Theodore the Studite (759–826) during a second wave of iconoclasm in the ninth century.[12] Theodore was abbot of a monastery in Studium in Constantinople (modern Istanbul) and, like John, wrote three short treatises defending icons. His arguments are like John's but he digs deeper, showing how the discussions that led to the affirmation at the Council of Chalcedon in 451 (that Jesus was both human and divine) could also be used in relation to icons. Just as the human and the divine come together in Christ, so the material and the divine are brought together in icons. Theodore's theology stresses the christological dimensions of icons and their use, bringing out the intertwining of the human and the divine. In classical Christian theology of the Trinity, which both John and Theodore employ, there is a living relation between the Logos (or rationality of God) and the human (material) element. This relational dynamic is a movement between the human and the divine elements, and praying with icons draws believers into this movement. Insights from both John and Theodore about the importance of icons continue to play an important part in Orthodox spirituality today.

Although John and Theodore do not use the word, we might say that in an icon, the human and the divine come together in "conversation." Far from being idolatrous, using icons in worship focuses on the way God relates to the world and enables worshipers to enter God's very presence. This interaction of the human with the divine in an icon, along with the engagement of the intellect and the emotion, constitutes the heart of the theology of icons. In the same way, heads and hearts come together, study and prayer are united, and the conversation is sustained by the fundamental experience

11. See Anderson, *Divine Images*.

12. See Roth, *Holy Icons*.

of the pilgrim moving into God's dynamic, living presence. The theology of icons offers a rich theological articulation of the experience of pilgrims on St. George's College courses.

CONCLUSION

My suggestion regarding how St. George's College courses might be understood in terms of education and theology, therefore, looks broadly like this. As course participants travel in the Holy Land, praying and studying together, they are on a pilgrim journey of "conversational faith seeking understanding." Sometimes in the process of engaging with archeology, history, and texts, and with a wide variety of people and places, they encounter questions that challenge familiar patterns of faith and images treasured since childhood.

When pilgrim expectations are challenged and intentions are shattered, images fracture, crack, and crumble. There is disorientation. But as this happens, new perceptions emerge through a process of reorientation. Through a greater understanding of the processes of history, and a more informed appreciation of the emergence of biblical texts, through an awareness of the stories told by stones, and through meeting people of other denominations and religions, faith itself can be refreshed and reimagined. Within the all-round conversation that develops among all these elements, deeper dimensions of religious experience are activated. Not all questions are answered, and many matters remain unsettled or unknown. But layers of learning expand, enabling greater and deeper experiences of the reality of God.

In the theology of icons, the human and the divine move together in relation. Icons lie at the center of this movement or conversation, typifying the way God relates to the world through incarnation. The pilgrim's quest for a deeper awareness of God resonates with this movement. On St. George's College courses, all experiences and conversations are brought together in a renewed awareness of God. The "study-pilgrimage" is a holistic, experiential, conversational journey of "faith seeking understanding." All the variables and revisions of learning are carried into the divine presence in faith. Indeed, enabling this process is St. George's overall purpose and aim.

PART 6

Appendixes, Bibliography, and Index

Appendix A

Deans and Bishops

DEANS OF ST GEORGE'S COLLEGE SINCE 1961

Richard M. Sewell (2018–present)

Richard M. LeSueur, Interim (2017–2018)

Gregory C. Jenks (2015–2017)

Graham M. Smith (2011–2015)

Stephen W. Need (2005–2011)

John H. Tidy, Acting (2005)

S. Ross Jones (2000–2004)

Bob G. Jones (1996–2000)

Management Team (1995–1996)

Frederick W. Schmidt (1994)

John L. Peterson (1983–1994)

Edward P. Todd (1975–1982)

John D. Wilkinson (1969–1975)

Felix V. A. Boyse—Principal (1961–1964)

APPENDIX A

ANGLICAN BISHOPS IN JERUSALEM

Hosam Elias Naoum (2021–present) (Archbishop)

Suheil Salman Ibrahim Dawani (2007–2021) (Archbishop from 2014)

Riah Hannah Abu El-Assal (1998–2007)

Samir Hanna Kafity (1984–1998)

Faik Ibrahim Haddad (1976–1984)

Robert Wright Stopford (1974–1976) (Vicar General under whom the diocese was restructured and the Province of the Episcopal Church in Jerusalem and the Middle East created)

George Frederick Appleton (1969–1974) (Archbishop)

(Najib A. Cubain, Bishop of Jordan, Lebanon, and Syria with jurisdiction over East Jerusalem, 1958–1976)

Angus Campbell MacInnes (1957–1968) (Archbishop)

Weston Henry Stewart (1943–1957)

George Francis Graham Brown (1932–1942)

Rennie Miles MacInnes (1914–1931)

George Francis Popham Blyth (1887–1914)

Vacant (1881–1887)

Joseph Barclay (1879–1881)

Samuel Gobat (1846–1879)

Michael Solomon Alexander (1841–1845)

NB

Anglican–Lutheran Bishops 1841–1881

Anglican only, from 1887

Archbishop 1957–1974 (when the title was dropped), and again from 2014 (when the title was revived)–present

Appendix B

Constitutions[1]

THE CONSTITUTION OF ST GEORGE'S COLLEGE JERUSALEM

Article 1: THE PURPOSE OF THE COLLEGE

Saint George's College shall serve as a centre for studies which draw on the unique resources available in the Holy Land. To this end it shall be a particular aim of the College to offer to clergy and lay people of the Christian Churches, courses designed to deepen their understanding of the geographical, cultural, and religious background of the Bible; and to introduce them to the life of the other communities, Christian and non-Christian, amongst which the college is placed.

Article 2: THE INTERNATIONAL GOVERNING COUNCIL

The College shall be governed by an International Governing Council (hereinafter called the Council) comprising ten members. They shall serve for a period of three years and shall be eligible for re-appointment for one additional term. The Council shall be constituted as follows:

Three members to be appointed by the Anglican Consultative Council or its Standing Committee;
The Anglican Bishop in Jerusalem;

1. The texts of this and other documents in the appendixes have been taken from the originals including inconsistences. All are available in the college archive and are reproduced here with permission.

One member to be appointed by the Episcopal Synod in the Middle East; and
Five other members to be appointed by the Council, of whom at least two shall be non-Anglicans.

The Council shall elect a Chairman from among its own members who shall serve for a period of three years.

It shall be the responsibility of the Council to determine all questions of policy relating to the College and its operation; to create a Management Committee and appoint a Dean of Studies for the college and to determine their duties and the policy they are to implement; to foster the creation of such bodies as shall encourage the execution of the policy so determined and forward the objects, interests, and support of the College. It shall draw up such Rules for the conduct of its business as are in accordance with this Constitution. In all matters of policy and management of the College, the Council shall be the final authority.

Article 3: THE MANAGEMENT COMMITTEE

The Council shall create a Management Committee which shall comprise not more than eleven members, namely:

The Anglican Bishop in Jerusalem, ex officio, who shall serve as Chairman, but may at his discretion appoint some other person to act in his stead;
Two members to be appointed by the Council;
Two members to be appointed by the Anglican Bishop in Jerusalem as diocesan bishop, in consultation with his Diocesan Council;
The Dean of Studies, ex officio, who shall serve as Secretary;
One member of the teaching staff of the college other than the Dean of Studies;
Four other members to be appointed by those appointed above, having regard to ecumenical considerations.

Unless serving ex officio, members shall serve for a term of three years and shall be eligible for re-appointment. The Management Committee shall meet at least twice a year. The quorum shall be any six members. All members shall have the right to vote. The Chairman shall have a casting vote in addition to his deliberative vote.

The Management Committee shall be responsible to the Council for executing the Council's policy, for adopting a budget, and for making annually a financial report to the Council, and shall send the members of the Council copies of its minutes. It is also responsible for liaison with those attending courses at the college.

The members of the Management Committee shall constitute St. George's College Foundation under the Ottoman Law of Societies, 1909, and shall send the members of the Council copies of the Minutes and Financial Reports of the Foundation.

Article 4: THE DEAN OF STUDIES

The Council shall appoint a Dean of Studies, and shall arrange the terms and conditions of his appointment and his salary, which shall be included in the annual budget of the college. With the Management Committee the Dean of Studies shall be responsible for the operation of the college as a centre for studies which shall draw on the unique resources available in the Holy Land, and shall plan and organise the courses.

He shall attend the meetings of the Council with a right to speak but not to vote, and shall act as its secretary. He shall be a member of the Management Committee which he shall serve as Secretary.

The Dean of Studies shall appoint all members of the college staff after consultation with the Management Committee, and shall invite scholars to Jerusalem to reside temporarily in the college and take part in its educational programme. Contracts with members of the College staff shall be signed by the Dean of Studies on behalf of St George's College Foundation.

If there should be a vacancy in the office of the Dean of Studies, the Management Committee shall arrange for the work of the College to continue until such time as the Council shall appoint a successor.

Article 5: AMENDMENTS

Notice of proposed amendments to this constitution shall be circulated to Council Members at least two months in advance of the meeting at which they are to be discussed, and no amendment shall be made which shall not be supported by a two-thirds majority of those present at the meeting before which such notice was duly given.

THE RULES OF THE INTERNATIONAL GOVERNING COUNCIL OF SAINT GEORGE'S COLLEGE, JERUSALEM

1. Meetings shall be held at least once in two years.
2. The quorum for a meeting shall be any six members.
3. Notification of regular meetings shall be sent to members by the Secretary. Other meetings may be called by the Chairman at the written request of any three members.
4. A member's term of service shall be three years from the date of the first meeting to which he was called. Members are eligible for one further term of service.
5. The Council shall elect its own Chairman who shall serve for a period of three years or at least for two successive meetings.
6. The Dean of Studies shall attend the meetings of the Council and act as Secretary, and shall have a right to speak but not to vote.
7. The Chairman shall have a casting vote in addition to his deliberative vote.
8. If a vote should need to be taken at a time when the Council cannot meet, the chairman may at his discretion request the members to vote by post.

(Constitution and Rules adopted by the International Governing Council at its first meeting held in Dublin on the 12th and 13th July, 1973.)

CONSTITUTION OF ST. GEORGE'S COLLEGE JERUSALEM

ARTICLE I

St. George's College, Jerusalem, is a continuing education institution located in the Cathedral Close of the Diocese of Jerusalem of the Evangelical Episcopal Church of Jerusalem and the Middle East.

ARTICLE II

The College is owned by the Diocese of Jerusalem of the Evangelical Episcopal Church in Jerusalem and the Middle East and operated as a ministry of the same Diocese.

ARTICLE III

The period of the College's duration is perpetual.

ARTICLE IV

The College is organized and shall be operated and administered exclusively for cultural, religious and charitable purposes as a college (sometimes referred to herein as the "College") in union with the Diocese of Jerusalem of the Evangelical Episcopal Church in Jerusalem and the Middle East (sometimes referred to herein as the "Diocese").

In the accomplishment of the above purposes and subject to the terms and conditions hereof, the College hereby recognizes and accedes to the authority of the Constitution and Canons of the Diocese of Jerusalem and agrees to conform solely to its Doctrine, Discipline, and Worship. In pursuit of the foregoing purposes, the College may (a) receive personal property and use and apply the income therefrom and the principal thereof; (b) receive real property, title to which shall be vested in accordance with the Constitution and Canons of the Diocese.

ARTICLE V

The street address of the College is: College Gate: 31 Salahedeen Street, Jerusalem.

ARTICLE VI

The group of persons vested with the administration of the College, the Foundation of the College, shall serve as and exercise the powers of the Board of Directors of the college.

The members constituting the Foundation of the College are:

The bishop of the Diocese of Jerusalem, Chair;
The dean of the college;
The Chair of the British Regional Committee;
The Chair of the Australian and New Zealand Regional Committee;
The President of the North American Regional Committee;
A representative appointed by the Anglican Consultative Council;
No fewer than two, but no greater than four appointees of the Bishop of the Diocese of Jerusalem.

ARTICLE VII

The college shall be governed, operated and administered in accordance with the Constitution and Bylaws of St. George's College Jerusalem.

ARTICLE VIII

The power to amend, modify, restate or repeal the Constitution and Canons of the College shall rest with the Foundation of the College; provided, no such amendment, modification, restatement or repeal shall become effective unless and until approved by a majority of the members of the Foundation in two separate meetings, and provided further that same has been approved in writing by the Bishop of the Diocese of Jerusalem; or, if the office of Bishop is vacant, by the Ecclesiastical Authority of the Diocese of Jerusalem, which approval shall be evidenced on any such amendment, modification, restatement or repeal.

ARTICLE IX

Each member of the Foundation, each former member, and other persons while serving at the request of the College may be indemnified by the Foundation for any act or omission in such person's capacity as a member of the Foundation.

ARTICLE X

The College shall not:

(a) Permit any part of the net earnings of the College to inure to the benefit of any private individual unless such benefit is incidental to and in accomplishment of the College's purposes as expressed in Article IV of the Constitution; provided, reasonable compensation may be paid for personal services rendered to or for the College, affecting one or more of its purposes;

(b) Devote any of its activities to attempting to influence legislation by propaganda or otherwise;

(c) Participate or intervene in (including the publication or distribution of statements), any political campaign on behalf of any candidate for public office; or

(d) Attempt to influence the outcome of any specific public election or to carry on, directly or indirectly, any voter registration drives.

ARTICLE XI

The Bylaws of the College shall be in compliance with the Constitution and Canons of the Diocese.

ARTICLE XII

Upon the dissolution of the College, or upon termination of the status of the College as an institution of the Diocese, the assets of the College remaining after payment or provision for payment of the College's liabilities belong exclusively to the Diocese of Jerusalem and should be used for educational purposes.

IN WITNESS WHEREOF, we have hereunto set our hands this 30th day of January, 2001.

St. George's College Jerusalem
By: The Very Rev. S. Ross Jones, Dean

Approved on the ____day of _____, 2001

____

The Rt. Rev. Riah H. Abu El-Assal
Bishop of the diocese of Jerusalem

Appendix C

Committees

THE RULES OF SAINT GEORGE'S COLLEGE FOUNDATION

1. NAME

   This Society shall be named Saint George's College Foundation hereinafter called the Foundation.

2. ADDRESS

   The address of the Foundation shall be Saint George's College, PO Box 1248, 31 Salah-ed-Din Road, Jerusalem.

3. OBJECTS

   The objects of the Foundation shall be to further the work of Saint George's College, Jerusalem, hereinafter called the college, as a centre of studies which shall draw on the unique resources available in the Holy Land, offering to Christian clergy and lay people courses designed to deepen their understanding of the geographical, cultural, and religious background of the Bible; and introducing them to the life of the other communities, non-Christian as well as Christian, amongst which the College is placed; and to raise funds for the College and collect for its use gifts, contributions, inheritances and other payments whether in cash or in kind, and also to exercise rights and receive preferences from any person, corporate body, governmental institution or local authority; provided always that the Foundation shall apply its income, property or assets solely for the objects aforesaid, as a nonprofit-making organization.

4. MEMBERSHIP

a. The Foundation shall comprise not more than eleven and not less than seven members of whom the majority shall not be related to each other by birth;

b. The members of the Foundation shall have power to elect honorary members who may attend meetings but shall not participate in the voting.

5. COMPOSITION

The membership of the Foundation shall be constituted as follows:

The Anglican Bishop in Jerusalem, ex officio;

Two members to be elected by a majority vote of the members of the Governing Council of the College;

Two members to be elected by the Anglican Bishop in Jerusalem in consultation with his diocesan council;

The Dean of Studies of the college, ex officio;

One member other than the Dean of Studies to be elected by a majority vote of the full-time teaching staff of the College other than the Dean of Studies;

Four other members to be elected by a majority vote of the members specified above, having regard to ecumenical considerations.

Each member shall be elected for a term of two years, unless a member ex officio, and shall be eligible for re-election for further terms, provided that for the first eight months after the Foundation is formed, the ex officio members and any six other members of the Jerusalem Advisory Committee of the College shall form the Founder members of the Foundation.

6. OFFICERS

The Officers of the Foundation shall be the Chairman, the Treasurer and the Secretary. The Chairman shall be the Anglican Bishop in Jerusalem, ex officio. The Treasurer shall be elected by a majority vote of the members of the Foundation from among their number to serve for a term of two years, and shall be eligible for re-election for further terms, provided that for the period immediately after the Foundation is formed, the Treasurer shall be elected for a term of eight months. The Secretary shall be the Dean of Studies of the college ex officio.

7. EXECUTIVE POWERS OF OFFICERS

Subject to Rule 8 the Chairman, the treasurer, and the secretary shall jointly or severally have power to represent the Foundation in all legal matters and act on its behalf and bind the Foundation in its legal transactions with third parties, and to sign and to affix the seal of the Foundation to all such documents as may require it.

8. FINANCIAL TRANSACTIONS

The cheques and other financial documents of the Foundation shall be signed by any two members from among the following:

- The Chairman
- The Treasurer
- The Secretary
- One member appointed for this function by the members of the Foundation.

9. DUTIES OF THE OFFICERS

a. The Chairman shall preside at the meetings of the Foundation;
b. The Treasurer shall ensure the preparation and production of an annual financial report and audited accounts;
c. The Secretary shall give notice of meetings and shall record the minutes of the meetings of the Foundation.

10. MEETINGS

a. The Chairman or in his absence the Secretary shall convene at least two meetings of the Foundation in each year, at one of which the Treasurer shall present the annual financial report and audited accounts of the Foundation;
b. An extraordinary meeting of the Foundation shall be convened at the written request to the Secretary of any three members of the Foundation;
c. The Secretary shall give at least a fortnight's notice of ordinary meetings to the members of the Foundation;
d. In the event that the Chairman is unable to preside at a meeting the members of the Foundation shall by a majority vote appoint one of their number to serve as Deputy Chairman for that meeting.

e. The quorum shall be five members of the Foundation. All members of the Foundation with the exception of honorary members shall have the right to vote. The Chairman or in his absence the Deputy Chairman shall have a casting vote in addition to his deliberative vote.

11. POWERS OF THE FOUNDATION

The Foundation is a legal entity and is inter alia entitled to purchase and sell assets, to act in respect of movables and immovables, to raise funds, to collect monies, to appear and act as claimant or defendant before any courts, legal tribunals and other legal bodies, to appear to represent and to be represented before all governmental, municipal, and other authorities, and offices. The Foundation is entitled to appoint a lawyer or lawyers to represent it, and shall have, inter alia, the following powers:

a. To receive gifts, contributions, and inheritances, whether in cash or in kind, and also rights and preferences from any person, corporate body, governmental institution or local authority;

b. To borrow monies for the purposes of the Foundation and to that end to pledge or mortgage the assets of the Foundation, and also to give such loans or guarantees as the Foundation may deem appropriate and to receive in exchange for such loans and guarantees appropriate securities;

c. To insure the assets of the Foundation;

d. To employ various officials and workers and also to make use of the services of other persons and pay them salaries, fees and various other payments.

e. To establish and manage funds and subsidiary bodies for the realisation of the objects of the Foundation whether wholly or in part, inclusive of funds and subsidiary bodies for the keeping and managing of enterprises and properties and also funds for the awarding of grants, stipends and prizes;

f. To invest the monies of the Foundation in securities or other investments as the Foundation may deem appropriate; provided always that any profits thus accruing to the Foundation be applied solely for the objects of the Foundation.

g. To open bank accounts for the Foundation, to manage the same, and to draw monies from such accounts.

h. To engage in any activity necessary or advantageous for the accomplishment of the objects of the Foundation.

The functions, activities and programmes of the Foundation and of its subsidiary bodies shall only be such as may be performed by tax-exempted organizations in Jerusalem.

12. DISSOLUTION OF THE FOUNDATION

The Foundation shall be dissolved by a resolution of a meeting of the Foundation supported by a two-thirds majority vote of all the members of the Foundation, subject to a resolution of the Governing Council of the college supported by a two-thirds majority vote of the members of the said Governing Council.

13. DISPOSAL OF ASSETS

In the event of the dissolution of the Foundation its property and assets shall be transferred by a resolution supported by a two-thirds majority vote of all the members of the Foundation to some similar body whose objects are religious or educational and shall in no case be distributed amongst its members.

14. ALTERATION OF RULES

Any meeting of the Foundation may by a two-thirds majority vote of all the members make new Rules and amend or add to the existing Rules.

SAINT GEORGE'S COLLEGE JERUSALEM

CONCERNING THE REGIONAL COMMITTEES

Adopted, 7 June 1985

I) ORIGINS

Two of the three existing Regional Committees were called into being by Dean John Wilkinson and the then Archbishop in Jerusalem more than a decade ago and before the establishment of the St. George's College Foundation; the third Regional Committee has recently been formed at the invitation of Dean Edward P. Todd.

II) STATUS AND GUIDELINES

Since their inception the Regional Committees have acted as autonomous, self-perpetuating bodies, which was the status originally accorded to them.

The "Terms of Reference" of the American Regional Committee (now the North American Regional Committee) are too vague to have been effective guidelines for that committee's work.

The first meeting of the British Regional Committee minutes do not spell out clearly the mandate and functions of the Committee.

No formal guidelines have been established for the Australian Regional Committee.

With the prospect of a major upgrading of the College's facilities and an increase in its full-time academic staff, it is time for a fresh evaluation of the role of the Regional Committees and for consideration to be given to providing them with constitutions which will link them in more relevant ways with the St. George's College Foundation.

To this end, the following has been adopted:

III) PROPOSALS

1. Formation

Regional Committees are formed at the invitation of the Chairman of the St. George's College Foundation together with the Foundation of the College, as prescribed under article 3 of this proposal. If not otherwise appointed, the following have a right to be represented with a voice,

At ARC: AMB, SSM, Australian Council of Churches.

At BRC: CMS, CMJ, JMECA.

At NARC: ECUSA, Anglican Church of Canada, NCCUSA, Program Agency of the Presbyterian Church.

2. Functions

Among the functions of a Regional Committee of St. George's College are:

(i) To support the college—its Foundation, its dean and his staff in Jerusalem, and its current and future programmes—in every way possible.

(ii) To inform the Foundation of St. George's College and its Dean of the relevant needs of the Churches and individuals in its area.

(iii) To publicize the College and its offerings in its area.

(iv) To recruit students to the College for its various courses and to facilitate correspondence between potential students and the College.

(v) To help the Foundation seek scholarship funds (or information about scholarship funds to which prospective students might apply) which will help prospective students from their area to come to St. George's College for a course.

(vi) To help the Foundation seek scholarship funds (or information about scholarship funds to which prospective students might apply) which will help prospective students from less affluent areas of the world to come to St. George's College for a course.

(vii) To advise the Dean of the College of possible Visiting Professors who will assist in the academic work of the College, and to advise the consultative committee in its search for new full-time members of the College staff when this is appropriate.

(viii) To provide an effective liaison between former students of the College in its own area and beyond, in cooperation with the Dean and the other Regional Committees;

(ix) The Regional Committees shall at all times work in close cooperation with the Dean of the College and his staff in Jerusalem.

3. Membership and Officers

As regional circumstances permit, each Regional Committee shall consist of:

(i) A chairperson, who shall report to the Chairman of the Foundation through the Dean of the College on the work of the Regional Committee and on ways of making this more effective.

(ii) An executive secretary, who shall be responsible to the Regional Committee for recruiting students to the College for its various courses and to the Dean of the College for facilitating correspondence between potential students and the College.

(iii) A public relations secretary, who shall be responsible to the Regional Committee for publicizing the College and its offering in the area for which the Regional Committee is responsible.

Note: At its discretion a Regional Committee may combine its responsibilities of the Executive and Public Relations Secretary.

(iv) A financial secretary, who shall be responsible to the Regional Committee for the finances of that Committee, and especially for seeking scholarship funds as set out in 2. v and 2. vi.

(v) An alumni/ae secretary, who shall be responsible to the Regional Committee for providing the liaison between former students and friends of the college as 2. viii envisages.

(vi) A recording secretary, who shall be responsible for keeping records of its meetings, and for maintaining communications between the members of the Committee, between the Committee and the Foundation, and between the Committee and the Dean of the College.

(vii) Further members, with special expertise or other contributions to make to the work of the Regional Committee, e.g., in relation to Theological Colleges/Seminaries; in relation to lay (theological) education; to ensure a balanced ecumenical representation on the Regional Committee; to include representatives of churches that have organizations related to the Diocese of Jerusalem.

4. The Appointment of members

(i) The chairperson, shall be invited to serve for a period of three years by the Consultative Committee on the nomination of the Chairman of the Foundation and the Dean of the College after consultation with the Regional Committee.

(ii) The other members (c.f. #3) shall be invited to serve for a period of three years by the Consultative Committee on the nomination of the Chairman of the Foundation and the Dean of the College after consultation with the Regional Committee.

(iii) The executive secretary, public relations secretary, financial secretary, and recording secretary shall be invited to serve for a period of three years by election from among the members of the Regional Committee.

(iv) In consultation with the Chairman of the Foundation and the Dean, the Regional Committee has the power to coopt further members for a period of three years with full rights of membership provided always that membership of the Regional Committee shall not exceed twelve.

(v) The Chairperson shall see to it that his committee appoints a member of the Regional Committee to be a constituent member of the Foundation.

(vi) The term of service of all members is renewable upon a decision of the Consultative Committee after consultation with the Chairperson of the Regional Committee.

IV) IMPLEMENTATION

1. It is suggested that, if accepted, these proposals be implemented over the next three years in such a way that the membership of the Regional Committee will rotate a few members at a time.

2. The Foundation proposes Committees for the following regions:

a. One Regional Committee for Australia

b. One Regional Committee for the United Kingdom

c. Two Regional Committees for North America (East and West).

These committees, if they choose, could have one executive secretary, one public relations secretary, and one alumni/ae secretary (as outlined in III.3).

d. In the next two years, it is hoped that a Canadian Regional Committee will be formed, thus dividing the NARC into two US Committees and one Canadian Committee. The logistics of the cooperation between the three resulting committees are for later discussion and resolution.

Adopted unanimously
St. George's College Foundation
7 June, 1985

Appendix D

Aims and Objectives of Courses (1988)

A. In planning a College Course, the Dean and his staff hope always to include each of the following components:

a) study of the Bible;

b) reflection on theological issues;

c) study of some aspects of Church History and of Liturgy;

d) introduction to the history of Judaism and of Islam in this land, and to the practice of these monotheistic faiths today; and, perhaps above all,

e) a study of the Geography of the Land as it has affected the development of the three great faiths and their religious literature.

While much of this study must be initiated in the form of lectures, a large proportion of time in each course is devoted to field trips—most of them preceded by briefings and some followed by summaries and reflection and, hopefully, by individual reading and study done by Course members in the College library. Naturally, visits to archeological sites are important to each course.

B. However, while each course has its own academic content, no course should simply be regarded as a series of intellectual exercises. Traditionally for Jews, Christians and Muslims alike, this land is a place of pilgrimage, rich in holy sites; and, through the ages, the goal of pilgrimage has been the confirming of commitment and the enrichment of faith and devotion. Hence, in planning our courses, we hope always to provide the setting and to allow adequate time for Course members to meditate, to reflect and to experience, individually and as a group, the sense of refreshment and renewal which this land can so richly give.

C. Inevitably, and indeed properly in a land so rich in history, much time is spent in contemplating the past (and this both for its own sake, and also because an understanding of the past can often illuminate the present); but in each Course, especially in the longer courses, the attempt is made to give time to a consideration of the present.

D. In the past sixteen years, students have enrolled in our courses from seventy-two countries, and 66 denominations have been represented. Students enrol in large numbers from the United Kingdom, the United States, Canada, Australia and New Zealand. Recently the numbers coming from the third world, especially on the ten-week course, have risen, to our great enrichment. Without doubt, the opportunity to meet, to live, to study and to travel with a group drawn from such diverse cultural and religious backgrounds is one of the facts which makes St. George's College so valuable to many students. Forty-three per cent of our students are priests or religious, while 57% are lay persons.

Appendix E

Course Calendars

Course calendars in this section have been included to provide a flavor of the college's offerings, indicating interests, fashions, and special focuses in different periods.

CALENDAR 1976

The Bible and Its Setting—1
Course for Seminarians and Lay Workers
22 December 1975–15 January 1976

The Palestine of Jesus—1
Course for Christ Church, Charlotte, North Carolina
5 February–19 February

The Palestine of Jesus—2
Course for Church Wardens and Lay Workers
4 March–19 March

The Palestine of Jesus—3
Course for Teachers
5 April–20 April

The Palestine of Jesus—4
6 May–21 May

The Bible and Its Setting—2
Continuing Education for Clergy and Bishops
9 June–21 July

The Bible and Its Setting—3
Course for Students and Teachers
4 August–1 September

The Bible and the Holy Land: Past and Present
Continuing Education for Clergy and Bishops
29 September–8 December

CALENDAR 1987

The Bible and the Holy Land Today
February 4–February 24

The Bible and Flowers
March 4–March 19

The Bible and Worship
April 4–April 20

The Bible and Its Setting
May 1–May 28

The Palestine of Jesus
June 3–June 18

The Palestine of Jesus
June 24–July 9

Youth Course
July 20–August 1

The Bible and Its Setting
August 4–August 31

The Bible and the Holy Land: Past and Present
September 23–December 1

CALENDAR 2000

The Palestine of Jesus
With Sinai experience
January 17–January 28

The Social Landscape of the Bible
February 5–February 25

The Palestine of Jesus
March 4–March 15

St. Paul and the Early Church:
From Jerusalem to Ephesus
including Turkey
March 23–April 5

Ways in the Wilderness: Desert Spirituality
including Judaean Desert, Negev, Sinai
and the monasteries of Egypt
April 8–April 19

The Bible and the Holy Land
including Sinai
May 3–May 30

The Palestine of Jesus
June 15–June 26

Youth Course
July 6–July 17

The Bible and the Holy Land
including Sinai
August 1–August 28

Pilgrimage and Spirituality
including Galilee retreat
September 4–September 13

The Bible and the Holy Land: Past and Present
including Sinai, Petra, Cairo, & Turkey
September 23–November 30

The Palestine of Jesus
December 1–December 12

CALENDAR 2024

Jerusalem Ministry Formation
January 8–January 22

Footsteps of Jesus
January 29–February 8

Footsteps of Jesus
February 12–February 22

Sharing Perspectives: Jews, Christians, and Muslims in the Holy Land
February 22–March 6

Easter in Jerusalem
March 19–April 2

Palestine of Jesus
April 9–April 23

Footsteps of Jesus
April 29–May 9

Palestine of Jesus
May 13–May 27

The Bible Lands Level 2
May 30–June 11

Holy Land and the Arts
June 16–June 28

Jerusalem Ministry Formation
July 2–July 12

Jerusalem Ministry Formation
July 16–July 26

Palestine of Jesus
September 2–September 16

Footsteps of Jesus
September 20–September 30

Palestine of Jesus
October 4–October 18

Footsteps of Jesus
October 21–October 31

Jerusalem Ministry Formation
November 4–November 15

Palestine of Jesus
November 19–December

Appendix F

A Note on St. George

Not much is known for certain about St. George, and there are numerous traditions and legends about him and the famous dragon. George probably came from Cappadocia (in modern Turkey) and served as a soldier in the Roman army in the third century. It is likely that he died a martyr's death in one of the great persecutions of Christians before Christianity became legal under Constantine. His mother may have come from Lod, or Lydda, in Palestine where George's own tomb is still marked today.[2] Some have suggested that George himself came from Lydda. In any case, he is acknowledged now as a Palestinian Christian saint and also as one of the holy men of Islam (known as Al-Khader: "the Green"). A tomb for this Islamic figure can be found in Beit Jala near Bethlehem in the West Bank. The cult of St. George became popular from the sixth century onwards.

The traditions relating to the dragon are later than George himself and were popularized along with those about George by Jacobus de Voragine in his work *The Golden Legend* in the thirteenth century.[3] This account tells of George in Libya, in the town of Silena, near a large lake from which the dragon rose up and breathed poisonous air on the people of the town and killed them. They calmed the dragon down by giving it two sheep a day to eat. When the sheep ran out, they gave it human beings. The daily sacrifice was decided by lot and it eventually fell on the local king's daughter. The king was greatly distressed, but as his daughter went to be eaten, George intervened and slew the dragon, saving her life. The town was converted to Christianity as a result. These and other stories about St. George have focused on his defeat of evil, typified by the dragon.

2. Lod is fifteen kilometers southeast of Tel Aviv.

3. See Stace, *Jacobus*.

The cult of St. George and the dragon grew widely in the Middle East and eventually throughout Europe. It was known in England by the eighth century. But it was during the period of the Crusades in the eleventh and twelfth centuries that George became popular with the English who took the legend back home with them from the Holy Land. In the fourteenth century, King Edward III established George as a patron saint of England by founding the Order of the Garter in George's name. The chapel at Windsor was later dedicated to the saint. George's popularity grew, and the celebration of his feast on April 23 cemented him into the Christian calendar of saints' days. St. George was reinforced as patron of England following the Battle of Agincourt as found in Shakespeare's *Henry V*. Eventually St. George replaced Edward the Confessor and Edmund of East Anglia as England's patron saint. His flag is a red cross on a white background. This is also the flag of England, the Union Jack being the flag of the United Kingdom.

Once George had become patron saint of England, his name was attached to numerous churches, schools, colleges, and hospitals not only in England but throughout the British Empire. Today, it is not at all unusual to find British institutions around the world dedicated to St. George. When it came to building an Anglican cathedral in Jerusalem in the nineteenth century, it is not surprising that the choice of saint for the dedication was St. George. It was inevitable, then, that the college, built in the twentieth century in the grounds of the cathedral, would follow suit by naming itself "St. George's College."

Bibliography

Aburish, Said K. *The Forgotten Faithful: The Christians of the Holy Land.* London: Quartet, 1993.

Aist, Rodney. *The Christian Topography of Early Islamic Jerusalem: The Evidence of Willibald of Eichstätt (700–787 CE).* Turnhout, Belgium: Brepols, 2009.

———. *From Topography to Text: The Image of Jerusalem in the Writings of Eucherius, Adomnan, and Bede.* Turnhout, Belgium: Brepols, 2019.

———. *Jerusalem Bound: How to Be a Pilgrim in the Holy Land.* Eugene, OR: Cascade, 2020.

———. *Pilgrim Spirituality: Defining Pilgrimage Again for the First Time.* Eugene, OR: Cascade, 2022.

Amos, Clare. *Peace-ing Together Jerusalem.* Geneva: WCC, 2014.

Anderson, David, trans. *On the Divine Images: Three Apologies Against Those Who Attack the Divine Images.* By St. John of Damascus. New York: St. Vladimir's Seminary, 2002.

Anglican Consultative Council. *Land of Promise? An Anglican Exploration of Christian Attitudes to the Holy Land, with Special Reference to "Christian Zionism."* London: ACC, 2012.

Appleton, George. *Jerusalem Prayers for the World Today.* London: SPCK, 1974.

Armstrong, Karen. *A History of Jerusalem: One City, Three Faiths.* London: HarperCollins, 1997.

Asher, Michael. *Lawrence: The Uncrowned King of Arabia.* London: Penguin, 1999.

Ateek, Naim Stifan. *Justice and Only Justice: A Palestinian Theology of Liberation.* New York: Orbis, 1989.

———. *A Palestinian Christian Cry for Reconciliation.* New York: Orbis, 2008.

———. *A Palestinian Theology of Liberation: The Bible, Justice, and the Palestine-Israel Conflict.* New York: Orbis, 2017.

Ateek, Naim, et al., eds. *The Forgotten Faithful: A Window into the Life and Witness of Christians in the Holy Land.* Jerusalem: Sabeel, 2007.

Avnery, Uri. *My Friend the Enemy.* London: Zed, 1986.

Barag, Dan, and John Wilkinson. "The Monza-Bobbio Flasks and the Holy Sepulcher." *Levant* 6:1 (1974) 179–87.

Barton, John. *A History of the Bible: The Book and Its Faiths.* London: Allen Lane, 2019.

Ben-Arieh, Yehoshua. *The Rediscovery of the Holy Land in the Nineteenth Century.* Jerusalem: Magnes, 1979.

Bible Lands. 1899–2022. Jerusalem and the Middle East Church Association Archive. Farnham, Surrey, UK.

Blyth, Estelle. *When We Lived in Jerusalem*. London: Murray, 1927.

Bond, Helen K. *The Historical Jesus: A Guide for the Perplexed*. London: Bloomsbury, 2012.

Bunton, Martin. *The Palestinian-Israeli Conflict: A Very Short Introduction*. Oxford: Oxford University Press, 2013.

Carse, Henry Ralph. "Creative Ambiguities in the Pilgrimage Process." PhD diss., University of Canterbury, 2003.

———. *No-One Land: Israel/Palestine 2000–2002*. London: Ziggurat, 2010.

———. *Sinai: The Abundant Emptiness*. London: Ziggurat, 2013.

Chadwick, Owen. *The Victorian Church, Part One: 1829–1859*. London: SCM, 1966.

———. *Victorian Miniature*. London: Hodder and Stoughton, 1960.

Chapman, Colin. *Whose Promised Land? The Continuing Crisis over Israel and Palestine*. Grand Rapids: Baker, 2002.

Cline, Eric H. *Biblical Archaeology: A Very Short Introduction*. Oxford: Oxford University Press, 2009.

Cohn-Sherbok, Dan, and Dawoud El-Alami. *The Palestine-Israeli Conflict*. Oxford: Oneworld, 2001.

Collins, Larry, and Dominique Lapierre. *O Jerusalem!* London: Weidenfeld and Nicolson, 1972.

Coombs, Richard, and Barbara Coombs. *Our Year in the Holy Land: A Chronicle of Service at St. George's College, Jerusalem in the Time of the Intifada*. El Sobrante, CA: T.H.C., 1992.

Corey, Muriel W. *From Rabbi to Bishop: The Biography of the Right Reverend Michael Solomon Alexander, Bishop in Jerusalem*. London: Olive, n.d.

Cragg, Kenneth. "The Anglican Church." In *Religion in the Middle East: Three Religions in Concord and Conflict*, vol. 1, *Judaism and Christianity*, edited by A. J. Arberry, 570–95. Cambridge: Cambridge University Press, 1969.

———. *The Arab Christian: A History in the Middle East*. London: Mowbray, 1992.

———. "Being Made Disciples—The Middle East." In *The Church Mission Society and World Christianity, 1799–1999*, edited by Kevin Ward and Brian Stanley, 120–43. Grand Rapids: Eerdmans, 2000.

———. *The Call of the Minaret*. New York: Oxford University Press, 1956.

———. *Faith and Life Negotiate: A Christian Story-Study*. Norwich: Canterbury, 1994.

———. *Sandals at the Mosque: Christian Presence amid Islam*. London: SCM 1959.

Crombie, Kelvin. *For the Love of Zion: Christian Witness and the Restoration of Israel*. London: Hodder and Stoughton, 1991.

———. *A Jewish Bishop in Jerusalem: The Life Story of Michael Solomon Alexander*. Jerusalem: Nicolayson's, 2006.

———. *A Prophetic Property: Celebrating 150 Years of CMJ's Work on Prophets Street in Jerusalem*. Jerusalem: Israel Trust of the Anglican Church, 2012.

———. *Restoring Israel: 200 Years of the CMJ Story*. Jerusalem: Nicolayson's, 2008.

Dalrymple, William. *The Anarchy: The Relentless Rise of the East India Company*. London: Bloomsbury, 2019.

———. *From the Holy Mountain: A Journey in the Shadow of Byzantium*. London: Flamingo, 1998.

Danby, Herbert, trans. *The Mishnah*. Oxford: Oxford University Press, 1933.

Danby, Herbert, and Moses Hirsch Segal. *A Concise English-Hebrew Dictionary with the English Pronunciation in Hebrew Transliteration*. Tel Aviv: Dvir, 1942.

Dark, Ken. *Archaeology of Jesus' Nazareth*. Oxford: Oxford University Press, 2023.

Davis, Miriam C. *Dame Kathleen Kenyon: Digging Up the Holy Land*. Walnut Creek, CA: Left Coast, 2008.

Dawood, N. J., trans. *The Koran*. London: Penguin, 2014.

Eliot, George. *Daniel Deronda*. London: Penguin, 1955.

Eliot, T. S. *The Complete Poems and Plays*. London: Faber and Faber, 1969.

Episcopal Church. *The Hymnal 1982: According to the Use of the Episcopal Church*. New York: Church Hymnal, 1985.

Everhart, Ruth. *Chasing the Divine in the Holy Land*. Grand Rapids: Eerdmans, 2012.

Farah, Rafiq A. *In Troubled Waters: A History of the Anglican Church in Jerusalem 1841–1998*. Leicester: Christians Aware, 2002.

Feiler, Bruce. *Abraham: A Journey to the Heart of Three Faiths*. New York: HarperCollins, 2002.

Frantzman, Seth J., and Ruth Kark. "General Gordon, the Palestine Exploration Fund, and the Origins of 'Gordon's Calvary' in the Holy Land." *Palestine Exploration Quarterly* 140:2 (2008) 119–36.

Freedman, David Noel, ed. *The Anchor Bible Dictionary*. 6 vols. New York: Doubleday, 1992.

French, Sally. "Becoming Pilgrims: Experience, Identity, and Virtue in the Context of a Holy Journey." DMin. diss., Virginia Theological Seminary, 2012.

Gadamer, Hans-Georg. *Truth and Method*. London: Sheed and Ward, 1975.

Genge, Ken. *How We Got Here from There*. Self-published, 2019.

Gibson, Shimon. "British Archaeological Institutions in Mandatory Palestine 1917–1948." *Palestine Exploration Quarterly* 131:2 (July–Dec. 1999) 115–43.

Gilmour, Calum. *A Pilgrim in Turkey: Visiting Classical and Early Christian Sites*. Auckland: Polygraphia, 2000.

Griffith, Bruce D. "Yearning: Gregory of Nyssa and the Vision of God." *Sewanee Theological Review* 43:3 (Pentecost 2000) 273–84.

Griffith, Bruce D., with Jason R. Radcliff. *Grace and Incarnation: The Oxford Movement's Shaping of the Character of Modern Anglicanism*. San Jose, CA: Pickwick, 2020.

Grimes, Daphne. *Journeys to Jerusalem: Troubling Times in a Holy Land*. Cody, WY: Wordsworth, 2009.

Harms, Gregory. *The Palestine-Israel Conflict: A Basic Introduction*. London: Pluto, 2005.

Hepper, F. Nigel. *St. George's College, Jerusalem: A Guide to the Bible Garden*. Jerusalem: St. George's College: 1993.

Herzl, Theodor. *The Jewish State*. New York: Dover, 1988.

Holloway, Richard. *Leaving Alexandria: A Memoir of Faith and Doubt*. Edinburgh: Canongate, 2012.

Huggett, Joyce. *Formed by the Desert, Heart-to-Heart Encounters with God*. Suffolk: Mayhew, 2004.

Hummel, Thomas. "Canon Bridgeman: An Anglican Emissary to the Eastern Church." In *Patterns of the Past, Prospects for the Future: The Christian Heritage in the Holy Land*, edited by Thomas Hummel et al., 105–13. London: Melisende, 1999.

Hummel, Thomas, et al., eds. *Patterns of the Past, Prospects for the Future: The Christian Heritage in the Holy Land*. London: Melisende, 1999.

Hunt E. D. *Holy Land Pilgrimage in the Later Roman Empire 312–460*. Oxford: Oxford University Press, 1982.

James, Serenhedd. *The Cowley Fathers: A History of the English Congregation of the Society of St. John the Evangelist*. Norwich: Canterbury, 2019.

Jenks, Gregory. *The Once and Future Bible: An Introduction to the Bible for Religious Progressives*. Eugene, OR: Wipf and Stock, 2011.

Jeremias, Joachim. *Jerusalem in the Time of Jesus: An Investigation into Economic and Social Conditions During the New Testament Period*. London: SCM, 1969.

Johnson, Sherman E. *Jesus and His Towns*. Wilmington, DE: Glazier, 1989.

Josephus. *The New Complete Works of Josephus*. Translated by William Whiston. Commentary by Paul L. Maier. Grand Rapids: Kregal, 1999.

Keble, John. *National Apostasy*. Steventon, UK: Rocket, 1983.

Kelly, Herbert. *An Idea in the Working: An Account of the Society of the Sacred Mission, Its History and Aims*. Nottingham: SSM, 1908.

Kenyon, Kathleen M. *Archaeology in the Holy Land*. 4th ed. London: Benn, 1979.

Khano, Delia. *By Eastern Windows*. Self-published, 1985.

Kroyanker, David. *Jerusalem Architecture*. London: Tauris Parke, 1994.

Larkin, Philip, ed. *The Oxford Book of Twentieth-Century English Verse*. London: Book Club Associates, 1978.

Lawrence, D. H. *Lady Chatterley's Lover*. London: SCM, 1963.

Lawrence, T. E. *Seven Pillars of Wisdom*. London: Penguin, 2000.

Lewis, Bernard. *The Middle East: 2000 Years of History from the Rise of Christianity to the Present Day*. London: Phoenix, 1995.

———. *The Multiple Identities of the Middle East*. New York: Schocken, 1998.

Macaulay, Rose. *The Towers of Trebizond*. London: Flamingo, 1995.

Mason, Alistair. *History of the Society of the Sacred Mission*. London: SPCK, 1993.

May, Herbert G., ed. *Oxford Bible Atlas*. 2nd ed. London: Oxford University Press 1974.

Mayes, Andrew D. *Holy Land? Challenging Questions from the Biblical Landscape*. London: SPCK, 2011.

———. *Spirituality in Ministerial Formation: The Dynamic of Prayer in Learning*, Cardiff: University of Wales, 2009.

McGowan, Anne, and Paul F. Bradshaw. *The Pilgrimage of Egeria: A New Translation of the* Itinerarium Egeriae *with Introduction and Commentary*. Collegeville, MN: Liturgical, 2018.

McKee, Dunstan. "Gilbert Sinden R.I.P." *SSM Chronicle* (1989–1996) Supplement XXI: The Directorship of Thomas Brown, 418–20. SSM_ACC_22. Society of the Sacred Mission Archive, Borthwick Institute for Archives, University of York, England.

Michener, James A. *The Source*. New York: Random House, 1965.

Montefiore, Simon Sebag. *Jerusalem: The Biography*. London: Weidenfeld and Nicolson, 2011.

Moorey, Roger. *A Century of Biblical Archaeology*. Cambridge: Lutterworth, 1991.

Morton, H. V. *In the Steps of the Master*. Boston: Da Capo, 2002.

Murphy-O'Connor, Jerome. *The Holy Land: An Oxford Archaeological Guide from Earliest Times to 1700*. 5th ed. Oxford: Oxford University Press, 2008.

———. *Paul: His Story*. Oxford: Oxford University Press, 2004.

Murray, Angela. *The Anglican Diocese of Cyprus and the Gulf: The Unfolding Story*. London: Gilgamesh, 2020.

Need, Stephen W. *Following Jesus in the Holy Land: Pathways of Discipleship Through Advent and Lent*. Durham, UK: Sacristy, 2019.

———. *The Gospels Today: Challenging Readings of John, Mark, Luke and Matthew*. Lanham, MD: Rowman and Littlefield, 2007.

———. *Jerusalem: Church of the Holy Sepulchre: An Introduction and Guide*. Jerusalem: Carta, 2016.

———. "Jerusalem Pilgrims: Spirituality, Rationality, and the Iconic in the Ministry of St. George's College." *International Journal of Religion and Spirituality in Society* 12:2 (2022) 1–14.

———. *Paul Today: Challenging Readings of Acts and the Epistles*. Lanham, MD: Rowman and Littlefield, 2007.

———. *Truly Divine and Truly Human: The Story of Christ and the Seven Ecumenical Councils*. London: SPCK, 2008.

Neill, Stephen. *A History of Christian Missions*. London: Penguin, 1990.

Newman, John Henry. *Apologia Pro Vita Sua*. Edited by Ian Ker. London: Penguin, 1994.

———. *The Letters and Diaries of John Henry Newman*. Vol. 8, *Tract 90 and the Jerusalem Bishopric January 1841–April 1842*. Edited by Gerard Tracey. Oxford: Clarendon, 1999.

———. *Tract One*. Blewbury, UK: Rocket, 1985.

O'Mahony, Anthony, ed. *Christianity and Jerusalem: Studies in Modern Theology and Politics in the Holy Land*. Leominster, UK: Gracewing, 2010.

———. *Palestinian Christians: Religion, Politics, and Society in the Holy Land*. London: Melisende, 1999.

O'Mahony, Anthony, et al., eds. *The Christian Heritage in the Holy Land*. London: Scorpion Cavendish, 1995.

Peterson, John L. "A Topographical Surface Survey of the Levitical 'Cities' of Joshua 21 and 1 Chronicles 6: Studies on the Levites in Israelite Life and Religion." PhD diss., Chicago Institute of Advanced Theological Studies and Seabury-Western Seminary, 1977.

———. *A Walk in Jerusalem: Stations of the Cross*. Harrisburg, PA: Morehouse, 1998.

Praill, David. *Return to the Desert: A Journey from Mount Hermon to Mount Sinai*. London: HarperCollins, 1995.

Prior, Michael. "Pilgrimage to the Holy Land, Yesterday and Today." In *Christians in the Holy Land*, edited by Michael Prior and William Taylor, 169–99. London: World of Islam Festival Trust, 1994.

Qleibo, Ali H. *Before the Mountains Disappear: An Ethnographic Chronicle of the Modern Palestinians*. Jerusalem: Kloreus, 1992.

———. *Jerusalem in the Heart*. Jerusalem: Kloreus, 2000.

Robinson, Edward, and Eli Smith. *Biblical Researches in Palestine and the Adjacent Regions*. 3 vols. Cambridge: Cambridge University Press, 2015.

Robinson, John. *Honest to God*. London: SCM, 1963.

Roth, Catherine P., trans. *On the Holy Icons: St. Theodore the Studite*. New York: St. Vladimir's Seminary, 2001.

Rowell, Geoffrey. *The Vision Glorious: Themes and Personalities of the Catholic Revival in Anglicanism*. Oxford: Oxford University Press, 1983.

Sadie, Stanley. *The New Grove Dictionary of Music and Musicians*. London: Macmillan, 1980.

Sanders, E. P. *The Historical Figure of Jesus*. London: Allen Lane, 1993.

Schweitzer, Albert. *The Quest of the Historical Jesus*. London: SCM, 1981.

Sewell, Richard. *River Through the Desert: A Lenten Journey in the Holy Land*. Jerusalem: St. George's College, 2022.

Shipler, David K. *Arab and Jew: Wounded Spirits in a Promised Land*. New York: Broadway, 2015.

Silberman, Neil Asher. *Digging for God and Country: Exploration in the Holy Land, 1799–1917*. New York: Doubleday, 1982.

Sinden, Gilbert. "The Jerusalem Experience." *SSM Chronicle* (1982–1989) Supplement XX: The Directorship of Edmund Wheat, 362–64. SSM_ACC_22. Society of the Sacred Mission Archive, Borthwick Institute for Archives, University of York, England.

———. "Ten Years in Jerusalem." *SSM Chronicle* (1989–1996) Supplement XXI: The Directorship of Thomas Brown, 411–13. SSM_ACC_22. Society of the Sacred Mission Archive, Borthwick Institute for Archives, University of York, England.

———. *Times and Seasons*. Sydney: Ambassador, 1980.

———. *When We Meet For Worship*. Adelaide: Lutheran, 1978.

Smith, George Adam. *The Historical Geography of the Holy Land*. London: Hodder and Stoughton, 1894.

Stace, Christopher, trans. *Jacobus de Voragine: The Golden Legend*. London: Penguin, 1998.

Stanley, Arthur Penrhyn. *Sinai and Palestine: In Connection with Their History*. London: Murray, 1868.

Stock, Eugene. *A History of the Church Missionary Society: Its Environment, Its Men, and Its Work*. 4 vols. London: CMS, 1899.

Thomas, David, with Clare Amos, eds. *A Faithful Presence: Essays for Kenneth Cragg*. London: Melisende, 2003.

Tibawi, A. L. *British Interests in Palestine 1800–1901: A Study of Religious and Educational Enterprise*. Oxford: Oxford University Press, 1961.

Tolan, Sandy. *The Lemon Tree*. New York: Black Swan, 2008.

Trocmé, Etienne. *The Passion as Liturgy: A Study in the Origin of the Passion Narratives in the Four Gospels*. London: SCM, 1983.

Tuchman, Barbara W. *Bible and Sword: England and Palestine from the Bronze Age to Balfour*. New York: Ballantine, 1956.

Turner, Victor, and Edith Turner. *Image and Pilgrimage in Christian Culture*. New York: Columbia University Press, 2011.

Twain, Mark. *The Innocents Abroad*. London: Penguin, 2002.

Vermes, Geza. *Jesus the Jew*. London: Collins, 1973.

Walker, Peter W. L. *Holy City: Holy Places? Christian Attitudes to Jerusalem and the Holy Land in the Fourth Century*. Oxford: Clarendon, 1990.

———. *In the Steps of Jesus: An Illustrated Guide to the Places of the Holy Land*. Oxford: Lion, 2006.

———. *In the Steps of Saint Paul: An Illustrated Guide to Paul's Journeys*. Oxford: Lion, 2008.

———. *Jesus and the Holy City: New Testament Perspectives on Jerusalem*. Grand Rapids: Eerdmans, 1996.

———. *The Weekend That Changed the World: The Mystery of Jerusalem's Empty Tomb*. London: Marshall Pickering, 1999.

Walker, Peter, and Graham Tomlin. *Walking in His Steps: A Guide to Exploring the Land of the Bible*. London: Marshall Pickering, 2001.

Ward, Benedicta, trans. *The Prayers and Meditations of St. Anselm*. Harmondsworth, UK: Penguin, 1973.

Warren, Charles, et al. *Survey of Western Palestine*. 7 vols. London: PEF, 1884.

Wilken, Robert L. *The Land Called Holy: Palestine in Christian History and Thought*. New Haven: Yale University Press, 1992.

Wilkinson, John, ed. *Catholic Anglicans Today*. London: Darton, Longman and Todd, 1968.

———. *Egeria's Travels*. London: SPCK, 1971.

———. *From Synagogue to Church: The Traditional Design; Its Beginning, Its Definition, Its End*. Oxford: Routledge, 2002.

———. *Interpretation and Community*. London: Macmillan, 1963.

———. *Jerusalem as Jesus Knew It: Archaeology as Evidence*. London: Thames and Hudson, 1978.

———. *The Jerusalem Jesus Knew: An Archaeological Guide to the Gospels*. Nashville: Thomas Nelson, 1983.

———. *Jerusalem Pilgrimage 1099–1185*. London: Hakluyt Society, 1988.

———. *Jerusalem Pilgrims Before the Crusades*. Jerusalem: Ariel, 1977.

———. *Jerusalem Prayers: Bible Readings and Prayers for the Holy Places*. Jerusalem: St. George's Cathedral, 1962.

———. *No Apology: A Handbook for Controversialists*. London: DLT, 1962.

———. *The Stations of the Cross in Jerusalem*. Jerusalem: St. George's Cathedral, 1963.

———. *The Supper and the Eucharist*. London: Macmillan, 1965.

Wybrew, Hugh. *Risen with Christ: Eastertide in the Orthodox Church*. London: SPCK, 2001.

Zimmerman, John D. "The Jerusalem Archbishopric." *Anglican Theological Review* 44:4 (Oct. 1962) 420–23.

Index

Note: Page numbers in *italics* indicate maps and photographs, and references following "n" refer to notes.

www.ingramcontent.com/pod-product-compliance
Lightning Source LLC
LaVergne TN
LVHW010539100826
845148LV00001B/234

* 9 7 9 8 3 8 5 2 3 7 5 9 3 *